HOP ADDITION

STEAM BOILER

To all our fellow beer hunters,
for following and letting us follow.

The Northern California Craft Beer Guide

KEN WEAVER

CAMERON + COMPANY

The Northern California Craft Beer Guide

©2012 by Ken Weaver
Photography ©2012 by Anneliese Schmidt
Book Design by vision road design

p. 37, SF Beer Week Logo, Courtesy of SF Brewers Guild, Design By Gamut
p. 50, Bay Area Beer Bloggers Logo, Courtesy of Jay Brooks
p. 139, Image Courtesy of Arne Frantzell
p. 140, Image Courtesy of Mitch Rice/Charbay Winery & Distillery

The author, photographer, and publisher strongly encourage the use of public transportation, a non-drinking designated driver, local accommodations, and common sense to safely and responsibly explore the contents of this book.

While all reasonable efforts have been made to ensure this guidebook contains only the most timely and accurate information available, please note that the details are subject to change, particularly given the rapidly changing nature of the region's craft beer scene. Important updates and instructions for submitting corrections can be found at:

www.northerncaliforniacraftbeer.com

Cameron + Company
6 Petaluma Blvd. North, Petaluma, CA 94952
info@cameronbooks.com   www.cameronbooks.com
800-779-5582

ISBN: 9781937359164
Library of Congress Control Number: 2012931516

Printed in China
10 9 8 7 6 5 4 3 2 1

THE NORTHERN CALIFORNIA
CRAFT BEER GUIDE

BY KEN WEAVER
PHOTOGRAPHY BY ANNELIESE SCHMIDT

FOREWORD BY KEN GROSSMAN

FOREWORD

Where It All Began

When I first started homebrewing back in 1970, it was impossible to imagine what would become of American brewing in the decades to follow. Back then, it was a bleak time for good beer. There were very few breweries left that hadn't been absorbed by other companies, or that hadn't just gone out of business altogether. With very few exceptions, the breweries that were left produced lots of similar beers: light American-style lagers, set apart from the beers next to them on the shelves only by differences in marketing strategies.

Thinking about that time, it stands in stark contrast to today—especially here in Northern California, where even the most humble corner stores and bodegas will feature staggering displays of craft beer from the West Coast and beyond.

When I made my first commercial batch of beer in 1980, the industry had hit a low point, and only about forty breweries remained; I recall listening to a talk by a highly respected industry analyst at the time, who predicted that in the next twenty years only two breweries would be left in America. I had invested every penny I had, and years of endless labor. I wondered whether I had made a huge mistake. What happened to change the tide? Exactly when did good enough stop being good enough?

Looking at the larger picture, Northern California in the late 1960s, early 1970s was really at the forefront of a lot of change. I think the craft beer revolution had a lot in common with the other movements sprouting up at the time. Suddenly it seemed like everyone had some sort of new consciousness. Renowned chef Alice Waters started the legendary Chez Panisse restaurant in Berkeley, which helped to usher in the movement for local, seasonal, and sustainable foods. People started to care about things that had been forgotten: new creameries making forgotten cheeses, artisan breadmakers, interesting wines. Every cultural movement paralleled what we were thinking when we started the brewery—and all here in Northern California!

Like the early days of anything, the going was never easy. I would literally go door to door to different bars and sell single bottles of Pale Ale. Back then, people thought I was nuts! It was several years and loads of good luck later that we began to see more people moving toward bolder beers.

Just as chefs were learning from Alice Waters, we were learning from some of the folks that came before us—Fritz Maytag at Anchor and Jack McAuliffe at New Albion—and the next generation was learning from us. Now, over three decades later, the community has grown so strong that it's hard to remember those lonely early days.

The fact that there is a need—much less the subject matter—for a guide to all the great beer and brewing spots in Northern California is a testament to the changing tastes of beer drinkers and to the tremendous support of the beer community. Building a movement isn't easy, and it wouldn't be possible without hundreds of people working collectively toward the same goal. We wouldn't be here today without hard work, luck, and standing in the right time and place— especially the right place!

KEN GROSSMAN, OWNER AND FOUNDER OF SIERRA NEVADA BREWING COMPANY

…Northern California, where even the most humble corner stores and bodegas will feature staggering displays of craft beer…

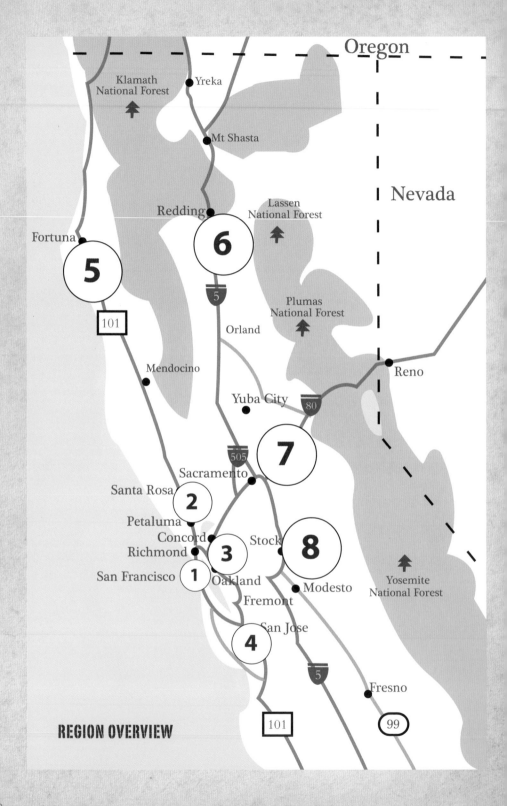

REGION OVERVIEW

Table of Contents

List of Styles

Beer people are good people

My wife, Anneliese (Ali), and I have been reminded of this truth many times over the past six months, when striking up conversations with the folks sitting next to us at the bar, being shown around small, hand-built brewing facilities by the energetic craft brewers at their helm, or sitting down over pints with seasoned craft-beer veterans who know (better than we possibly could) how far we've come since 1965.

When Ali and I were first approached about doing this guide, it seemed both a natural fit and terrifying. We've traveled across the country hitting up brewpubs and national parks. We've sampled thousands of commercial beers. And we've certainly put together our share of unwieldy reports over the years. But Northern California is truly something special in the craft beer world, and, being familiar with many of the regional craft beer guides that have come before ours, we realized and accepted that we would need to do something different.

If this book were a movie, it would be some ambitiously sprawling epic that went heinously over budget. Northern California is home to over 150 breweries, approaching one-tenth of the nation's total, and the number of notable beer bars, bottle shops, and other craft beer-centric venues is of similar magnitude. Over the six months of focused work leading up to the completion of this project, Ali and I ventured into every corner of Northern California where good beer was to be found: at best enjoying a leisurely trip out to the Central Valley and Yosemite (the first semblance of a real vacation I'd managed in over a year), but more frequently traveling at a frenetic pace and wondering how we were going to get everything finished. I was still consulting part time, while Ali was doing so full time and budgeting her limited vacation days.

The fact is, there's so much great beer stuff going on in Northern California that the only possible way to make any sense of it was to tackle it head-on. We'd often start early on travel days, hitting up a brewery or two before noon, leaving plenty of beer on the table and interspersing important brewery visits with time spent at bars and bottle shops, where we weren't obliged to sample. We had personalized Google Maps to shape our days, as well as standardized printouts to streamline our visits. It was an adventure of the most delicious sort, but it was also an enormous amount of work and took a great deal of organization. The people we met along the way, our fellow beer hunters, were a continuous source of energy and encouragement.

At the end of things, our ultimate hope is that we've given this beer scene the guidebook it deserves.

So much of the craft beer industry's evolution in this country has been an uphill battle, and people often ask me why I choose to spend my time writing about a fermented beverage. I think the craft beer world, at the core of things, asks a person a very simple question: What do you really want? And I believe that's one of the more important questions we can ask ourselves—whether framed in terms of taste, or how we choose to consume things, or how we interact with the communities around us, or (in the most immediate sense) how willing we are to savor what's directly in front of us. That's what I see in my glass, and having met so many enthusiastic beer lovers as of late, I think many of them see it in theirs as well.

But let's not get too far ahead of ourselves. I mean, it's just beer. Right?

In this introductory chapter, you'll find all of the information you need to confidently situate yourself in Northern California's craft beer culture. You'll find out how to best negotiate the various features of this guide, avoid some of the most common pitfalls, learn about important updates, and learn how to get in touch in case I happened to screw anything up. Safe travels, always, and we hope this book serves you well.

Beer Country

Brewing first began in California in 1849 with the opening of the Adam Schuppert Brewery in San Francisco. This was right around the peak of the California Gold Rush, that massive influx of fortune-seeking forty-niners, and, let's be honest, I get thirsty just thinking about basic yard work. Demand for inexpensive alcohol in the area led to a rapid increase in the number of breweries and saloons in the region, particularly in the boomtown of San Francisco. While the gold didn't last, the thirst for beer did.

By the beginning of the 1900s, Northern California was home to flourishing beer scenes in San Francisco, Oakland, Sacramento, and elsewhere, and America as a whole was home to over 1,700 breweries (this figure was even higher in years previous). While the beer industry wasn't nearly as refined as our current craft beer selection—quality and temperature controls, for instance, were still pretty iffy—it was a robust local industry that had major ties with the surrounding communities. "Steam" beers (essentially lagers fermented at warmer temperatures due to a lack of refrigeration) had become quite common. Sonoma County had grown into a major hop-producing region. And Buffalo Brewing Company in Sacramento was brewing more beer than anyone else west of the Mississippi River.

By the middle of the twentieth century—following over thirteen years of Prohibition ("the Noble Experiment," if you're into sarcasm), two World Wars, and a long list of further setbacks—almost the entire industry was gone. By the end of the 1970s, those original 1,700 breweries had been reduced to fewer than fifty, and those that had survived were generally national and regional breweries that predominantly brewed

Largest Northern California Craft Breweries

The Brewers Association (www.brewersassociation.org) annually releases its list of the largest fifty craft breweries in the country. Based on the most recently available sales volume data (from 2010), seven of these breweries are located in Northern California, including the second largest one in the country. The national rankings of the largest craft breweries that call Northern California home are as follows:

- **2** Sierra Nevada Brewing Co. (Chico)
- **17** Lagunitas Brewing Co. (Petaluma)
- **23** Anchor Brewing Co. (San Francisco)
- **30** Gordon Biersch Brewing Co. (San Jose)
- **38** Lost Coast Brewery and Cafe (Eureka)
- **40** North Coast Brewing Co. (Fort Bragg)
- **43** Bear Republic Brewing Co. (Cloverdale/Healdsburg)

bland pale lagers and "lite" beers. We'd lost something, both in terms of flavorful beer and the culture it fosters.

The Return of Beer Country

Having reviewed any number of articles on the subject, I haven't seen any more concise or precious a phrasing for what grew afterward than fellow beer writer Jay Brooks' reference to San Francisco as "the birthplace of the modern craft beer movement." That's everything in a nutshell—but I'll tweak it slightly to be a bit more inclusive. Northern California is the birthplace of the modern craft beer movement.

In 1958, a brewing program was established at the University of California, Davis, and many of the brewers who would later be at the forefront of the craft beer movement graduated from that program. It's currently one of the most esteemed professional brewing schools in the world (see Beer Education sidebar on page 215).

In 1965, Fritz Maytag purchased and began revamping Anchor Brewing Company in San Francisco, what would later become (once the term came into existence) the first "craft brewery" in the entire country. Fritz would rekindle a number of robust, abandoned beer styles, and Anchor's quality-driven approach would be an inspiration to the next generation of innovative craft brewers (see Anchor Brewery Tour sidebar on page 47).

In 1976, the first "microbrewery" in the U.S. opened in Sonoma. The New Albion Brewing Company was headed by Jack McAuliffe, who had been inspired by the expressive beers he'd sampled while traveling abroad (few of which were imported back

Safe Travels

Getting there and back safely is the most important part of any beer hunting expedition, and nowhere in Northern California is that easier than in San Francisco and the immediate surroundings. Bay Area Rapid Transit (BART) provides public transportation throughout San Francisco and the East Bay, putting numerous Beer Destinations within easy walking distance of a BART station. Beer By BART (www.beerbybart.com) provides in-depth information regarding how to use public transportation to get to more than fifty top-notch breweries, bars, and bottle shops in the Bay Area—including how far you'll have to walk.

There are also a number of alternative tours and tasting opportunities, particularly in the Bay Area. Brewery Adventures (www.breweryadventures.com) offers plush monthly bus tours to San Francisco breweries, which include beer education elements and two enthusiastic tour guides. They also offer occasional trips to North Bay destinations, as well as the option to schedule private tours. Another beer venture to check out is the new brewtruc (www.brewtrucsf.com), billed as San Francisco's "first taproom on wheels."

then). That brewery wouldn't last beyond 1983, but Jack and New Albion had demonstrated that small operations could make inroads against the monopolization of the larger corporate breweries, which had swallowed up many earlier small breweries.

In 1979, legislation signed by President Jimmy Carter (admittedly not from Northern California) went into effect, making homebrewing legal in the U.S. The section that actually involved homebrewing, though, was put forth by U.S. Senator Alan Cranston (who most certainly was from Northern California).

In traditional historian parlance: that's when shit got real.

The 1980s saw the emergence of Ken Grossman's Sierra Nevada Brewing Company in Chico, as well as its iconic pale ale, with an assertive, citrusy hop character that took the country by storm. Sierra Nevada's since grown into the second largest U.S. craft brewery and the sixth largest in the country overall. Of the first handful of new brewpubs to open up since Prohibition, three of them were based in Northern California: Hopland Brewery (now Mendocino), Buffalo Bill's Brewery, and Triple Rock. Eel River and Ukiah Brewing lay claim to the titles of first certified-organic brewery and brewpub in the U.S., respectively. And there's really no way to measure the impact of innovative brewers like Vinnie Cilurzo at Russian River, generally credited with inventing the double IPA style and changing the landscape of sour-ale brewing worldwide.

In 2010, the Brewers Association reported that the total number of breweries in the U.S. had swelled to over 1,700—returning to and surpassing the number from the early 1900s. How many of those brewers have cited Anchor, New Albion, Sierra Nevada, or Russian River as their sources of inspiration? I wouldn't know where to begin counting. And I haven't even touched upon influential beer bars like San Francisco's Toronado.

Are you thirsty yet?

A Brief Overview of Everything

The chapters that follow break down Northern California into eight regions, starting with San Francisco, three regions to the north, east, and south, then four additional

Regarding Chains

In an effort to streamline the listings (and not quadruple the book's length by including all of the BevMo! locations in Northern California), we chose not to include individual listings of the following chain stores:

BevMo!
(WWW.BEVMO.COM)

BJ's Restaurant and Brewhouse
(WWW.BJSBREWHOUSE.COM)

Cost Plus World Market
(WWW.WORLDMARKET.COM)

Mary's Pizza Shack
(WWW.MARYSPIZZASHACK.COM)

Pete's Restaurant & Brewhouse
(WWW.PETESRANDB.COM)

Trader Joe's
(WWW.TRADERJOES.COM)

Whole Foods Market
(WWW.WHOLEFOODSMARKET.COM)

However, all of these places typically have excellent selections of craft beer. If you're looking for bottles in a pinch, you can always check out the nearest BevMo!, Cost Plus, Trader Joe's (especially Mission Street Pale Ale), and Whole Foods. We were impressed by the general quality of BJ's beers at the locations we visited, and all three of the aforementioned restaurant chains will typically feature a solid lineup of Northern California craft beer.

regions beyond those. For each geographic region you'll find a lot of different information, including our top beer suggestions, individual place listings, style discussions, and other points of interest. These key features are outlined in brief detail below. The last chapters of the book provide a calendar of major beer events and a glossary.

It's ultimately up to you how you want to approach these chapters. While we do single out a number of Beer Destinations in each one, pretty much everything that gets a listing is worth a stop (we've been to a lot of places that we left out). There are at least a few breweries we don't have any interest in revisiting ourselves, but that doesn't mean your experiences there will be identical. People have different palates and preferences, recipes and brewing situations change, and I've really tried to be as kind and cognizant of these things as possible throughout the book without undermining the critical goal of being useful.

Tip your bartenders. Treat your hosts well. Hug your favorite brewers (ask first). Don't be afraid to leave unfinished beer behind. Taste first, drink later, etc. Above all: Get there and back safely, and have fun.

Key Features

Five to Try

Looking back, these are five of our absolute favorite beers in the region. Either a unique experience, or a textbook rendition of a certain beer style, or just something you won't want to miss. In summary: yum.

Uncharted Territory

These breweries either hadn't yet opened or had opened so recently that we weren't able to track them down before the manuscript was due. Some may still not be open. Some may never open. Call ahead.

Place Listings

These comprise the central content of the book: nearly three hundred breweries, restaurants, beer bars, bottle shops, homebrew shops, etc. Contact info, hours, and directions are generally provided for each listing, as well as tasting notes, recommendations, and useful details (see Explanation of Symbols sidebar). For breweries, in particular, we made a point to try and recommend one year-round beer that's particularly worth a taste, as well as any seasonal beers that we've tried and recommend. (If no address is provided, it's because they don't have a physical location to visit.) There's plenty of tasty beer in

FiftyFifty Brewing

Northern California, and we hope the listings will help you find what you're looking for. Note that we elected not to clutter the place listings with the major chains (see Regarding Chains sidebar for details). A full alphabetical index of the place listings can be found on page 285.

Sidebars

There are so many cool elements to Northern California's craft beer culture that simply wouldn't fit into a standard listing. From useful web sites to bierschnaps to bottle cap art, you'll find them in the sidebars.

Style Sidebars

Any time one attempts to group beers together into style categories (whether for judging homebrews, historical discussion, or whatever), it's crucially important to ask two questions: (1) do I really want to do this? and (2) what am I hoping to get out of this thankless endeavor (which will almost certainly devolve into argument and heartbreak)? For the purposes of this guide, I wanted something tangible that people could take away from the book (IPAs are a showcase of hops, barley wines will be higher in alcohol, etc.) without being too restrictive in the process. I think the most interesting quality of style categories is that they tend to represent something that works, when done correctly, again and again in a variety of commercial examples, like a classic pairing or harmonious chord.

For each style sidebar, I've chosen a bottled Northern California beer that embodies the style well, and Ali's put together similarly composed studio shots for each. We limited ourselves to a mere eighteen broad style categories in total, focusing on the things you'll find most often in Northern California (see List of Styles sidebar on page 5).

Disclaimers Galore

Though highlighting one's inadequacies is generally frowned upon in books like this, our time machine remains scattered in bits and pieces throughout the garage. Things change. While I'm sure it may feel like I've purposefully sent you on a wild goose chase for IPA when you're standing in front of that closed used-hot-tub lot wondering how on Earth I mistook this for a world-class bottle shop, I can guarantee you this wasn't intentional. I've made a point to save all my misleading copies for personal nemeses.

Details

Are subject to change. Hours may fluctuate seasonally. Brewers may leave for greener pastures. The tap lines may not always be as clean/not-so-clean as when we visited. If it's a detail that matters greatly, it matters enough to double-check it. Whatever you do, please don't take this book up to a bartender or manager and say, "But Ken Weaver said so, goddamn it!" I'm already running low on nemesis copies.

Check the web site provided at the end of this section for important updates: openings, closings, etc.

Directions

Should be taken with a boulder of salt. I've tried to make them as straightforward as possible, but these aren't meant to be anything other than abbreviated directions to get you close to your destination (so GPS is encouraged). I haven't triple-checked them, and you know how directions go. Use common sense.

Drinking and Driving

With great power comes great responsibility. This beer guide is neither an encouragement nor an excuse to drink and drive. Even if you're under the legal limit, even if you've only had one drink (and particularly if you're my size), alcohol impairs your ability to do things safely. Know your limits, and make yourself at home well below them. Stay locally, call a cab, use public transportation whenever possible. Buy a growler to enjoy later on. Look into a good breathalyzer (we own two). Become close friends with teetotalers. Be safe, please. We take no responsibility for your actions—but you most certainly should.

Updates, Corrections, and Feedback

The realities of print publishing guarantee that something in this book will be out of date. The realities of being human guarantee that something in this book I'll have screwed up. At least Ali's pictures look nice!

Taking the above limitations as a given, I'll be keeping the following web site updated regarding closures, openings, major corrections, and anything else that seems appropriate. From there you can submit updates, corrections, or (in a perfect world) just let us know how much you're enjoying the book. WWW.NORTHERNCALIFORNIACRAFTBEER.COM

You can also find us on Facebook: NORCAL CRAFT BEER GUIDE

Explanation of Symbols

Certain things are self-explanatory. Breweries, brewpubs, and nanobreweries sell their own beer on tap. Bottle shops, grocery stores, and convenience stores sell bottles to go. For everything else: symbols.

Places bearing this symbol are our chosen Beer Destinations: the crème de la crème. Breweries, beer bars, bottle shops, etc. designated with this symbol represent, for us, the very best that Northern California has to offer. While the exact rubric for choosing Beer Destinations was an inexact science at best and subject to personal preference, each of these places offers a wide range of magnificent beers and (often) an ideal environment for enjoying them. There are many great places without this symbol.

While some craft beer stops will allow a small taste or two if you're undecided, this symbol designates establishments that offer samplers or flights of different beers, either in sets or individually, and usually at a modest price (generally $10 or less for a full flight, or a buck or two for a sample). This is a great way to try a variety of beers, limit your consumption, and, at a brewery, get a better feel for the brewer's abilities and vision. Think winetasting without the extended pinkies and the expensive sampling fees.

This symbol indicates a place other than the aforementioned bottle shops, grocery stores, and convenience stores that sells bottles (or cans) to go.

This potbellied symbol designates breweries that offer "growlers." A growler, generally, is a 64-ounce (1/2-gallon) glass container filled directly from a tap, allowing beer lovers to transport a beer that often isn't bottled or otherwise available outside of the brewery. Nearly all California breweries require you use their own brewery-branded growlers. Occasionally, this symbol will represent slightly different vessels that work toward the same end (taking draft beer home), as a few breweries instead offer 1-gallon growlers, five-liter mini kegs, etc. In all cases, keep them cold and drink the contents as soon as possible, as they aren't meant to hold up.

Only used for brewery listings, this symbol indicates breweries that will sell kegs of their beers to customers directly (usually keg sales happen through bottle shops, etc., often with limited selection). It isn't especially useful when traveling to distant breweries, as one is generally required to leave a deposit and return the keg within a set time period. But since we're keeping track of everything else…

Cask-conditioned beer is an integral part of England's good beer culture and, in the most general of definitions, consists of beers that are unfiltered and naturally carbonated by yeast in the same vessels they're then served from (most often wooden barrels or stainless-steel kegs). Traditional kegged beer, in contrast, is filtered of yeast, artificially carbonated, and served cold. Cask-conditioned beers will be lightly carbonated and served at a warmer temperature—though they should be neither warm nor flat. It can be tough to find true cask-conditioned beer in the U.S., and even the beer spots bearing this symbol often won't have it all the time or properly handled.

Only used for brewery listings, this symbol designates beer production sites that have (in one way or another) gone above and beyond in limiting their environmental impact. This can include offsetting electricity usage with renewable sources, running delivery vehicles on alternative fuels, etc. A broader discussion of this topic can be found in the Environment and Sustainability sidebar on page 191.

Only used for brewery listings, each of these places offers anywhere from one to a full lineup of organic beer. The vast majority of places bearing this symbol have been certified organic by the CCOF organization in Santa Cruz. More information can be found in the Organic Brewing sidebar on page 105.

Places bearing this symbol sell food (anything from typical pub fare to fine dining).

Places bearing this symbol sell snacks (though nothing that would qualify as a full meal).

Only used for homebrew shop listings, these stores offer online shopping and shipping.

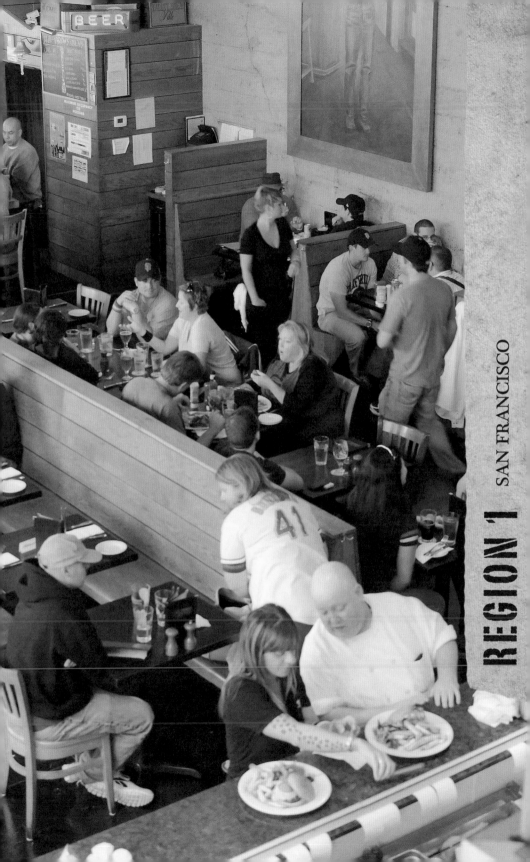

Beer Stats

	O.g	I.B.U	aBV%
PolaR BeaR	13.5	35	5.7
BRown BeaR	14.5	27	6.3
golden Vanilla	11.0	15	4.5
Howard St. I.P.A	17.5	65	7.0
Valencia Wheat	12.0	17	5.0
MeYeR e.S.B	15.0	30	6.4
KozLov Stout	14.5	35	6.3

★ oRiginal gravity ★
★ International bittering units ★
★ aLcohol by VoLume ★

San Francisco, like much of the Bay Area, is awash with great craft beer. You can't throw a rock without knocking over somebody's bottle of Anchor Steam. If you do happen to knock over somebody's bottle of Anchor Steam, we would advise taking them to any one of this chapter's numerous Beer Destinations to make up for it. You might even get your rock back.

Nowhere in Northern California (even North Bay, and we're biased) can quite keep up with what the City has to offer, both in terms of craft beer and in terms of just about everything else. Whether venturing to touristy destinations like Alcatraz, Fisherman's Wharf, and Ghirardelli Square, or just lounging around on a blanket in Dolores Park, there's something worth doing (at least once) in every corner of San Francisco.

The City's culinary expertise, in particular, carries over into many of the region's best beer spots. While a person can technically survive on standard pub fare, in San Francisco you're allowed to expect more.

Anchor Brewing Company and Toronado stand as the two main craft beer fixtures in the City, and a visit to both is standard for most beer lovers visiting the region (at least the ones who plan ahead, as tours of Anchor can be booked up months in advance). Our other Beer Destinations include 21st Amendment Brewery, Speakeasy Ales & Lagers, and the recently expanded City Beer Store, where I hope to take up residence one day. Food-minded folks—the term "foodie" sounds like a plush monster to me—will find appetizing pairing options at The Monk's Kettle, Social Kitchen, Magnolia Gastropub, La Trappe Cafe, and Suppenküche. And you might want to set a beer budget before visiting Healthy Spirits or Ales Unlimited. Overall, it proved difficult to limit ourselves in choosing Beer Destinations in this region.

San Francisco also happens to be your best region for taking advantage of public transportation options (East Bay is also reasonably accessible). Enjoy yourself safely and, in the timeless motto of City Beer Store: sip, sip, sip.

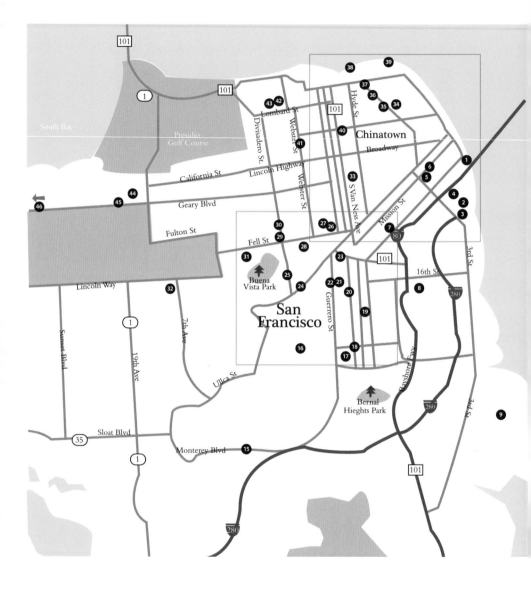

5 to try

21st Amendment Brew Free or Die IPA Anchor Liberty Ale Magnolia Bonnie Lee's Bitter Social Kitchen Rapscallion Speakeasy Prohibition Ale

1 Gordon Biersch   Brewpub

2 Paragon Restaurant   Restaurant

3 Public House   Beer Bar

4 21st Amendment Brewery   Brewpub

5 Thirsty Bear Brewing Company   Brewpub

6 Anchor & Hope   Restaurant/Beer Bar

7 City Beer Store   Beer Bar/Bottle Shop

8 Anchor Brewing Company   Brewery

9 Speakeasy Ales & Lagers   Brewery

10 Almanac Beer Co.   Brewery

11 MateVeza   Brewery

12 Pacific Brewing Laboratories   Brewery

13 Shmaltz Brewing Company   Brewery

14 Triple Voodoo Brewing   Brewery

15 Monterey Deli   Convenience Store

16 Plumpjack Wines   Bottle Shop

17 Pi Bar   Beer Bar

18 Rosamunde Sausage Grill   Restaurant/Beer Bar

19 Shotwell's   Beer Bar

20 The Sycamore   Beer Bar

21 The Monk's Kettle   Beer Bar/Restaurant

22 Gestalt Haus   Beer Bar

23 Zeitgeist   Beer Bar

24 Starbelly   Restaurant

uncharted territory

Bosworth Brewery Elizabeth Street Brewery Local Brewing Co. Mission Rock Brewery & Oyster Bar

- **25** Healthy Spirits   Bottle Shop
- **26** Biergarten   Beer Garden
- **27** Suppenküche   Restaurant/Beer Bar
- **28** Toronado   Beer Bar
- **29** New Star-Ell Liquor   Convenience Store
- **30** Bar Crudo   Restaurant
- **31** Magnolia Gastropub & Brewery   Brewpub
- **32** Social Kitchen & Brewery   Brewpub
- **33** Amsterdam Cafe   Beer Bar
- **34** Church Key   Beer Bar
- **35** Rogue Ales Public House   Beer Bar
- **36** La Trappe Cafe   Beer Bar/Restaurant
- **37** Kennedy's Irish Pub & Indian Curry House Restaurant   Beer Bar/Restaurant
- **38** Jack's Cannery Bar   Beer Bar/Restaurant
- **39** Beer 39   Beer Bar
- **40** The Jug Shop   Bottle Shop
- **41** Ales Unlimited   Bottle Shop
- **42** Delarosa   Restaurant
- **43** The Tipsy Pig   Restaurant/Beer Bar
- **44** San Francisco Brewcraft   Homebrew Shop
- **45** Blackwell's Wines & Spirits   Bottle Shop
- **46** The Beach Chalet Brewery & Restaurant   Brewpub

While a person can technically survive on standard pub fare, in San Francisco you're allowed to expect more.

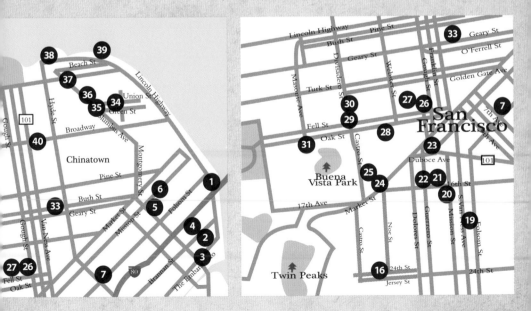

① Gordon Biersch
Brewpub

WWW.GORDONBIERSCH.COM

2 Harrison St., San Francisco, CA 94105, (415) 243-8246—A short walk from the Embarcadero BART station. By Pier 24 on The Embarcadero, near the corner of Spear St. and Harrison St.

OPEN Su-Th: 11:30 a.m.–midnight, F-Sa: 11:30 a.m.–2 a.m.

Chain location (for details, see main listing: Gordon Biersch – San Jose on page 147).

② Paragon Restaurant
Restaurant

WWW.PARAGONRESTAURANT.COM

701 Second St., San Francisco, CA 94107, (415) 537-9020—Close to Pier 38 and AT&T Park, near the corner of Townsend St. and Second St.

OPEN M-F: 11:30 a.m.–closing, Sa: 5:30 p.m.–closing (also open for Giants home games)

Slightly upscale restaurant between 21st Amendment Brewery and AT&T Park. Paragon featured a dozen taps and a dozen bottles when we had dinner there—mostly West Coast taps, with a more geographically diverse bottle list. Craft only. Their appetizing menu included house-smoked almonds and wild boar enchiladas.

③ Public House
Beer Bar

WWW.PUBLICHOUSESF.COM

24 Willie Mays Plaza, San Francisco, CA 94107, (415) 644-0240—AT&T Park, near the corner of Third St. and King St., Willie Mays Plaza.

OPEN Su-Th: 4 p.m.–10 p.m., F-Sa: 4 p.m.–11 p.m. (game-day hours vary; check web site)

Public House was a surprisingly geeked-out beer bar right next to AT&T Park. Their twenty taps included some limited-release California beers, and they regularly offer selections from Magnolia Brewery on cask. Serious beer place, enthusiastic staff, and a small, well-chosen bottle list. The wall of kegs is a nice touch. We're going to have a difficult time choosing between this place and 21st Amendment before a ballgame.

4 21st Amendment Brewery
Brewpub

WWW.21ST-AMENDMENT.COM

563 Second St., San Francisco, CA 94107, (415) 369-0900—Close to Pier 38 and AT&T Park, near the corner of Brannan St. and Second St.

OPEN M-Th: 11:30 a.m.–midnight, F-Sa: 11:30 a.m.–1 a.m., Su: 10 a.m.–midnight

21st Amendment was actually our first stop when putting this book together, as we happened to be headed to a Giants game for a friend's birthday. The brewpub is a two-story building with a seat-yourself section upstairs, which is especially handy when there's a ballgame about to start just down the street. Their beers are excellent across the board, whether on site or in cans. Brew Free or Die IPA is our shared favorite, with juicy orange and pink grapefruit hop contributions that simply pop: fresh and tangy and tongue-numbing. We've consumed more than our fair share of this beer. Other highlights include Bitter American (a rustic, citrusy session beer

weighing in well under 5%) and Crisis! (an assertive double IPA with American hops and slight touches of oak). The pub itself is an excellent stop for beer, and they've got an outdoor beer garden of sorts as well. Get a plastic cup or can, find a seat, and if it's a game day, watch a steady parade of orange and black pass by.

BREWMASTER: Shaun O'Sullivan
ESTABLISHED: 2000
BE SURE TO TRY: Brew Free or Die IPA
ELSEWHERE: Bottles, Draft

5 Thirsty Bear Brewing Company
Brewpub

WWW.THIRSTYBEAR.COM

661 Howard St., San Francisco, CA 94105, (415) 974-0905—A short walk from the Montgomery St. BART station. Just east of Yerba Buena Gardens/Center for the Arts, on Howard St. between Third St. and Hawthorne St.

OPEN M-Th: 11:30 a.m.–10 p.m.+, F: 11:30 a.m.–11 p.m.+, Sa: noon–11 p.m.+, Su: 5 p.m.–10 p.m.+

Thirsty Bear is San Francisco's first CCOF-certified organic brewery, and they typically have a pretty big lineup of house-made brews for sampling in addition to weekly cask ale specials and a tapas-style menu (pretty atypical for brewpubs). Their Polar Bear is a nicely done Bohemian-style Pilsner, providing herbal and mineral hops and a toasty Pils malt core, while Brown Bear Ale shows roasted malts along with solid caramel and biscuity notes. A few local places offer their beer on tap, including nearby Anchor & Hope. A few blocks away is Press Club, which also offers a high-end selection of California and international beer but didn't really warrant an additional entry.

BREWERS: Brenden Dobel (Brewmaster),
Ron Silberstein (Head Brewer)
ESTABLISHED: 1996
BE SURE TO TRY: Brown Bear Ale
SEASONALS: Bearly Legal Barley Wine (occasional)
ELSEWHERE: Draft

City Beer

⑥ Anchor & Hope
Restaurant/Beer Bar

WWW.ANCHORANDHOPESF.COM

83 Minna St., San Francisco, CA 94107, (415) 501-9100—A short walk from the Montgomery St. BART station. About three blocks northeast of Yerba Buena Gardens/Center for the Arts, near the corner of Second St. and Minna St.

OPEN M-Th: 11:30 a.m.–2 p.m., 5:30 p.m.–10 p.m., F: 11:30 a.m. –2 p.m., 5:30 p.m. –11 p.m., Sa: 5:30 p.m. –11 p.m., Su: 5:30 p.m. –10 p.m.

Shellfish and seafood–minded restaurant with an excellent selection of beer. The fifteen taps included some pretty geeked-out selections when we stopped

Anchor Brewing

by (Lost Abbey, Jolly Pumpkin, Stillwater, Linden Street), and their bottle list, with just over fifty entries, was broken down by style and beautifully chosen. Anchor & Hope also organizes occasional oyster and dry stout pairings.

7 City Beer Store
Beer Bar/Bottle Shop

WWW.CITYBEERSTORE.COM

1168 Folsom St., Suite 101, San Francisco, CA 94103, (415) 503-1033—A short walk from the Civic Center/UN Plaza BART station. South of Market neighborhood, near the corner of Eighth St. and Folsom St.

OPEN Tu-Sa: noon–10 p.m., Su: noon–6 p.m.

Even before their expansion in late 2011, City Beer was one of the best stops in San Francisco. Now, is there anything that compares? I'm not sure there is. Beth and Craig have done a fantastic job compiling not only fifteen amazing taps and hundreds of bottles (most available refrigerated to go), but I've been to a few beer places and have never seen anything quite like their onsite-only cooler behind the bar. "Absurd" is the appropriate word here. Alesmith's rare barrel-aged beers, older vintages of FiftyFifty Imperial Eclipse, Sacramento barrel-aged beers that I thought were extinct, plus some brews made especially for City Beer. A beer-literate, enthusiastic young crowd. Along with Beer Revolution, this is the best location for Bay Area beer-release events. Weekly flight nights.

8 Anchor Brewing Company
Brewery

WWW.ANCHORBREWING.COM

1705 Mariposa St., San Francisco, CA 94107, (415) 863-8350—Close to Jackson Playground in eastern SF, at the corner of De Haro St. and Mariposa St.

OPEN For tours only.

A beer-centric trip to San Francisco isn't fully complete without a tour of Anchor's brewery (Anchor Brewery Tour sidebar on page 47) and a fresh pint of Anchor Steam (see sidebar Style: California Common on page 34). So much of the craft beer world today has its beginnings in 1965, when Fritz Maytag purchased the then-floundering Anchor Brewing Company. The opening of the first new "microbrewery" in the country (New Albion Brewing Company in Sonoma) was still eleven years off, and in the meanwhile Fritz would turn Anchor around, return to brewing traditions that focused on flavor, and revitalize classic beer styles with products like Anchor Steam, Anchor Porter, and Anchor Liberty Ale. The clearest start to the craft beer movement occurred right here in San Francisco in 1965, and each of us owes a debt of gratitude—and a raised pint—to Fritz Maytag and Anchor Brewing. Today, even after the retirement of Fritz in 2010, Anchor Brewing continues to make some of the finest beer in the world. Anchor Porter remains one of the most complex porters we've ever tasted. Anchor Old Foghorn Barleywine Ale is a potent example that's perfect for cellaring. And their modestly spiced Christmas Ale has

CALIFORNIA COMMON ANCHOR STEAM

"Steam beer" is perhaps one of the better current-day reminders of this country's rich brewing history—a history occasionally overlooked in today's craft beer narrative, which specifically counterpoints the dismal state of U.S. brewing in the 1970s and 80s. While there were indeed only eight (eight!) craft breweries in America in 1980, there were over 1,700 breweries making beer here in the early 1900s, and even more before then. While much of our brewing history has been lost or forgotten in the time since, much remains, and I'd recommend Maureen Ogle's Ambitious Brew: The Story of American Beer for anyone interested in following the history back even further.

Steam beer, as it was called, was a popular style of beer in California in the late 1800s, particularly around San Francisco. There remains some historical uncertainty regarding the origin of the name—whether from the highly effervescent nature of the style (such that over-pressurized kegs would need to let off some "steam"), or from the large quantities of steam that resulted from transferring recently boiled wort into shallow troughs to cool, or from something else entirely. In the absence of consistent refrigeration, lager yeast was used but at higher-than-normal temperatures, resulting in what's generally regarded as a hybrid style between a lager and an ale. Today, use of the word "steam" in regard to beer is trademarked by Anchor Brewing Company; examples from other breweries are called "California Commons."

First brewed back in 1896, Anchor Steam remains the archetype of the style: orange-amber in color, lightly effervescent (think of it as "steam"), and well balanced between a crackly pale-ale maltiness and a non-citrusy hop character often described as minty or woody. The use of lager yeast at higher temperatures gives it a light fruitiness. While not dissimilar from an American pale ale, it won't have that citrus hop assertiveness and is more of a balanced, crisp style. Lucky Hand Cali Common is another solid local rendering, while numerous other Northern California breweries will occasionally release their own versions of California Common, often (not surprisingly) named with a creative riff on the word "steam."

Currently, Linden Street Brewery in Oakland is doing as much as anyone with traditional "steam beer" techniques in the Bay Area, as their entire lineup is fermented with lager yeast at warmer temperatures. Be sure to check out Urban People's Common Lager, Burning Oak Black Lager, and pretty much anything else they make.

continued to surprise year after year since 1975 (each year's recipe remains a closely kept secret). Did I mention they have a distillery, too?

BREWMASTER: Mark Carpenter
ESTABLISHED: 1896
BE SURE TO TRY: Anchor Steam
SEASONALS: Humming Ale (summer-fall), Christmas Ale (winter)
TOURS: Two tours each weekday, by reservation only.
ELSEWHERE: Bottles, Draft

9 Speakeasy Ales & Lagers ⭐
Brewery

WWW.GOODBEER.COM

1195 Evans Ave., San Francisco, CA 94124, (415) 642-3371—Close to India Basin and Hunters Point in southeast San Francisco, near the corner of Keith St. and Evans Ave.

OPEN F: 4 p.m.–9p.m., Sa: 1 p.m.–6 p.m. (likely to change—check web site)

While Speakeasy kept limited weekly hours for much of 2011, they're planning to have an expanded taproom in 2012. Their standard bottled lineup includes some pretty magnificent things like Prohibition Ale (a textbook cola- and caramel-tinged amber ale) and Payback Porter, but visiting the brewery allows access to limited-release beers you're not likely to find anywhere else. We ordered cups of the Vendetta IPA (developed with Craig of City Beer Store), which showed juicy orange notes and perfectly integrated grapefruit and piney hop bitterness; look for it as a seasonal bottle

release in 2012. Same goes for Sutro Stout, made with TCHO cocoa nibs, which offers coffee notes and seemingly endless layers of milk chocolate.

HEAD OF BREWING OPS: Kushal Hall
ESTABLISHED: 1997
BE SURE TO TRY: Prohibition Ale
SEASONALS: Vendetta IPA (spring)
ELSEWHERE: Bottles, Draft

⑩ Almanac Beer Co.
Brewery

WWW.ALMANACBEER.COM

San Francisco, CA

Jesse and Damian are producing some of the most interesting and challenging brews coming out of the Bay Area, highlighting locally grown fruit in their seasonal releases. Their initial offering, Summer 2010, included Sonoma County blackberries and was aged for eleven months in red wine barrels, giving a Belgian-style ale with pronounced white pepper and toasted barrel notes, plus an undercurrent of darker fruits. Their follow-up release, Autumn 2011 Farmhouse Pale, was made with organic San Joaquin Valley plums and showed a softer yeast character, husky wheat, and raisiny notes. Each release is unique and crafted to be paired with food. Look for their beers in San Francisco and at select spots around the Bay Area.

> BREWERS: Jesse Friedman, Damian Fagan
> ESTABLISHED: 2010
> BE SURE TO TRY: Autumn 2011 Farmhouse Pale
> ELSEWHERE: Bottles, Draft

⑪ MateVeza
Brewery

WWW.MATEVEZA.COM

San Francisco, CA

MateVeza produces beer using organic yerba maté, the leaves of a South American plant generally used in tea making. Their India Pale Ale pairs yerba maté with a significant dose of American hops, while the Black Lager switches the focus to darker specialty malts. All of their beers are naturally caffeinated from the yerba maté. Morpho—made with organic hibiscus flowers and bay leaves—was a collaboration beer done with Mill Valley Beerworks, which is where we sampled it. Herbaceous, floral, and firmly textured, the maté contribution was soft and showed no tea-like astringency. Definitely an interesting beer to try.

MateVeza plans to open up a brewpub, Cervecería de MateVeza, in the Mission District in 2012.

> FOUNDER: Jim Woods
> ESTABLISHED: 2006
> BE SURE TO TRY: Morpho
> ELSEWHERE: Bottles, Draft

⑫ Pacific Brewing Laboratories
Brewery

WWW.PACBREWLAB.COM

San Francisco, CA

As much as I enjoyed sampling Pac Brew Lab beer in Patrick and Bryan's garage, their recent transition to professional brewing operations means I'll be able to drink their beers a lot more often. Squid Ink was their first release in late 2011, a robust black IPA with zesty citrusy hops and a cocoa-like center, and this will probably be their most traditional offering. Look for Hibiscus Saison and Crazy Ivan (brewed with beet sugars) in 2012. While Pac Brew Lab's current arrangement puts them closer to the upper end of the nanobrewing categorization (by annual volume), they're planning to expand beyond that soon.

FOUNDERS: Patrick M. Horn,
Bryan Hermannsson
ESTABLISHED: 2011
BE SURE TO TRY: Squid Ink Black IPA
ELSEWHERE: Bottles, Draft

13 Shmaltz Brewing Company
Brewery

WWW.SHMALTZBREWING.COM

San Francisco, CA

While their production brewing
operations are currently centered
in upstate New York, Shmaltz
Brewing got its start in San
Francisco and maintains an active,
engaging presence in the region.
They currently produce two
different brands: HE'BREW: The
Chosen Beer and Coney Island
Craft Lagers. The Coney Island line
is partnered with nonprofit Coney Island
USA, and that sideshow vibe carries
over into much of Shmaltz's commercial
presence, including the 2011 opening
of Coney Island Brewing Company in
Brooklyn: "The World's Smallest Brewery,"
producing one-gallon batches of brew at
a time. Their limited-release beers (with
names like Genesis, Jewbelation, and
Rejewvenator) are particularly worth
checking out. HE'BREW and Coney
Island fans can also look for Jeremy
Cowan's small-business memoir, Craft
Beer Bar Mitzvah.

FOUNDER: Jeremy Cowan
ESTABLISHED: 1996
BE SURE TO TRY: Their limited-release
beers (Jewbelation, Genesis, etc.)
ELSEWHERE: Bottles, Draft

San Francisco Beer Week

Spanning ten glorious days each February,
San Francisco Beer Week (www.sfbeerweek.
org) is an annual celebration of all things
beer in the Bay Area, featuring events at
breweries, craft beer bars, restaurants, bottle
shops, homebrew shops, and even ice cream
parlors. One of the largest of its kind in the
country, it's the sort of week that makes your
normal week seem empty by comparison

and three days too short.

The San Francisco Brewers Guild,
a nonprofit affiliation of local breweries,
organizes the event each year with help
from numerous members of the craft beer
community. Since its debut in 2009, SF Beer
Week has already expanded to include nearly
four hundred events throughout the week,
including beer-and-food pairing dinners,
themed tasting events, collaborative beer
releases, beer-focused cocktail nights, and
hands-on brewing demonstrations—which
is to say nothing of Toronado's longstanding
Barleywine Festival, the Opening Gala, the
release of Russian River's Pliny the Younger
in the weeks beforehand, or Sacramento
Beer Week shortly thereafter. You might
want to start stockpiling vacation days now.

The Northern California Craft Beer Guide

Triple Voodoo Brewing
Brewery

WWW.TRIPLEVOODOOBREWING.COM

San Francisco, CA, (415) 598-8811

Triple Voodoo is a newer addition to San Francisco's craft beer scene, with their first major release being Inception, a potent Belgian IPA hybrid showing peppery Belgian yeast contributions and plenty of zesty hops. Look for their ambitious set of upcoming releases in bottles and on draft throughout the Bay Area.

> BREW MASTER: Yuri Green
> ESTABLISHED: 2010
> BE SURE TO TRY: Inception Belgian Style Ale
> ELSEWHERE: Bottles, Draft

Monterey Deli
Convenience Store

499 Monterey Blvd., San Francisco, CA 94127, (415) 337-8447—Sunnyside neighborhood in south-central SF, at the corner of Edna St. and Monterey Blvd.

OPEN M-F: 7 a.m.–11 p.m.,
Sa-Su: 9 a.m.–10 p.m.

Small corner store in southern San Francisco. Monterey Deli has a modest selection and featured Almanac, Russian River, Firestone Walker, and BrewDog (including some über-pricey bottles behind the front counter).

Plumpjack Wines
Bottle Shop

WWW.PLUMPJACKWINES.COM

4011 24th St., San Francisco, CA 94114, (415) 282-3841—Noe Valley neighborhood, near the corner of Noe St. and 24th St.

OPEN M-Th: 11 a.m.–8 p.m., F-Sa: 11 a.m.–9 p.m., Su: noon–6 p.m.

While the overall focus at Plumpjack is obviously wine, the Noe Valley location offers a small selection of top-tier bottles: Midnight Sun, Jolly Pumpkin, Fantôme, Russian River, etc. More singles than six-packs.

Pi Bar
Beer Bar

WWW.PIBARSF.COM

1432 Valencia St., San Francisco, CA 94110, (415) 970-9670—A short walk from the 24th St. Mission BART station. Mission District, near the corner of 25th St. and Valencia St.

OPEN Every day: 3:14 p.m.–midnight

As someone who memorized way too many digits of pi as a child, I'm inclined to have a slight bias here. But their thin-crust pizza's excellent (the large was huge), and they've got twelve stellar, craft-only taps, along with a very descriptive, page-per-beer bottle menu that angles toward Belgian and sour beers.

18 Rosamunde Sausage Grill
Restaurant/Beer Bar

WWW.ROSAMUNDESAUSAGEGRILL.COM

2832 Mission St., San Francisco, CA 94110, (415) 970-9015—A short walk from the 24th St. Mission BART station. Mission District, near the corner of 24th St. and Mission St.

OPEN M: 11:30 a.m.–11 p.m., Tu-F: 11:30 a.m.–midnight, Sa: 10 a.m.–midnight, Su: 10 a.m.–11 p.m.

Craft beer lovers are probably more familiar with the original Rosamunde location, which is right next to Toronado. If you're drinking there and wondering where most people's food came from, now you know. The first location focuses solely on delicious sausages, but this one adds twenty-plus taps and a selection of bottles.

19 Shotwell's
Beer Bar

WWW.SHOTWELLSBAR.COM

3349 20th St., San Francisco, CA 94110, (415) 648-4104—Between 16th St. Mission and 24th St. Mission BART stations. Mission District, at the corner of Shotwell St. and 20th St.

OPEN M-Sa: 4:30 p.m.–2 a.m., Su: 4 p.m.–1 a.m.

Dark, cozy corner bar with a friendly pub atmosphere. Shotwell's has about a dozen taps and upward of thirty bottles, heavily

focused on Northern California and Belgian-style beers. Pool table, pinball, cash only.

20 The Sycamore
Beer Bar

WWW.THESYCAMORESF.COM

2140 Mission St., San Francisco, CA 94110, (415) 252-7704—A short walk from the 16th St. Mission BART station. Mission District, at the corner of Sycamore St. and Mission St.

OPEN Every day: 11:30 a.m.–midnight

Neighborhood bar in the Mission offering sandwiches, sliders, weekend brunch, and a focused craft beer selection. Within reasonable walking distance of Gestalt Haus, Monk's Kettle, and Shotwell's.

21 The Monk's Kettle
Beer Bar/Restaurant

WWW.MONKSKETTLE.COM

3141 16th St., San Francisco, CA 94103, (415) 865-9523—A short walk from the 16th St. Mission BART station. Mission District, near the corner of Albion St. and 16th St.

OPEN Every day: noon–2 a.m.

A very cozy bistro and beer bar renowned for its farm-to-table menu and popular beer-pairing dinners. This place fills up—seriously. Phenomenal selection of California and Belgian beers, comparable to La Trappe but with harder-to-find beers and significantly less space. They offer both horizontal (all same style) and vertical (same beer, different vintages) flights, and a very knowledgeable, friendly staff that pretty impressively handles the space constraints. One of the best spots for beer in San Francisco, though most certainly on the pricier side. They offer a challenging, non-traditional collection of wines as well.

㉒ Gestalt Haus
Beer Bar

WWW.GESTALTSF.COM

3159 16th St., San Francisco, CA 94103, (415) 655-9935—A short walk from the 16th St. Mission BART station. Mission District, near the corner of Guerrero St. and 16th St.

OPEN Every day: 11:30 a.m.–2 a.m.

"Beer, Brats and Bikes." A comfortable neighborhood bar with twenty taps highlighting German and Bay Area beers, a limited food menu (sausages, sandwiches, etc.), and the option to park one's bicycle indoors.

㉓ Zeitgeist
Beer Bar

WWW.ZEITGEISTSF.COM

199 Valencia St., San Francisco, CA 94103, (415) 255-7505—A short walk from the 16th St. Mission BART station. At the corner of Duboce Ave. and Valencia St.

OPEN Every day: 9 a.m.–2 a.m.

Craft-focused beer bar with a punk vibe somewhat similar to Toronado, albeit with more room, fewer rarities, and a huge outdoor patio (long benches, scattered trees, Franziskaner umbrellas). Cash only. The sizable tap list has red and blue markers to distinguish the Bay Area and German beers. A fun, low-key neighborhood bar.

24 Starbelly
Restaurant

WWW.STARBELLYSF.COM

3583 16th St., San Francisco, CA 94114, (415) 252-7500—Close to Corona Heights Park in central SF, near the corner of Market St. and 16th St.

OPEN M–Th: 11:30 a.m.–11 p.m., F: 11:30 a.m.–midnight, Sa: 10:30 a.m.–midnight, Su: 10:30 a.m.–11 p.m.

Rich Higgins (Brewmaster at Social Kitchen and one of a very small number of Master Cicerones in the country, trained in the art of beer and food pairing) is responsible for the beer menus at both Starbelly and Delarosa, and both offer endearing lineups of diverse, food-friendly brews. Sip a small pour of something from the East Bay while perusing Starbelly's casual California-minded menu.

Biergarten

25 Healthy Spirits
Bottle Shop

HEALTHY-SPIRITS.BLOGSPOT.COM

2299 15th St., San Francisco, CA 94114, (415) 255-0610—Close to Corona Heights Park in central SF, near the corner of Castro St. and 15th St.

OPEN M–Th: 10 a.m.–10 p.m., F: 10 a.m.–11 p.m., Sa: 11 a.m.–11 p.m., Su: 11 a.m.–9 p.m.

One of the three main bottle shops in San Francisco, along with City Beer and Ales Unlimited. Hands-on service, beer-fluent staff, and over seven hundred bottles in stock. Healthy Spirits gets basically everything cool that makes it into the city, and they're right on top of things with the latest coveted beer releases. Their Beer of the Month Club, featuring three to six beers monthly, is well curated and supplemented by their head beer buyer's cellar reports, letting folks know how previously featured bottles are aging. They also have a selection of 150+ bourbons.

26 Biergarten
Beer Garden

WWW.BIERGARTENSF.COM

424 Octavia St., San Francisco, CA
94102—Close to Patricia's Green, just
east of Hayes Valley Playground, near the
corner of Fell St. and Octavia St.

OPEN W-Su: 2 p.m.–8 p.m. (check web
site—varies by season and weather)

Brought to you by Suppenküche (just
a few blocks away), Biergarten is a very
recent addition to the San Francisco
beer scene. This industrial beer garden
overlooks Patricia's Green in an endearing
neighborhood of specialty stores and
restaurants. Serving half and full liters of
traditional German beer, it's a fun place to
meet up with friends, enjoy the open air,
and munch some German-inclined food
(pretzels, sausages, pickles) at Biergarten's
communal tables. Shopping goes so much
more smoothly after a liter of beer.

27 Suppenküche ★
Restaurant/Beer Bar

WWW.SUPPENKUCHE.COM

525 Laguna St., San Francisco, CA 94102,
(415) 252-9289—Between Hayes Valley
Playground and Patricia's Green, near the
corner of Hayes St. and Laguna St.

OPEN M-Sa: 5 p.m.–10 p.m., Su: 10 a.m.–
2:30 p.m., 5 p.m.–10 p.m.

While there are a number of other

German restaurants in San Francisco
(including Leopold's, Schmidt's, Walzwerk,
and the eldest, Schroeder's), the beer
selection and expertise at Suppenküche is
unmatched. Their significant beer menu
is organized by style and emphasizes
the diversity of German brewing: Bock,
Hefeweizen, Helles, Pilsener, Schwarzbier,
etc. They offer a selection of Belgian ales
as well. The interior minimalist design
(light walls, stencil work, whimsical ceiling
art) accents the attention to detail, and
the food here is highly regarded: there's
usually a line outside every Saturday
waiting for them to open. This is the
best spot we've found for limited-release
German seasonals from Weihenstephaner
and Schlenkerla. Suppenküche also
operates the open-air Biergarten just a
few blocks away.

28 Toronado ★
Beer Bar

WWW.TORONADO.COM

547 Haight St., San Francisco, CA 94117,
(415) 863-2276—Lower Haight, on
Haight St. between Steiner St.
and Fillmore St.

OPEN Every day: 11:30 a.m.–2 a.m.

Along with Anchor Brewing, Toronado
is one of San Francisco's most firmly
established beer institutions. Toronado
owner David "Big Daddy" Keene has
been one of the most formative influences
on the region's craft beer scene for over
twenty years, and I don't think one can
overstate Toronado's role in supporting
burgeoning Northern California craft

breweries in those earliest days. The number of tribute beers made in honor of David and Toronado is mind-boggling and puts things into perspective (Speakeasy Big Daddy, Pizza Port 547 Haight, Anderson Valley Brother David's Double, Russian River Toronado 20th Anniversary, Lost Abbey Cable Car, and so on). There's little argument that Toronado consistently ranks as one of the very best craft beer bars in the country. In addition to upward of fifty taps featuring plenty of limited-release brews, their bottle menu regularly has things you just won't see available anywhere else. How they do this remains one of life's tasty mysteries.

Bring cash. Know what you want to order before you get the bartender's attention. Stop by Rosamunde Sausage Grill next door. Stare in awe at decades of Anchor Christmas Ale tap handles. Ditto their lineup of dusty Belgian magnums. And don't miss Toronado's annual Barleywine Festival, held each February.

29 New Star-Ell Liquor

Convenience Store

WWW.NEWSTARELL.COM

501 Divisadero St., San Francisco, CA 94117, (415) 567-7900—Near the Panhandle in central SF, at the corner of Fell St. and Divisadero St.

OPEN Every day: 9 a.m.–1:45 a.m.

It looks like a typical convenience store, but New Star-Ell Liquor has thirteen coolers of great beer conquering most of the back of the store, including a thorough selection of Belgian and Northern California singles.

30 Bar Crudo

Restaurant

WWW.BARCRUDO.COM

655 Divisadero St., San Francisco, CA 94117, (415) 409-0679—One block west of Alamo Square in central SF, near the corner of Grove St. and Divisadero St.

OPEN Tu-Sa: 5 p.m.–11 p.m., Su: 5 p.m.–10 p.m.

A "modern raw bar" featuring fresh seafood and a solid accompanying craft beer selection. Half a dozen well-chosen taps, plus a bottle menu of about fifty entries broken into thoughtful, pairing-minded categories like "Floral, Fruity, Spice" and "Sour, Acid, Fruit." Nothing particularly difficult to find beer-wise, but excellent choices.

31 Magnolia Gastropub & Brewery
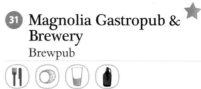
Brewpub

WWW.MAGNOLIAPUB.COM

1398 Haight St., San Francisco, CA 94117, (415) 864-7468—Haight-Ashbury District, at the corner of Masonic Ave. and Haight St.

OPEN M-Th: 11 a.m.–midnight, F: 11 a.m.–1 a.m., Sa: 10 a.m.–1 a.m., Su: 10 a.m.–midnight

Less than a mile down Haight Street from Toronado, Magnolia Gastropub & Brewery is one of the major brewing landmarks in San Francisco. The brewpub's focus tends to be English styles (milds, bitters, expertly conditioned cask ales, etc.), but they also venture well beyond that territory. Their German-influenced Kalifornia Kolsch and Belgian-style Deep Elem Dubbel, for instance, were both exceptional. The English styles are where they shine, though; the only other brewery in Northern California that comes to mind for similar excellence is Dying Vines in East Bay. Magnolia took a silver and bronze medal in the Ordinary/Special Bitter category at the Great American Beer Festival in 2011, and the Bonnie Lee's Bitter (earning bronze) is just beautiful, with soft caramel and butterscotch notes, a perimeter of English hop bitterness, and a lasting toasty finish. Huge amounts of flavor for a 4.1%-ABV beer. Their best-selling Proving Ground IPA is an excellent English-style IPA, while their cask-conditioned Winter Warmer, with its vinous red fruitiness, slight warmth, and light carbonation, is

The Northern California Craft Beer Guide

Anchor Brewery Tour

I would say that the Anchor tour should be on every beer lover's agenda when visiting San Francisco, but apparently it already is. The tour of Anchor Brewery often books up months in advance. Plan well ahead.

This is one of the best tour experiences we've ever been on: charismatic guides, beautiful setting, a well-organized operation, and a tour program that's particularly inclusive in terms of appealing to a wide range of beer lovers, from first-time samplers to, well…people writing books about the subject. There's no better place to learn about the origins of the craft beer movement, hear about the different theories on where the term "steam beer" came from, or just see a beautiful and historic brewing facility creating some absolutely top-shelf beers, which you get to sample after the tour. Be sure to check out the large-format bottle of Anchor Steam with its name replaced by that of immortal beer hunter Michael Jackson. The whole building's a showcase of craft beer memorabilia.

exactly what we want in cool weather. In the event you happen to be visiting at a particularly busy time, Magnolia does have a few off-site draft accounts. Alembic (no listing) is just down the street, and had four Magnolia beers on tap when we last checked.

BREWERS: Dave McLean (Brewmaster), Ben Spencer (Head Brewer)
ESTABLISHED: 1997
BE SURE TO TRY: Bonnie Lee's Best Bitter
SEASONALS: Strong Beer Month beers (February), Winter Warmer (fall-winter)
ELSEWHERE: Draft

32 Social Kitchen & Brewery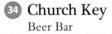
Brewpub

WWW.SOCIALKITCHENANDBREWERY.COM

1326 Ninth Ave., San Francisco, CA 94122, (415) 681-0330—Sunset District, a block and a half south of Golden Gate Park, near the corner of Ninth Ave. and Irving St.

OPEN M-Th: 5 p.m.–midnight, F: 5 p.m.–2 a.m., Sa: 11:30 a.m.–2 a.m., Su: 11:30 a.m.–midnight

This was an ideal stop for us: delicious food, attentive staff, and a great selection of Belgian-style brews (plus a bready and crackery Kölsch thrown in for good measure). The "cuisine a la bière" approach here is evident in the food-friendly offerings, particularly the Kölsch and the 4.4% L'Enfant Terrible, a Belgian-style "table beer." The latter is fluffy, fruity, and light enough in alcohol not to skew the conversation. In addition to two solid, peppery seasonals on the menu, the Rapscallion was our favorite of the lineup: its yeast character of white pepper and toast precisely mingled with a soft, dried-fruit sweetness. Social Kitchen is a short walk from Golden Gate Park, which may be a better parking option depending on the time of day. The limited parking spots surrounding the brewpub can fill up pretty quickly.

BREWMASTER: Rich Higgins
ESTABLISHED: 2010
BE SURE TO TRY: Rapscallion
LAST-MINUTE UPDATE: Rich Higgins departing in early 2012.

33 Amsterdam Cafe
Beer Bar

WWW.AMSTERDAMCAFESF.COM

937 Geary St., San Francisco, CA 94109, (415) 409-1111—Tenderloin neighborhood, on Geary St. between Polk St. and Larkin St.

OPEN M-Sa: 10 a.m.–2 a.m., Su: 11 a.m.–2 a.m.

This craft beer bar in the Tenderloin neighborhood features a wide range of bottles from California and beyond. While the in-house menu is limited, imbibers are welcome to bring in food from elsewhere.

34 Church Key
Beer Bar

1402 Grant Ave., San Francisco, CA 94133—Just southeast of Washington

ocial Kitchen & Brewery

Square off Columbus Ave., near the corner of Green St. and Grant Ave.

OPEN Every day: 5 p.m.–2 a.m.

The southernmost stop in a series of beer bars along Columbus Ave., Church Key is a more subdued and modestly priced alternative to La Trappe. Features ten thoughtful taps, plus a bottle menu highlighting American and Belgian styles that include some limited-release, barrel-aged beers from Marin and North Coast.

35 Rogue Ales Public House
Beer Bar

WWW.ROGUE.COM

673 Union St., San Francisco, CA 94133,

Social Kitchen & Brewery

(415) 362-7880—Close to Washington Square, near the intersections of Columbus Ave., Powell St., and Union St.

OPEN Su-Th: noon–midnight, F-Sa: noon–2 a.m.

Despite the power of suggestion, there's no brewing happening here; all the Rogue beer is coming down from Oregon. The Public House has thirty-five-plus taps, half of them an excellent selection of Rogue offerings and the other half a nice bunch of Northern California beers, including some limited releases. Loads of Rogue bottles for purchase, and they can do growlers of the Rogue taps. Coit Liquor (no listing) is right around the corner.

The Northern California Craft Beer Guide

BAY AREA
BEER
BLOGGERS

Bay Area Beer Bloggers

In putting together any sort of semi-comprehensive beer guide, it becomes immediately apparent that certain elements of craft beer culture (smaller-scale events, new beer releases, time-sensitive brewery news, etc.) simply don't fit. What you really need is a small army of enthusiastic beer-loving individuals spread throughout the Bay Area, each contributing their own unique take on news in the craft beer world, perhaps even blogging about it...you've probably noticed the logo by now.

The Bay Area Beer Bloggers group began in 2008 and has since grown to include approximately fifty area beer bloggers covering a wide variety of topics. Particularly vital blogs to the local beer culture include (but are by no means limited to) Beer 47, Beer By BART, Better Beer Blog, Brewed For Thought, and Jay Brooks' Brookston Beer Bulletin. Personally, I'm a fan of the eccentric, mustache-minded Ünnecessary Ümlaut. Jay Brooks is deservedly one of the most highly regarded print beer writers in the region, and—in addition to serving as a manager of the Bay Area Beer Bloggers group—currently writes the syndicated column "Brooks on Beer," serves as media director for San Francisco Beer Week, and is an all-around kickass dad. A full list of BABB members can be found at Jay's web site (www.brookstonbeerbulletin.com/babb/). John Heylin (NorCal Beer Guide) also manages the group.

Perhaps the most comprehensive coverage of the Bay Area craft beer scene, though, is coming from Bay Area Craft Beer (www.bayareacraftbeer.com), a recently begun cooperative blog featuring a number of talented writers. Brian Stechschulte serves as the web site's editor as well as a frequent contributor, and (in addition to running a tight ship) he's one of the most talented beer-minded photographers out there. Their site offers regularly updated beer news and brewery profiles, plus a calendar of upcoming events.

---

36 La Trappe Cafe ★
Beer Bar/Restaurant

🍴

WWW.LATRAPPECAFE.COM

800 Greenwich St., San Francisco, CA 94133, (415) 440-8727—North Beach neighborhood, near the intersections of Mason St., Greenwich St., and Columbus Ave.

OPEN Tu-W: 6 p.m.–11 p.m.+, Th-Sa: 5 p.m.–11 p.m.+

Strongly Belgian-focused beer bar that definitely caters to the beer-geek crowd; its offerings included multiple sours and special releases the last time I visited. Attractive downstairs bar and dining area. Knowledgeable staff. Proper glassware. Most importantly: an enormous bottle menu, organized alphabetically and by style.

37 Kennedy's Irish Pub & Indian Curry House Restaurant
Beer Bar/Restaurant

🍴 🥛 🍾

WWW.KENNEDYSCURRY.COM

1040 Columbus Ave., San Francisco, CA 94133, (415) 441-8855—Just south of Fisherman's Wharf, directly off Columbus Ave. between Francisco St. and Chestnut St.

OPEN Daily: 10:30 a.m.–1 a.m.+

As the name suggests, an Irish-inclined pub attached to a curry house. My first time drinking El Toro Poppy Jasper was over a bowl of bhelpuri, and it all seemed kind of magical. About fifty taps, 130+ bottles. A good mixture of Belgian-focused taps, Irish pub regulars, and specialty California and Oregon beers.

Jack's Cannery Bar
Beer Bar/Restaurant

2801 Leavenworth St., San Francisco, CA 94133, (415) 931-6400—In The Cannery near Fisherman's Wharf, near the corner of Jefferson St. and Leavenworth St.

OPEN Every day: 6 a.m.–midnight

Inside The Cannery (the historic site of Del Monte's Plant No. 1), Jack's offers dozens of craft beer taps, including upward of six or seven dedicated to Anchor brews. Something of a hybrid between a storied pub and a bank hall, particularly the dining section. The second bar in the back focuses on Belgian styles.

39 Beer 39
Beer Bar

Pier 39, The Embarcadero, San Francisco, CA 94133, (415) 421-2913—On the second-floor shopping level of Pier 39 along The Embarcadero.

OPEN M–F: 11 a.m.–9:30 p.m., Sa–Su: 11 a.m.–10 p.m.

Newly opened in 2011, Beer 39 is basically a tourist-angled tasting bar on Pier 39 offering a dozen taps, two dozen bottles, and a wide range of beer-centric merchandise. They had Speakeasy and Anchor gear when I stopped by, a nice range of Northern California brews, and a variety of (rare!) neon signs and brewery paraphernalia.

40 The Jug Shop
Bottle Shop

WWW.THEJUGSHOP.COM

1590 Pacific Ave., San Francisco, CA 94109, (415) 885-2922—Nob Hill neighborhood, near the corner of Polk St. and Pacific Ave.

OPEN M–Sa: 9 a.m.–9 p.m., Su: 10 a.m.–7 p.m.

The Jug Shop hosts some fun ticketed beer tastings throughout the year and offers upward of a few hundred bottles, including some less-common Italian, Danish, and German beers. The focus is on singles and top-shelf offerings, though the selection isn't as filled out or as organized as the main bottle shop Beer Destinations in San Francisco. Their free parking lot is a major plus.

41 Ales Unlimited
Bottle Shop

WWW.ALESUNLIMITED.COM

2398 Webster St., San Francisco, CA 94115, (415) 346-6849—North-central SF, between Alta Plaza Park and Lafayette

Ales Unlimited

Park, near the corner of Jackson St. and Webster St.

OPEN M–Th: 9 a.m.–10:30 p.m., F–Sa: 9 a.m.–midnight, Su: 9 a.m.–7 p.m.

42 Delarosa
Restaurant

WWW.DELAROSASF.COM

2175 Chestnut St., San Francisco, CA 94123, (415) 673-7100—Marina District, near the corner of Pierce St. and Chestnut St.

OPEN Every day: 11:30 a.m.–1 a.m.

Casual Roman-style pizza and pasta eatery with an engaging beer menu. Their fifteen taps had some harder-to-find Bay Area breweries (Linden Street, Dying Vines), and the eclectic bottle menu has something for everybody. A block from The Tipsy Pig, the beer menu here seemed more interesting to us.

43 The Tipsy Pig
Restaurant/Beer Bar

WWW.THETIPSYPIGSF.COM

2231 Chestnut St., San Francisco, CA 94123, (415) 292-2300—Marina District, near the corner of Pierce St. and Chestnut St.

OPEN M–Tu: 5 p.m.–2 a.m., W–F: 11:30 a.m.–2 a.m., Sa–Su: 11 a.m.–2 a.m.

A well-regarded "American Gastrotavern" in the Marina District, The Tipsy Pig offers sustainably sourced comfort food, sweet digs, and solid craft beer options. Definitely check out their smoked bacon mac n' cheese.

44 San Francisco Brewcraft
Homebrew Shop

WWW.SANFRANCISCOBREWCRAFT.COM

1555 Clement St., San Francisco, CA
94118, (415) 751-9338/(800) 513-5196—
Five blocks north of Golden Gate Park, at
the corner of 17th Ave. and Clement St.

OPEN Su-W: noon–6 p.m., Th-F: noon–
8 p.m., Sa: 10 a.m.–6 p.m.

The main stop for homebrew supplies in
San Francisco, this shop has apparently
been in business since 1978. They
offer regular homebrewing classes, plus
equipment and supplies for making beer,
wine, soda, and more.

45 Blackwell's Wines & Spirits
Bottle Shop

WWW.BLACKWELLSWINES.COM

5620 Geary Blvd., San Francisco, CA
94121, (415) 386-9463—Richmond
District, four blocks north of Golden
Gate Park, on Geary Blvd. between 20th
and 21st Ave.

OPEN M-Sa: 10:30 a.m.–9 p.m., Su:
noon–6 p.m.

While generally wine-focused, Blackwell's
has an admirable selection from U.S. and
international breweries alike. Predominantly
larger-format singles (bombers and 750-
mL bottles), highlights included a variety
of Lost Abbey, Ninkasi, The Bruery, and
Hair of the Dog selections. This bottle shop
can also ship beer.

46 The Beach Chalet Brewery & Restaurant
Brewpub

WWW.BEACHCHALET.COM

1000 Great Highway, San Francisco, CA
94121, (415) 386-8439—Right along
the water in northwestern SF, directly off
Great Hwy.

OPEN M-Th: 9 a.m.–11 p.m., F: 9 a.m.–
midnight, Sa: 8 a.m.–midnight, Su:
8 a.m.–11 p.m.

Located above the historic Golden Gate
Park Visitor's Center, Beach Chalet likely
holds the best brewpub view in all of
Northern California (Half Moon Bay
and Gold Hill are the only places that
could compete). Their standard lineup is
of varying quality, with the Fleishhacker
Stout being their most precise, showing
robust roasted and milk chocolate notes.
Their seasonal Rip Curl Imperial Red
was outstanding, probably the best
beer I've ever had from Beach Chalet,
weighing in at 7.5% and offering chewy
caramel and red fruits with perfectly
matched surrounding bitterness. You'll
occasionally see Beach Chalet kegs and
bottles at venues outside the pub.

BREWMASTER: Aron Deorsey
ESTABLISHED: 1997
BE SURE TO TRY: Fleishhacker Stout
SEASONALS: Rip Curl Imperial Red
(occasional)
ELSEWHERE: Bottles, Draft

The North Bay and Wine Country region consists of three counties just north of San Francisco: Sonoma, Napa, and Marin. This is our home turf, and one of the world's most exciting regions for innovative craft beer. Ali grew up in Marin, and when we had the option of relocating basically anywhere in the country, we chose Sonoma County.

We didn't move here for the wine.

That said, we can't complain…and should you somehow feel the need for another alcohol option, I hear there are some vineyards around here somewhere. (A shout-out to our friends at Meeker and Chateau St. Jean, who we doubt would argue with the aphorism that it takes a lot of great beer to make great wine.) Whether exploring the endless nooks of Point Reyes National Seashore and Bodega Bay, walking around Sausalito and Mill Valley, or just looking for a great spot for sunset snapshots of the Golden Gate Bridge, North Bay wholly encourages the laidback enjoyment of life. I'm pretty sure we're starting to get the hang of it.

For beer-loving folks coming from near and far, North Bay has Beer Destinations like Russian River, Napa Smith, Marin, Moylan's, Moonlight, Lagunitas, and Bear Republic, plus a bunch of other top-notch breweries worthy of one's most focused attention. We have taprooms inside our grocery stores. Even grocery stores without their own listings—Andy's, Oliver's, Paradise Foods, to name a few—stock great brews. We host weekly beer events like we were born to. We cook with beer, we write about beer, we run major international beer web sites. We have superb lagers and sour ales and hoppy beers and—somehow—we make it all look easy. Come visit.

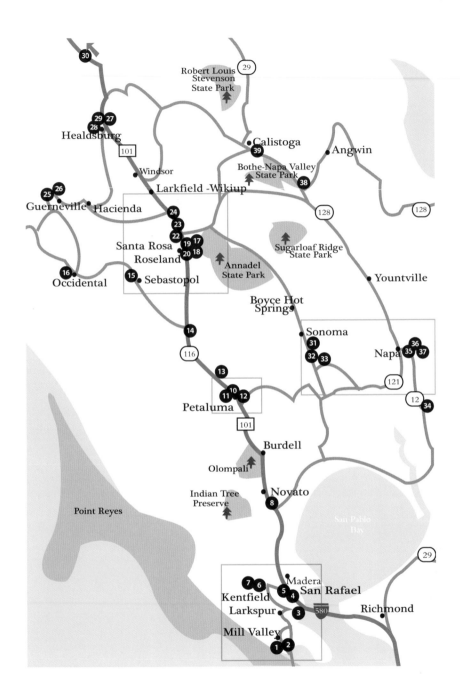

5 to try

Bear Republic Racer 5 Iron Springs Kent Lake Kolsch Moonlight Lunatic Lager
Napa Smith Organic IPA Russian River Supplication

1. Mill Valley Beerworks – Mill Valley   Brewpub
2. Mill Valley Market – Mill Valley   Grocery Store/Bottle Shop
3. Marin Brewing Co. – Larkspur   Brewpub
4. Pizza Orgasmica & Brewing Co. – San Rafael   Brewpub
5. Broken Drum Brewery & Wood Grill – San Rafael   Brewpub
6. Iron Springs Pub and Brewery – Fairfax   Brewpub
7. Gestalt Haus – Fairfax   Beer Bar
8. Moylan's Brewery and Restaurant – Novato   Brewpub
9. Lucky Hand Brewing Company – Novato   Brewery
10. TAPS – Petaluma   Beer Bar/Restaurant
11. Petaluma Market – Petaluma   Grocery Store
12. Dempsey's Restaurant & Brewery – Petaluma   Brewpub
13. Lagunitas Brewing Company – Petaluma   Brewpub

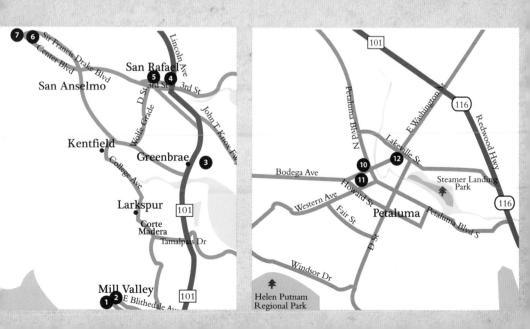

uncharted territory

8-Bit Brewing Company (Sebastopol) Beltane Brewing Beer Cafe and Brewery (Novato) Carnero
Old Redwood Brewing Company (Windsor) Petaluma Hills Brewing Company (Petaluma)

(14) Bubble Berri Home Brew and Smoke Shop – Cotati   Homebrew Shop

(15) Hopmonk Tavern – Sebastopol   Restaurant/Beer Bar

(16) Barley and Hops Tavern – Occidental   Restaurant

(17) Russian River Brewing Company – Santa Rosa   Brewpub

(18) Flavor Bistro – Santa Rosa   Restaurant

(19) Third Street Aleworks Restaurant & Brewery – Santa Rosa   Brewpub

(20) The Toad in the Hole – Santa Rosa   Beer Bar

(21) Moonlight Brewing Company – Santa Rosa   Brewery

(22) The Tap Room at Whole Foods Market – Santa Rosa   Beer Bar/
Grocery Store/Homebrew Shop

(23) The Beverage People – Santa Rosa   Homebrew Shop

(24) Bottle Barn – Santa Rosa   Bottle Shop

(25) Rio Nido Roadhouse – Rio Nido   Beer Bar/Restaurant/Roadhouse

(26) Stumptown Brewery – Guerneville   Brewpub

(27) The Wurst: Sausage Grill & Beer Garden – Healdsburg   Restaurant

(28) Bear Republic Brewing Co. – Healdsburg   Brewpub

(29) Healdsburg Beer Company – Healdsburg   Nanobrewery

(30) Ruth McGowan's Brewpub – Cloverdale   Brewpub

Brewing Company (Sonoma) Divine Brewing (Sonoma) HenHouse Brewing Company (Petaluma) Tavern McHugh's (Guerneville) Van Houten Brewing Co. (San Anselmo)

31 Olde Sonoma Public House – Sonoma   Beer Bar

32 Sonoma Springs Brewing Co. – Sonoma   Brewery

33 Hopmonk Tavern – Sonoma   Restaurant/Beer Bar

34 Napa Smith Brewery – Napa   Brewery

35 Billco's Billiards and Darts – Napa   Beer Bar/Pool Hall

36 Downtown Joe's Brewery and Restaurant – Napa   Brewpub

37 JV Wine & Spirits – Napa   Bottle Shop

38 Silverado Brewing Company – St. Helena   Brewpub

39 Napa Valley Brewing Co./Calistoga Inn – Calistoga   Brewpub

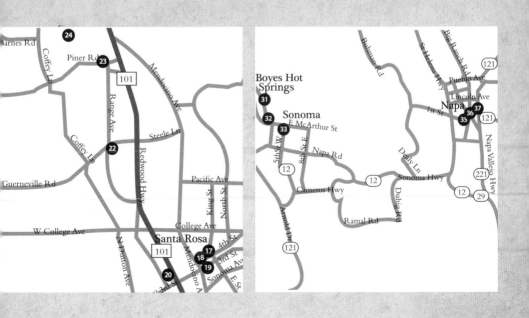

❶ Mill Valley Beerworks
Brewpub

WWW.MILLVALLEYBEERWORKS.COM

173 Throckmorton Ave., Mill Valley, CA 94941 (415) 888-8218—GOING N: 101 Exit 447 (Hwy 131/Tiburon Blvd./E Blithedale Ave.), L@ Tiburon Blvd. (2.0), L@ Throckmorton Ave. GOING S: 101 Exit 447 (E Blithedale Ave.), R@ E Blithedale Ave. (1.8), L@ Throckmorton Ave.

OPEN Every day: 11 a.m.–midnight

Mill Valley Beerworks was in the process of expanding the last time we checked in, but they're already off to a great start. Their collaboration beer with MateVeza, Morpho (an organic beer made with yerba maté, hibiscus flowers, and bay leaves), was quite nice, showing plenty of herbal and floral notes and a mineral firmness. They also have a fantastic selection of high-end guest bottles that included BrewDog (Scotland), Cascade (Portland), Mikkeller (Denmark), Hitachino (Japan), and Almanac's limited-release beers from San Francisco. They plan to expand to twenty-two taps in 2012, six of which will be pouring their own house-brewed beers.

> BREWERS: Justin and Tyler Catalana
> ESTABLISHED: 2010
> ELSEWHERE: Bottles, Draft

❷ Mill Valley Market
Grocery Store/Bottle Shop

WWW.MILLVALLEYMARKET.COM

12 Corte Madera Ave., Mill Valley, CA

94941, (415) 388-3222—GOING N: 101 Exit 447 (Hwy 131/Tiburon Blvd./E Blithedale Ave.), L@ Tiburon Blvd. (2.0), L@ Throckmorton Ave., R@ Corte Madera Ave. GOING S: 101 Exit 447 (E Blithedale Ave.), R@ E Blithedale Ave. (1.8), L@ Throckmorton Ave., R@ Corte Madera Ave.

OPEN M-Sa: 7 a.m.–7:30 p.m., Su: 8 a.m.–7 p.m.

The bottle shop section of Mill Valley Market offers about six coolers full of craft beer. The Northern California highlights included various brews from Iron Springs, Lucky Hand, MateVeza, and Russian River, while the small but well-chosen import selection was particularly unique: Rochefort's full lineup, Traquair Jacobite, plus bottles from Panil Barriquée and Abbaye des Rocs (both quite rare in North Bay).

❸ Marin Brewing Co. ⭐
Brewpub

WWW.MARINBREWING.COM

1809 Larkspur Landing Cir., Larkspur, CA 94939, (415) 461-4677—GOING N: 101 Exit 450B (Richmond Bridge, keep right), L@ Larkspur Landing Cir. GOING S: 101 Exit 450B (Sir Francis Drake Blvd., keep left), L@ Sir Francis Drake Blvd., L@ Larkspur Landing Cir.

OPEN Su-Th: 11:30 a.m.–midnight, F-Sa: 11:30 a.m.–1 a.m.

Marin Brewing Co. and Moylan's are both ventures spearheaded by Brendan

Moylan, and both are making delicious brews in Marin county. While Marin Brewing Co. typically has a smaller lineup of draft beers than Moylan's, Marin also tends to produce some really nice limited-release beers that are worth a special trip. Brass Knuckle is one (an amped-up version of their already stellar White Knuckle Double IPA), as well as different treatments of their Old Dipsea Barleywine. This relaxed, well-run brewpub has plenty of Marin merchandise for sale, standard bottles available to go, a "Barrel-O-Meter" tallying annual production, and brews like Three Flowers IPA, which earned a gold medal at the 2011 Great American Beer Festival.

BREWERS: Arne Johnson, Brendan Moylan

ESTABLISHED: 1989

BE SURE TO TRY: White Knuckle Double IPA

SEASONALS: Brass Knuckle Imperial IPA (occasional), Old Dipsea Barleywine variations (occasional), Three Flowers IPA (occasional)

ELSEWHERE: Bottles, Draft

④ **Pizza Orgasmica & Brewing Co.**
Brewpub

WWW.PIZZAORGASMICA.COM

812 Fourth St., San Rafael, CA 94901, (415) 457-2337—GOING N: 101 Exit 452 (Central San Rafael), L@ 4th St. GOING S: 101 Exit 452 (Central San Rafael), R@ 4th St.

OPEN Su-Th: 11 a.m.–midnight, F-Sa: 11 a.m.–2 a.m.

The San Rafael location brews the beer for all of the Pizza Orgasmica locations around the Bay Area (four going on five, with a new spot opening near the existing Filmore location in the near future; check their web site). Their beers were decent, if generally tending toward the sweet side, with the IPA being one standout. Its tongue-numbing earthy and citrus bitterness pair well with the majority of their amorously named pizzas.

BREWMASTER: Rev Jackson

ESTABLISHED: 2011

BE SURE TO TRY: IPA

Moylan's Brewery

5 Broken Drum Brewery & Wood Grill

Brewpub

WWW.BROKENDRUM.COM

1132 Fourth St., San Rafael, CA 94901, (415) 456-4677—GOING N: 101 Exit 452 (Central San Rafael), L@ 4th St. (0.5). GOING S: 101 Exit 452 (Central San Rafael), R@ 4th St.

OPEN Every day: 11:30 a.m.–11 p.m.+

Walking distance from Pizza Orgasmica's San Rafael location, Broken Drum Brewery offers a comparable lineup overall: a reasonably wide range of styles, some off-base renditions, and a few popular beers that are quite good. Their best-selling Whamber was the standout: rich caramel, biscuity notes, and red fruit.

BE SURE TO TRY: Whamber

6 Iron Springs Pub and Brewery
Brewpub

WWW.IRONSPRINGSPUB.COM

765 Center Blvd., Fairfax, CA 94930, (415) 485-1005—GOING N: 101 Exit 452 (Central San Rafael), L@ 3rd St., keep straight (3.7). GOING S: 101 Exit 452 (Central San Rafael), R@ 3rd St., keep straight (3.7).

OPEN M-Th: opens at 4 p.m., F-Su: opens at noon

While a bottle of Iron Springs Kent Lake Kolsch (see sidebar) was what most immediately attracted to us to Iron Springs, their lineup is pretty delicious throughout. We've had a couple of misfired seasonals, but it doesn't really matter all that much when there are frequently over a dozen great house-brewed beers on tap. Their Epiphany Ale is a robust, well-hopped amber ale featuring whole-leaf Cascade hops, while the Casey Jones Imperial IPA shows plenty of orangey citrus and soft crystalline sugars. Their JC Flyer IPA is a less-bitter alternative, with more of a grapefruit focus. Honestly, though, I'm not sure anything sounds better than pulling up a stool beneath their Iron Springs Road sign, ordering black bean nachos and pints of the Kolsch (or Czechered Past Pilsner, if it's on), and catching a Niners game.

HEAD BREWER: Christian Alexander Kazakoff

ESTABLISHED: 2004

BE SURE TO TRY: Kent Lake Kolsch

ELSEWHERE: Bottles, Draft

STYLE:
KÖLSCH
IRON SPRINGS KENT LAKE KOLSCH

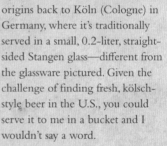

Though we weren't able to make it to the Great American Beer Festival in 2011, I'll admit to doing a little dance at home when I saw Iron Springs win bronze for Kent Lake Kolsch in the Golden/Blonde Category. The kölsch style traces its origins back to Köln (Cologne) in Germany, where it's traditionally served in a small, 0.2-liter, straight-sided Stangen glass—different from the glassware pictured. Given the challenge of finding fresh, kölsch-style beer in the U.S., you could serve it to me in a bucket and I wouldn't say a word.

Iron Springs Kent Lake Kolsch makes one wish the traditional serving size was, in fact, one bucketful. This is a challenging style to brew well, and many American versions tend toward too much sweetness and fruitiness from the yeast. In contrast, Kent Lake Kolsch hits a fantastic drinkability: soft Pilsner malt, light fruitiness, a medium-light body, and some noble-hop bitterness on the perimeter. Lively, refreshing, and a stellar example of what kölsch-style beers bring to the glass. Also check out Sutter Buttes' take on the style.

Gestalt Haus
Beer Bar

WWW.GESTALTHAUSFAIRFAX.COM

28 Bolinas Rd., Fairfax, CA 94930, (415) 721-7895—GOING N: 101 Exit 452 (Central San Rafael), L@ 3rd St., keep straight (4.0), L@ Bolinas Rd. GOING S: 101 Exit 452 (Central San Rafael), R@ 3rd St., keep straight (4.0), L@ Bolinas Rd.

OPEN Su-M: 11:30 a.m.–11 p.m., Tu-W: 11:30 a.m.–midnight, Th-Sa: 11:30 a.m.–2 a.m.

Second location (for details, see main listing: Gestalt Haus – San Francisco on page 41).

8 Moylan's Brewery and Restaurant
Brewpub

WWW.MOYLANS.COM

15 Rowland Way, Novato, CA 94945, (415) 898-4677—GOING N: 101 Exit 462A (Rowland Blvd.), R@ Rowland Blvd., L@ Rowland Way. GOING S: 101 Exit 462A (Rowland Blvd.), L@ Rowland Blvd., L@ Rowland Way.

OPEN M-Th: 11:30 a.m.–midnight, F: 11:30 a.m.–1 a.m., Sa-Su: 11:30 a.m.–midnight

Denise Jones is one of the few female brewers in the region, and she's kicking ass and taking names (though I'm pretty certain this is not how Denise would describe herself). The last time we stopped in we sampled about a dozen brews, and everything was solid, from the Celts Golden Ale (toast, cereal, mineral hops) to the robust Ryan Sullivan's Imperial Stout, showing rich roasted notes and plenty of chocolate. Giants fans have been drinking plenty of their Orange and Black Congrats Ale, which offers brown sugar and molasses notes with a touch of orange zest. Along with the Kilt Lifter, be sure to try the potent Hopsickle Triple IPA (in moderation): a dank, grapefruity giant.

BREWERS: Denise Jones (Brewmaster), Brendan Moylan (Owner)
ESTABLISHED: 1995
BE SURE TO TRY: Hopsickle Triple IPA
SEASONALS: Harvest IPA (fall)
ELSEWHERE: Bottles, Draft

9 Lucky Hand Brewing Co.
Brewery

WWW.IWANTALUCKYHAND.COM

Novato, CA

Lucky Hand currently has two bottled beers available, with distribution predominantly within the Bay Area. Both the Cali Common and Black Lager were solid brews, with the latter offering notes of cocoa, chocolate, restrained roast, and a prominent mineral quality. A tasty dark lager with a dry finish.

HEAD BREWER: Adam Krammer
ESTABLISHED: 2009
BE SURE TO TRY: Cali Common

⑩ TAPS ⭐
Beer Bar/Restaurant

WWW.PETALUMATAPS.COM

205 Kentucky St., Petaluma, CA 94952,
(707) 763-6700—GOING N: 101 Exit 474
(E Washington St./Central Petaluma), L@
E Washington St. (1.3), R@ Kentucky St.
GOING S: 101 Exit 474 (E Washington St./
Central Petaluma), R@ E Washington St.
(1.0), R@ Kentucky St.

OPEN M-Sa: 11:30 a.m.–close, Su:
10 a.m.–11:30 p.m.

I've elsewhere referred to TAPS as the
best beer bar in North Bay, and my
opinion hasn't really changed in the time
since. Eric Lafranchi and company run
a tight ship here, offering weekly pint
nights that feature local breweries with
local beer writer Mario Rubio, who
writes the beer blog Brewed for Thought,
and generally pouring thirty taps of
everything from masterfully brewed
German-style lagers (Hofbräu München
regularly appears) to the newest über-
potent, one-off, barrel-aged California
releases. TAPS offers samplers of their
most popular beers, and both the brews
and their kid-friendly American menu are
reasonably priced.

⑪ Petaluma Market
Grocery Store

WWW.PETALUMAMARKET.COM

210 Western Ave., Petaluma, CA 94952,
(707) 762-5464—GOING N: 101 Exit 472A
(Petaluma Blvd. S) (2.4), L@ Western Ave.

TAPS

GOING S: 101 Exit 474 (E Washington St./
Central Petaluma), R@ E Washington St.
(1.1), L@ Keller St.

OPEN Every day: 7 a.m.–9 p.m.

While they don't offer an enormous
selection, Petaluma Market carries a better
high-end selection than most grocery
stores in the area, including beers from
Russian River, Lost Abbey, Allagash, The
Bruery, and Oskar Blues.

FAIRFAX–NOVATO–PETALUMA

The Northern California Craft Beer Guide

⑫ Dempsey's Restaurant & Brewery
Brewpub

WWW.DEMPSEYS.COM

50 East Washington St., Petaluma, CA 94952, (707) 765-9694—GOING N: 101 Exit 474 (E Washington St./Central Petaluma), L@ E Washington St. (1.1). GOING S: 101 Exit 474 (E Washington St./ Central Petaluma), R@ E Washington St. (0.9).

OPEN Su-Th: 11:30 a.m.–9 p.m., F-Sa: 11:30 a.m.–10 p.m.

Dempsey's Brewery offers lighter-bodied, easy-drinking craft beers, with a patio view that overlooks the waterfront in downtown Petaluma. The Red Rooster Ale is one of the more potent offerings, along with the roasted maltiness of the Ugly Dog Stout. The regulars tend to order their own blends.

BREWMASTER: Peter Burrell
ESTABLISHED: 1991

⑬ Lagunitas Brewing Company ⭐
Brewpub

WWW.LAGUNITAS.COM

1280 N. McDowell Blvd., Petaluma, CA 94954, (707) 769-4495—GOING N: 101 Exit 476 (Old Redwood Hwy/Penngrove), R@ Old Redwood Hwy N, R@ N McDowell Blvd. GOING S: 101 Exit 476 (Petaluma Blvd. N/Penngrove), L@ Old Redwood Hwy N, R@ N McDowell Blvd.

Lagunitas Brewing

OPEN W-F: 2 p.m.–9 p.m., Sa-Su: 11:30 a.m.–8 p.m.

Lagunitas is a heavily hop-centric brewery, from their assertively bitter Pils to their well-handled IPA (see sidebar), to their huge library of hopped-up strong ales: Undercover Investigation Shut-down, Lucky #13, Hop Stoopid, The Hairy Eyeball Ale, etc. They do potent, lingering hop bitterness, and they consistently do it well. Their deviations from this core focus serve as a nice counterpoint. The relatively new Our Own Bavarian-Style DoppelWeizen (made with yeast provided by the Bavarian folks who built their new brew system) is a juicy, no-punches-pulled wheat beer that goes down far too easily for 8.5% ABV. A Little Sumpin' Sumpin' Ale, in contrast to much of their standard lineup, focuses on soft, orange-driven hop flavor. This brewpub offers one of the more comfortable beer-sipping locations in Northern California, and they recently added an outdoor stage to better host live music. Lagunitas has also been hugely generous in its support of local nonprofit and fundraising events (although they generally refrain from tooting their own horn).

HEAD BREWER: Jeremy Marshall
ESTABLISHED: 1993
BE SURE TO TRY: Lagunitas IPA
SEASONALS: Undercover Investigation Shut-down Ale (spring), Brown Shugga' (fall), Olde Gnarly Wine (winter)
TOURS: Available daily. Check web site.
ELSEWHERE: Bottles, Draft

(14) Bubble Berri Home Brew and Smoke Shop
Homebrew Shop

WWW.BUBBLEBERRI.COM

8579 Gravenstein Hwy, Cotati, CA 94931, (707) 792-2259—
GOING N: 101 Exit 481B (Hwy 116 W/Rohnert Park/Sebastopol), R@ Gravenstein Hwy. GOING S: 101 Exit 481 (Gravenstein Hwy/Hwy 116 W/Cotati), L@ Gravenstein Hwy.

INDIA PALE ALE (IPA)
LAGUNITAS IPA

India Pale Ale gets its name from pale ale that was imported to India from England, beginning around the early 1700s, for the benefit of the merchants and troops stationed there. Well-researched historical accounts tend to debunk the notion that IPA was developed specifically for this journey, as a number of different styles were already making the voyage by the time a pale ale reached India. Today, a decent distinction can be made between English and American IPAs, with the former tending to show maltiness to a greater degree (and English hop varieties) and the latter typically focusing on citrusy American hops. It bears remarking that history doesn't technically taste like anything, and IPAs today are delicious hoppy things.

IPAs and pale ales are currently the most popular craft beer styles in the U.S., with IPAs generally distinguished from pale ales by amped-up alcohol levels and a more hop-forward approach. They are frequently 6% ABV or more (above 8% usually puts them into imperial/double IPA territory), and can offer a multitude of different hop flavors and aromas: lemon, grapefruit, orange, tropical fruits, grass, pine, etc. The hugely popular Lagunitas IPA is often just referred to as "IPA" at certain spots in North Bay, and it's a great example of the style. In addition to citrus, I often find a unique and delicious Concord grape note. American IPA is one of the styles Northern California is best known for, and excellent examples can be found from Russian River, High Water, Bear Republic, Loomis Basin, and a number of other local breweries.

PETALUMA–COTATI

The Northern California Craft Beer Guide

OPEN M–Sa: 11 a.m.–8 p.m., Su: 11 a.m.–3 p.m.

Bubble Berri is a very Northern California amalgam of homebrewing and smoking, and offers homebrew supplies, occasional beer-making classes, and some pretty phenomenal pieces of artisanal glassware.

15 Hopmonk Tavern
Restaurant/Beer Bar

WWW.HOPMONK.COM

230 Petaluma Ave., Sebastopol, CA 95472, (707) 829-7300—Directly off Hwy 116/Petaluma Ave. in Sebastopol.

OPEN Su–W: 11:30 a.m.–11 p.m.+, Th–Sa: 11:30 a.m.–midnight+

In addition to being the best place in Sebastopol for live music (check out their event calendar), Hopmonk has an excellent selection of Northern California beers, including a number of delicious German-style house brands brewed by Gordon Biersch. In addition to a significant bottle list, they offer sampler

flights of the Hopmonk-brand beers and (very occasionally) serve cask ale. There's a sweet beer garden out back, and this was definitely our go-to drinking spot when we lived in Sebastopol.

16 Barley and Hops Tavern
Restaurant

WWW.BARLEYNHOPS.COM

3688 Bohemian Hwy, Occidental, CA 95465, (707) 874-9037—About 30 minutes off Hwy 101 (Exit 488B). Head W on Hwy 12 (12.5), R@ Bohemian Hwy (3.7).

OPEN M–Th: 4 p.m.–9:30 p.m., F: 4 p.m.–10 p.m., Sa: 11 a.m.–10 p.m., Su: 11 a.m.–9:30 p.m.

Casual, friendly pub in the heart of Occidental. Barley and Hops offers about ten well-chosen taps, along with an impressively detailed "User Guide" highlighting their bottle selections (chapters include Smooth & Creamy, Hop-tastic, and The Vault). A sweet guide to some great bottles. There's plenty of live music on the weekends, including regular appearances by popular local groups like The Jen Tucker Band. As of early 2012, plans were in the works to open up a production brewery and tasting room in Sebastopol.

17 Russian River Brewing Company
Brewpub

WWW.RUSSIANRIVERBREWING.COM

725 Fourth St., Santa Rosa, CA 95404, (707) 545-2337—Going N: 101 Exit @ Downtown Santa Rosa, R@ 3rd St., L@ Santa Rosa Ave., R@ 4th St. Going S: 101 Exit 489 (Downtown Santa Rosa), L@ 3rd St., L@ Santa Rosa Ave., R@ 4th St.

OPEN Su–Th: 11 a.m.–midnight, F-Sa: 11 a.m.–1 a.m.

In my experience, whenever beer-loving folks fly into San Francisco, the crucial travel decision is typically whether to make the trip up to Russian River Brewing Company, owned by husband-and-wife team Vinnie and Natalie Cilurzo. Vinnie is generally credited with inventing the double/

SOUR/WILD ALE RUSSIAN RIVER TEMPTATION

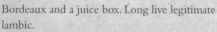

American sour ales have frequently found their inspiration in traditional styles overseas, including the various delicious tart traditions of both Belgium (lambic, Flanders Red, Oud Bruin) and Germany (Berliner weisse). Just because this comes up quite frequently: thinking of Lindemans Framboise as a good example of traditional lambic is sort of like drawing parallels between first-growth Bordeaux and a juice box. Long live legitimate lambic.

Well-crafted sour ales can offer a bracing acidity, vibrant carbonation, and layers of surprising flavors that can include everything from tart lemons to balsamic vinegars to bleu cheese. These beers can be all over the map flavor-wise, with the common denominators being that (1) they're usually fermented with a combination of wild yeast and/or bacteria (benevolent ones!), (2) they can take some getting used to with that first sip, and (3) they may eventually be all you want to drink.

Russian River Temptation is a prime example of the complexity and refreshing qualities that a sour beer can offer, and it's worth mentioning that the success of Russian River's Vinnie Cilurzo and other sour ale brewers in the U.S. has helped rekindle some of the aforementioned traditional styles abroad. Temptation is a blonde ale fermented with Brettanomyces, Lactobacillus, and Pediococcus (which taste much better than they sound) and aged in Chardonnay barrels. The result is one of the most unique and engaging beers out there: lemony tartness, touches of vanilla-tinged oak, and sturdy acidity.

These beers deserve far more attention than I have space. For those who also catch the sour bug, Wild Brews by Jeff Sparrow offers a thoughtful introduction to these historical, challenging beer styles.

SEBASTOPOL-OCCIDENTAL-SANTA ROSA

The Northern California Craft Beer Guide

STYLE:
DOUBLE/IMPERIAL IPA RUSSIAN RIVER PLINY THE ELDER

Double (or Imperial) IPAs are a relatively recent phenomenon in the craft beer world, their origins in the mid-1990s. The progression generally goes as follows: pale ale, to India pale ale (IPA), to double IPA. More hops, more alcohol, and often a touch more malt flavor to help balance the increasing hop bitterness. While you'll occasionally hear talk of "triple IPAs," double IPAs are essentially the uppermost echelon of hoppy beers.

They can take some getting used to (pale ales tend to be more approachable), but offer huge amounts of hop flavor and aroma, with a potent alcohol punch.

There's probably no better example than the main double IPA developed by Vinnie Cilurzo, brewmaster at Russian River Brewing Company and the man generally regarded as the inventor of the style. Pliny the Elder is everything one could want in a double IPA: perfectly rendered citrus and tropical fruit flavor and aromatics, enough soft alcohol to help cut through the bitterness, and a quiet maltiness that stays out of the way. (If I had a nickel for every time I complained about the overuse of darker crystal malts in hoppy beers, I'd currently be swimming in my nickel vault.) Pliny's a hugely bitter, hop-forward beer, while still a pleasure to drink.

Other great local examples are 21st Amendment Hop Crisis! (with its touch of oak) and Drake's Denogginizer. And if the idea of a "triple IPA" sounded like liquid awesome, February is when Russian River's Pliny the Younger is released. Important reminder: As they're typically 8% ABV or higher, double IPAs will pair poorly with both light dishes and movement.

imperial IPA style (see sidebar Style: Double/Imperial IPA) back in 1994, and over the years his Pliny the Elder has inspired countless brewers and won every big award I could think to look up, including back-to-back gold medals at the Great American Beer Festival and the "Best Beer in America" title three years running (between 2009 and 2011), as voted on by the homebrewing readers of Zymurgy magazine. He also makes some of the most masterful sour beers in the world (see sidebar Style: Sour/Wild Ale on page 71), and even their lightest beer, the 4.5% Aud Blonde, is stunning. I appear to have drooled on my keyboard again. If there's anything negative or tempering to say about this brewpub, it's that it's understandably popular and live music events on the weekends can sometimes make it difficult to get a table in the evening. Just keep that in mind when making travel plans, especially with any sort of a group. If you've already sipped through the enormous sampler platter (truly a sight to behold), an illuminating exercise is to sample one of their Belgian beers on tap side by side with its bottled version. The latter are bottle-conditioned (i.e., bottled with live yeast), and the differences can be pretty eye-opening. Sundays they offer all-day happy hour. Their live music is among the best in Santa Rosa, and Hyatt Vineyard Creek down

Third Street is an easy walk.

BREWMASTER: Vinnie Cilurzo
ESTABLISHED: 1997
BE SURE TO TRY: Everything
SEASONALS: Beatification
(occasional),
Compunction (occasional),
Huge Large Sound Czech
Pils (occasional), Pliny the
Younger (winter)
ELSEWHERE: Bottles, Draft

(18) Flavor Bistro
Restaurant

WWW.FLAVORBISTRO.COM

96 Old Courthouse Square,
Santa Rosa, CA 95404, (707)
573-9600—GOING N: 101 Exit
@ Downtown Santa Rosa, R@
3rd St. GOING S: 101 Exit 489
(Downtown Santa Rosa), L@
3rd St.

OPEN M-Th: 11 a.m.–10 p.m., F:
11 a.m.–11 p.m., Sa: 8 a.m.–11
p.m., Su: 8 a.m.–10 p.m.

While ostensibly a wine bar and
Italian bistro (with an impressive
burger menu), Flavor is also your
best bet for sampling Moonlight
beers. The establishment has
six taps, five of which include
Moonlight standards like
Lunatic Lager, Death & Taxes,
and Reality Czeck. The sixth
tap is reserved for the brewery's
rotating seasonals. Flavor is two
blocks from Russian River
Brewing, they offer half pints

Flavor Bistro

Lagers in America

Basically every beer in the world can be put into one of two main categories, distinguished by what type of yeast was used to ferment it—in the simplest delineation, ale yeast or lager yeast. While most mass-produced beer in America falls into the lager category, the majority of craft beer in this country is brewed with ale yeast. There are many reasons for that, not limited to (1) craft beer has always had an interest in distinguishing itself from the corporate pale lager tradition, (2) many craft brewers got involved in the industry by pursuing their homebrewing hobby (which often didn't include a budget for the extra temperature-controlling equipment needed in lager brewing), and (3) ales are delicious anyway.

But the reality is also this: brewing a good lager is freaking hard. You don't have an ale yeast's fruitiness to hide small flaws, and lagers frequently take significantly more time, space, and money to brew. Lagers, from the German verb lagern ("to store"), are stored at cool temperatures for weeks or months following the initial ferment to let coarser flavors dissipate and allow their subtler notes to predominate and balance. When you find craft brewers making great lager, they're more than worthy of your fanciest high-five.

I didn't ask Brian Hunt of Moonlight Brewing Company how many high-fives he receives on a daily basis—though knowing Brian, he probably wouldn't tell me anyway. Brian's lager selection includes some of the finest examples in the country: Reality Czeck-style Pils, Death & Taxes Black Beer, and Lunatic Lager, to name a few. This lager focus arises partly from the fact that Brian came into craft beer from a slightly different angle than most. He wasn't a homebrewer beforehand (although he's been experimenting with fermentation since high school). He studied at UC Davis when their brewing program's focus was more lager-centric, and he previously spent time brewing at Schlitz. His background in biochemistry probably doesn't hurt, either.

While great craft lagers may take a bit of extra effort to track down, it helps to know where to look. Some of the most consistent places to sample Moonlight's lagers include Flavor Bistro in Santa Rosa and Toronado in San Francisco. Brian's distribution is generally limited to the Bay Area. Other regional breweries making excellent lagers include Linden Street, Sudwerk Brewery, and Trumer.

of everything, and in our experience the service has always been excellent.

19 Third Street Aleworks Restaurant & Brewery
Brewpub

WWW.THIRDSTREETALEWORKS.COM

610 Third St., Santa Rosa, CA 95404, (707) 523-3060—GOING N: 101 Exit @ Downtown Santa Rosa, R@ Third St. GOING S: 101 Exit 489 (Downtown Santa Rosa), L@ Third St.

OPEN Su-Th: 11:30 a.m.–midnight, F-Sa: 11:30 a.m.–1 a.m.

Third Street's biggest setback, through the eyes of the beer-geek community, is that it happens to be located in the same city as Russian River and Moonlight, which cast long shadows. I'll admit that I don't make it over here all that often, but when we're looking for something that isn't hoppy, sour, or a lager, this is a reliable place to get some food and enjoy a pint. The stouts tend to be especially good, and both the Stonyfly Oatmeal Stout and Blarney Sisters' Dry Irish Stout recently medaled at the Great American Beer Festival.

> BREWMASTER: Randy Gremp
> ESTABLISHED: 1996
> BE SURE TO TRY: Stonefly Oatmeal Stout

20 The Toad in the Hole
Beer Bar

WWW.THETOADPUB.COM

116 Fifth St., Santa Rosa, CA 95401, (707) 544-8623—GOING N: 101 Exit @ Downtown Santa Rosa, L@ Fifth St. GOING S: 101 Exit 489 (Downtown Santa Rosa), R@ Fifth St.

OPEN M-Th: 4 p.m.–12 a.m., F-Su: noon–1:45 a.m.

One of my favorite places to drink in Santa Rosa, Toad includes a solid lineup of Northern California beer, including North Coast Scrimshaw, Moonlight Death & Taxes, and Bear Republic Racer 5. Paul Stokeld and company host a number of community events throughout the year (their eccentric "Mostly Python" festival of silliness is one good example), and the British pub fare is generally spot-on. The Toad also hosts weekly cask events supported by Mario Rubio, who writes the blog Brewed for Thought (see sidebar Imbibing Online and Off on page 81), and we try to attend these events as often as possible.

21 Moonlight Brewing Company
Brewery

WWW.MOONLIGHTBREWING.COM

Santa Rosa, CA, (707) 528-2537

Between Russian River for hoppy and sour beers and Moonlight for lagers (see sidebar), one can pretty easily see through any flimsy reasoning we might offer for our moving to Santa Rosa that doesn't involve beer. Our first brew pouring in the new digs was a pony keg of Lunatic Lager: a crisp pale lager with touches of honey, a firm mineral and herbal bitterness, and a perfectly integrated hint of green olives. Like most of Brian Hunt's beer, it's brewed to be particularly food-friendly. Lunatic Lager was part of the brewery's original lineup, along with Twist of Fate Bitter Ale and Death & Taxes Black Beer, a popular lighter-bodied lager that's a perfect example of why dark, flavorful beer doesn't necessarily mean a liquid meal. Reality Czeck-style Pils was added in 2002, following a trip Brian took to Prague, and it's one of the tastiest Bohemian-style Pilsners out there. Brian's attention to detail and hands-on approach are highly renowned within the craft beer community, and he delivers most of the beer to accounts himself. Jeff Barkley (son of industry veteran Don Barkley at Napa Smith) has been assuming some of the brewing workload as of late, and together they're looking at some expansion for Moonlight in the very near future. During the fall, be sure to check out the Homegrown Fresh Hop Ale, made with hops grown on site at the brewery.

BREWER: Brian Hunt
ESTABLISHED: 1992
BE SURE TO TRY: Reality Czeck-style Pils
SEASONALS: Homegrown Fresh Hop Ale (fall), Bony Fingers Strong Lager (around Halloween), Winter Tipple Ale (after Thanksgiving), Toast (Slightly Burned) Strong Lager (around New Year's)
ELSEWHERE: Draft

22 The Tap Room at Whole Foods Market
Beer Bar/Grocery Store/ Homebrew Shop

WWW.WHOLEFOODSMARKET.COM

390 Coddingtown Mall, Santa Rosa, CA 95401, (707) 542-7411—GOING N: 101 Exit 491 (Steele Ln./Guerneville Rd.), L@ Guerneville Rd./Steele Ln., L@ Coddingtown Mall. GOING S: 101 Exit 491 (Steele Ln./Guerneville Rd.), R@ Guerneville Rd., L@ Coddingtown Mall.

OPEN M-F: noon–9 p.m., Sa-Su: 11 a.m.– 9 p.m. (Tap Room). Every day: 8 a.m.– 9 p.m. (Whole Foods).

Is it concerning that I do a fair percentage of my beer sampling in a grocery store? Let me rephrase that question. How magnificent is it that I finally manage to consistently find time to go grocery shopping? The knowledgeable beer folks at Whole Foods' Tap Room have done wonders for my domestic participation, offering about twenty taps featuring everything from the latest high-end releases from Mikkeller to brewery night events spotlighting Northern California brewers. While the bottle selection isn't as massive as Bottle Barn's, it's all refrigerated and they occasionally carry beers Bottle Barn overlooks. The homebrew supply section is a recent addition, and includes basic equipment, ingredients, and homebrewing books. There's nothing quite like sipping Cantillon in a little wooden room in the middle of a grocery store, watching first-time shoppers do double-takes as they pass.

Bottle Barn

23 The Beverage People
Homebrew Shop

(www)

WWW.THEBEVERAGEPEOPLE.COM

840 Piner Rd. #14, Santa Rosa, CA
95403, (800) 544-1867/(707) 544-2520—
GOING N: 101 Exit 491B (Bicentennial
Way, keep left) (0.6), R@ Range Ave.,
L@ Piner Rd. GOING S: 101 Exit @
Mendocino Ave., L@ Cleveland Ave.
(0.6), R@ Piner Rd.

OPEN Tu-F: 10 a.m.–5:30 p.m., Sa: 10
a.m.–5 p.m. (Aug-Dec: also open M)

The Beverage People is one of the better
homebrew shops in Northern California
and their skilled, experienced staff cater
to essentially all of one's beer, wine, soda,
vinegar, cheese, mead, and cider-making
needs (I probably missed a few). The
shop has served the region's brewing
community for close to thirty years,
and led the local homebrew club to ten
(!) consecutive national championships
from 1986 to 1995. Noted homebrewing

author Byron Burch, a partner at The Beverage People, played a significant role in this success. The shop hosts regular educational workshops and offers fixed-rate shipping for most West Coast orders.

LAST-MINUTE UPDATE: They will be moving to a nearby location in early 2012

24 Bottle Barn ⭐
Bottle Shop

WWW.BOTTLEBARN.COM

3331 A Industrial Dr., Santa Rosa, CA 95403, (707) 528-1161—GOING N: 101 Exit 491B (Bicentennial Way, keep left) (0.6), R@ Range Ave., L@ Piner Rd., R@ Industrial Dr. GOING S: 101 Exit @ Hopper Ave./Mendocino Ave., R@ Hopper Ave., L@ Airway Dr., R@ Industrial Dr.

OPEN M-Sa: 9 a.m.–7:30 p.m., Su: 9 a.m.–6 p.m.

Bottle Barn is the most comprehensive bottle shop in North Bay, about ten minutes north of downtown Santa Rosa. There's a huge California selection (including solid lineups from Lost Abbey, Alesmith, Stone, and The Bruery from the southern half of the state), plus an extensive range of both Belgian and Danish brews. If you're thirsting for a keg of a particular Moonlight beer (and who isn't?), this is a good place to go.

25 Rio Nido Roadhouse
Beer Bar/Restaurant/Roadhouse

🍴

WWW.RIONIDOROADHOUSE.COM

14540 Canyon Two, Rio Nido, CA 95471, (707) 869-0821—About 25 minutes off Hwy 101 (Exit 494). Head W on River Rd. (13.6), R@ Canyon Two Rd.

OPEN M-F: 11:30 a.m.–midnight, Sa-Su: 9 a.m.–midnight

A spacious roadhouse hideaway down the street from Stumptown Brewery (see below) and Tavern McHugh's (no listing). Family-friendly, outdoor pool, live music, and fifteen regional craft beers on tap.

㉖ Stumptown Brewery
Brewpub

WWW.STUMPTOWN.COM

15045 River Rd., Guerneville, CA 95446, (707) 869-0705—About 25 minutes off Hwy 101 (Exit 494). Head W on River Rd. (14.4).

OPEN Su-Th: 11 a.m.–midnight, F-Sa: 11 a.m.–2 a.m.

Stumptown Brewery has a prime location overlooking the river in Guerneville, and a large outdoor patio fitted with a pool table, BBQ area, an additional bar, and plenty of seating. They typically offer between two and three house beers, as well as five guest taps (Moonlight Death & Taxes and Bear Republic Racer 5 tend to be regulars). Stumptown's Rat Bastard Pale Ale shows zesty grapefruit with a crackly malt core, while their Bushwhacker Wheat is a fruity, effervescent wheat ale. Both are well-handled brews. Tavern McHugh (no listing) is apparently another brewery located right near Stumptown, but they were in flux as of early 2012.

BREWER: Peter
ESTABLISHED: Late 1990s

㉗ The Wurst: Sausage Grill & Beer Garden
Restaurant

22 Matheson St., Healdsburg, CA 95448, (707) 694-0770—GOING N: 101 Exit 503 (Central Healdsburg) (0.7), L@ Matheson St. GOING S: 101 Exit 504 (Westside Rd./ Guerneville), L@ Westside Rd., L@ Healdsburg Ave., L@ Matheson St.

OPEN Every day: 11 a.m.–9 p.m.

An excellent casual beer stop in Healdsburg, The Wurst specializes in authentic sausage, sauerkraut, and sauces. Nothing from a package here except the olive oil and base ketchup. Particularly good were their Wisconsin-style Sheboygan Brat, Sweet Hot Mustard, and the rich Truffle Aioli, made in-house from fresh eggs. The eight taps focus on Northern California, and the bottles included Allagash White, Victory Prima Pils, and Schneider Weisse. Digging into their ice cream puff dessert was almost a religious experience.

㉘ Bear Republic Brewing Co.
Brewpub

WWW.BEARREPUBLIC.COM

345 Healdsburg Ave., Healdsburg, CA 95448, (707) 433-2337—GOING N: 101 Exit 503 (Central Healdsburg) (0.7). GOING S: 101 Exit 504 (Westside Rd./ Guerneville), L@ Westside Rd., L@ Healdsburg Ave.

Bear Republic Production Facility

Bear Republic's Racer 5 is one of the more ubiquitous craft tap handles in Northern California (for good reason), and their standard lineup is fantastic across the board, from the earthy rye notes and citrus bitterness of Hop Rod Rye to the dark chocolate and toastiness of Big Bear Black Stout (a modest-sized imperial stout, at 8.1%).

In addition to keeping a regular supply of their standard bottled offerings on tap, the brewpub in central Healdsburg also generally offers a pretty wide selection of their draft-only releases. Racer X is an amped-up relation of Racer 5, weighing in at 8.9%, while the El Oso Lager offers toastiness and light caramel in a very clean, crisp lager packaging. The outdoor patio area looks out onto an open field of green grass and a tucked-away stream, while heading out in the opposite direction leads right into Healdsburg Plaza.

Bear Republic holds a ticketed Cellar Party before the Great American Beer Festival each year, where one can sample all the beers they've entered. Their Black Racer won a bronze medal in 2011.

HEAD BREWERS: Richard G. Norgrove (Brewmaster), Peter Kruger (Master Brewer)
ESTABLISHED: 1996
BE SURE TO TRY: Racer 5
SEASONALS: Racer X (occasional)
ELSEWHERE: Bottles, Draft

Healdsburg Beer Company
Nanobrewery

WWW.HEALDSBURGBEERCO.COM

Healdsburg, CA

Founded in 2007, Healdsburg Beer Company was one of the first of a handful of nanobreweries in the country (see sidebar). Creating small-batch artisan brews out of his garage, Kevin McGee distributes almost entirely within Healdsburg and the immediate surroundings. We've enjoyed everything we've managed to track down, particularly the spicy English-style IPA (which won a bronze medal at the 2009 U.S. Open Beer Championship) and the nontraditional, peppery California Golden Ale (which earned a silver medal in 2010). Healdsburg Beer produces less than 1,000 gallons annually, and the best places to check for Kevin's beers include the Healdsburg Bar & Grill, The Wurst, and Affronti—all right near Healdsburg Plaza.

BREWER: Kevin McGee
ESTABLISHED: 2007
BE SURE TO TRY: California Golden Ale
ELSEWHERE: Draft

30 Ruth McGowan's Brewpub
Brewpub

WWW.RUTHMCGOWANSBREWPUB.COM

131 E First St., Cloverdale, CA 95425, (707) 894-9610—GOING N: 101 Exit 520 (Citrus Fair Dr.), L@ Citrus Fair Dr., R@ S Cloverdale Blvd., R@ E 1st St. GOING S: 101 Exit 520 (Citrus Fair Dr.), R@ Citrus

Imbibing Online and Off

Fermented beverages have served a fundamental community-building role in societies for thousands of years, though we've come a long way from glugging alcoholic porridge and jovially bonking each other with wooden clubs. Today, beer communities appear in countless different forms, and North Bay is home to two excellent examples of the diversity of these shared worlds and how far we, as imbibers, have evolved.

Mario Rubio (www.brewedforthought. com) is a beer writer, blogger, and event organizer based in Santa Rosa. In addition to his regular contributions to Northwest Brewing News, Examiner.com, and Hop Press (where he serves as editor for a talented group of American and international beer bloggers), Mario also hosts some of the best regular beer events in North Bay. His weekly brewery-highlighting nights at Toad in the Hole in Santa Rosa and TAPS in Petaluma offer excellent opportunities to meet the brewers and other members of the beer industry of Northern California while sipping their latest beer releases.

Mario also frequently works with Joe Tucker, the Executive Director of RateBeer (www.ratebeer.com), which is one of the largest online beer communities in the world, currently boasting over 3 million user-submitted reviews of commercial beers. (Full disclosure: approximately 0.1% of those are mine.) It is, in many ways, the yin to this book's yang. Joe's site aggregates reviews from thousands of members, offering an overall picture of the community's take on pretty much any brew you come across. It's also one of the best ways to get involved in beer trading, or just meet fellow enthusiasts.

Fair Dr., R@ S Cloverdale Blvd., R@ E 1st St.

OPEN M–Th: 3 p.m.–9 p.m., F: 11:30 a.m.–10 p.m., Sa–Su: 10 a.m.–10 p.m.

The northernmost beer stop in North Bay, Ruth McGowan's house-made lineup includes brown, amber, and blonde ales, along with an IPA. They also offer a few Northern California guest taps. But our favorite of the bunch is their Irish Dry Stout: a creamy, chocolatey usurper of Guinness, weighing in at just 4.2%.

BREWER: Tim Gallagher
ESTABLISHED: 2002
BE SURE TO TRY: Irish Dry Stout
ELSEWHERE: Bottles, Draft

31 Olde Sonoma Public House
Beer Bar

WWW.OLDESONOMAPUB.COM

18615 Sonoma Hwy, Ste 110, Sonoma, CA 95476, (707) 938-7587—Directly off Hwy 12/Sonoma Hwy, northwest of central Sonoma.

OPEN Su–Th: 11 a.m.–midnight, F–Sa: 11 a.m.–1 a.m.

A relatively new stop in the area, Olde Sonoma Public House is about two miles out from Sonoma Plaza. They've got thirty-two taps pouring a pretty stellar selection of international and Northern California beers, with plenty of limited-release ones mixed in. While they don't serve food, patrons are encouraged to bring in their own or order from neighboring establishments. Add a younger, beer-savvy crowd, and you can see why we dug this place.

32 Sonoma Springs Brewing Co.
Brewery

WWW.SONOMASPRINGSBREWERY.COM

750 W. Napa St., Sonoma, CA 95476, (707) 938-7422—Directly off Hwy 12/W Napa St. in Sonoma.

OPEN M: 3 p.m.–8 p.m., Th–Sa: 1 p.m.– 8 p.m., Su: 1 p.m.–6 p.m.

Sonoma Springs is six or seven blocks from Sonoma Plaza, a calm respite from the city's main shops, tasting rooms and restaurants. While it's a modest space, Tim Goeppinger's got a ton of brewing experience (with time spent at Goose Island, Firestone Walker, Lagunitas, and Russian River), and he's making some excellent and creative beers here. Mission Bell Sour Wheat was our immediate favorite: wheat, lemons, and a modest tartness and acidity, with a touch of toast and vanilla from its time in a Chardonnay barrel. Lil' Chief Pale Ale is one of the heftiest pale ales you'll find (at 7.0% ABV), while the more recently added Enchanted Forest black IPA is an excellent example of the style, with lots of citrus, pine, and bitter chocolate notes.

BREWMASTER: Tim Goeppinger
ESTABLISHED: 2009
BE SURE TO TRY: Lil' Chief Pale Ale
SEASONALS: Mission Bell Sour Wheat (occasional)
ELSEWHERE: Draft

Hopmonk Tavern
Restaurant/Beer Bar

WWW.HOPMONK.COM

691 Broadway, Sonoma, CA
95476, (707) 935-9100—
Directly off Hwy 12/Broadway
in Sonoma.

OPEN Su–W: 11:30 a.m.–11
p.m.+, Th–Sa: 11:30 a.m.–
midnight+

Second, slightly fancier location
(for details, see main listing:
Hopmonk Tavern – Sebastopol
on page 70). Two blocks south
of Sonoma Plaza and City Hall.
Hopmonk Sonoma also offers
custom beer samplers.

**34 Napa Smith
Brewery**
Brewery

WWW.NAPASMITHBREWERY.COM

1 Executive Way, Napa, CA
94558, (707) 255-2912—Near
the intersection of Hwy 12 and
Hwy 29 in southern Napa.

OPEN Every day: 10 a.m.–5 p.m.

Napa Smith Brewery (&
Winery) instills in one a sense
of how far the craft brewing
industry has come in the last
thirty years. Master Brewer
Don Barkley traces his roots

Napa Smith Brewery

Napa Smith Brewery

back to New Albion Brewing Company, which opened in 1976 in Sonoma and is generally regarded as the first American microbrewery since Prohibition. Though New Albion closed in 1983, Don has since racked up over thirty years' worth of experience in the craft beer industry, and the quality of the brews at Napa Smith is a testament to this.

The huge relative size of the brewery's tasting room to their winetasting room gives one a warm, fuzzy feeling. The paler Napa Smith selections (particularly the Pale Ale and Amber) offer an endearing, crackly malt character throughout, and the Ginger Wheat shows a well-placed spicy ginger quality without being overwhelming. Their seasonals are dialed-in as well, including their piney, rustic,

almost minty Cool Brew (which lives up to its name) and toasty Crush amber lager—a tribute to Napa Valley's annual grape harvest. Their Organic IPA earned a silver medal at the Great American Beer Festival in 2011, and might very well make one reconsider his or her general opinion on organic beers. Nothing half-hearted here.

MASTER BREWER: Don Barkley
ESTABLISHED: 2007
BE SURE TO TRY: Organic IPA
SEASONALS: Cool Brew (spring/summer), Crush (fall), Bonfire (winter)
TOURS: Two scheduled tours daily
ELSEWHERE: Bottles, Draft

Billco's Billiards and Darts
Beer Bar/Pool Hall

WWW.BILLCOS.COM

1234 Third St., Napa, CA 94559, (707) 226-7506—Near the corner of Third St. and Randolph St. in downtown Napa.

OPEN Every day: noon–close

Pool and darts in downtown Napa, with about sixty craft-focused taps and plenty of bottles. If I'm going to embarrass myself at pool, I might as well be sipping a glass of Hair of the Dog Fred. They've also got plenty of suggested beer mixes on the blackboard, from a standard "Snake Bite" to the aptly named "Nagging Mother-in-Law" (half Moylan's Kilt Lifter, half North Coast Old Rasputin).

36 Downtown Joe's Brewery and Restaurant
Brewpub

WWW.DOWNTOWNJOES.COM

902 Main St., Napa, CA 94559, (707) 258-2337—Near the corner of Main St. and Second St. in downtown Napa.

OPEN Every day: 8:30 a.m.–1:00 a.m.

This was one of our more disappointing beer and food experiences, and I'm hoping we caught them at an off time. A number of the beers were overtly flawed, though their Tail Waggin' Amber and Golden Thistle Very Bitter (the latter showing earthiness and mineral-like hop

Nanobrewing

While "microbrewery" has traditionally been the common term for a small brewery in the U.S. (defined as a brewery that makes less than 10,000 barrels of beer annually), "nanobrewery" is a relatively new term indicating the smallest of the small. There isn't a universally agreed-upon definition, but Healdsburg Beer Company produces less than 20 barrels of beer each year, which equates to less than 620 gallons. Hence, "nano."

For Kevin McGee, owner and brewer of Healdsburg Beer, the brewery came about as part of a business plan he discussed with winemaker Jess Jackson, with whom Kevin worked closely at Kendall-Jackson. It was originally just a business exercise—until he realized he could actually make it work. Today Kevin brews Healdsburg Beer in the family garage with his assistant Gordie (the family dog), shuffling full kegs around with a skateboard and working with a semi-automated brewing system he wired himself.

Time is one major limiting factor in operating a nanobrewery, and Kevin's quick to thank Brian Hunt of Moonlight for lending him the use of his industrial keg cleaner, which significantly cuts down his cleaning time. He added, "I've gotten nothing but love and encouragement from every professional I've talked to." While it's taken Kevin time to get the work down to a manageable level, the small-batch results are exceptional.

Other nanobreweries currently operating in Northern California include Chappell Brewery in Mariposa and Old Hangtown Beer Works in Placerville. There will very likely be more on the scene soon, including Beltane Brewing, Van Houten Brewing, and Petaluma Hills Brewing Co. And that's just in the North Bay.

bitterness) were both worth a sample.
BREW MASTER: Colin Kaminski
ESTABLISHED: 1993

③⑦ JV Wine & Spirits
Bottle Shop

WWW.JVWINE.COM

301 First St., Napa, CA 94559, (707) 253-2624—Near the corner of First St. and Hwy 121/Silverado Trail near downtown Napa.

OPEN M-Sa: 8 a.m.–9 p.m., Su: 9 a.m.–8 p.m.

Hosting a solid beer selection in the heart of wine country, JV Wine & Spirits featured particularly large selections from Napa Smith, Anderson Valley, and Russian River when we stopped in. Some international highlights are stocked as well (Belgian, Japanese, German, etc.), although wine remains the predominant focus.

③⑧ Silverado Brewing Company
Brewpub

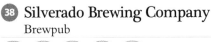

WWW.SILVERADOBREWINGCOMPANY.COM

3020 St. Helena Hwy, St. Helena, CA 94574, (707) 967-9876—Directly off St. Helena Hwy/Hwy 29/Hwy 128 in northern St. Helena.

OPEN Su-Th: 11:30 a.m.–9 p.m., F-Sa: 11:30 a.m.–9:30 p.m.

Silverado Brewing Company makes its home in what was once the Freemark

Abbey Winery, a historical building built in 1895, and the general vibe inside is a calmer version of the surrounding wine country. The "Certifiably" Blonde Ale (brewed with certified-organic malts) is a spritzy, effervescent blonde—an excellent alternative to sparkling wine—and their Coffee Stout, which is the Oatmeal Stout transformed by organic Sumatra coffee, shows a deliciously well-presented roasted coffee character. Everything on tap typically ranges between 4.5% and 5.5% ABV, a welcome divergence from many of the recent, alcohol-heavy brewery lineups. Silverado also offers tasty house-made root beer, plus a cocktail called "The Orange Blondeshell," made with Charbay, blood oranges, fresh juices, and a bit of the "Certifiably" Blonde Ale on top.
HEAD BREWER: Ken Mee
ESTABLISHED: 2000
BE SURE TO TRY: "Certifiably" Blonde Ale
SEASONALS: Oktoberfest (fall)

③⑨ Napa Valley Brewing Co., Calistoga Inn
Brewpub

WWW.NAPABEER.COM

1250 Lincoln Ave., Calistoga, CA 94515, (707) 942-4101—Directly off Hwy 29/Lincoln Ave. in Calistoga.

OPEN M-F: 11:30 a.m.–closing, Sa-Su: 11 a.m.–closing

Napa Valley Brewing Company operates out of the Calistoga Inn, which means the closest hotel room is just upstairs. In addition to a darkened bar area and a generally casual interior dining spot, the outdoor patio offers an upscale, white-tablecloth dining experience. Entrees range from about $10 to $30 (remember, you're technically in wine country). The four house beers—Wheat Ale, Porter, Red Ale, and Calistoga Pilsner—were quite good, with the lattermost being the standout. Spicy and herbal hops, a quietly honeyed maltiness, and well-handled fermentation made the Calistoga Pilsner a refreshing, toasty lager. Their seasonals, a Witbier and an American Special Bitter, were equally well handled. We really enjoyed having dinner here, from the precise décor and nearby stream to the attentive service. Definitely not your everyday brewpub.

BREWMASTER: Brad Smisloff
ESTABLISHED: 1987
BE SURE TO TRY: Calistoga Pilsner

NAPA–ST. HELENA–CALISTOGA

The Northern California Craft Beer Guide

Cooking and Pairing with Beer

Northern California just happens to be home to two of the most recognized beer-minded chefs in the country: Sean Z. Paxton (The Homebrew Chef) and Bruce Paton (The Beer Chef). Both are professionally trained chefs who have, over the past ten years or so, helped improve the American mindset toward beer's role at the dinner table. Bruce (www.beer-chef.com) often hosts beer and food pairing dinners in the Bay Area and beyond, while Sean (www.homebrewchef.com) has become one of the country's most recognized figures in the art of cooking with beer as a talented chef, beer writer, and the host of a monthly show, "The Home Brewed Chef," on The Brewing Network. As my own culinary capabilities are usually limited to sandwich preparation and staying out of Ali's way, Sean was kind enough to offer one of his own recipes using a local beer. He wrote:

When cooking with beer, it's good to think about the style of beer being used to cook with and what flavors that beer brings to the dish. Take note of its International Bittering Units (IBUs) and the complexity of the malt, and how they work together and separately in the brew. The Sierra Nevada Tumbler seasonal brown ale is great to cook with, as it has a nice toasty malt flavor with a hint of smoke but isn't overpowering or astringent. These flavors boost the natural earthiness of the chanterelle mushrooms in this recipe and combine with the herbs, highlighting the lighter hopping of the ale. Try pairing this dish with a similar brown ale, smoked porter or bock-style lager.

When cooking with beer, it's good to think about the style of beer being used to cook with and what flavors that beer brings to the dish.

Pearl Barley Risotto with Chanterelle Mushrooms, Bacon, Sierra Nevada Tumbler and Goat Cheese

SERVES: SIX GUESTS AS AN ENTRÉE OR EIGHT TO TEN GUESTS AS A SIDE DISH

Ingredients:

6 ounces bacon, applewood smoked, sliced into lardons

1 cup cippolini onion, peeled and sliced (or substitute shallots)

8 ounces chanterelle mushrooms, fresh, brushed clean, sliced

4 each garlic cloves, peeled and sliced thin

2 tablespoons thyme leaves, fresh

1 teaspoon rosemary, fresh, minced

1 cup pearl barley

24 ounces Sierra Nevada Tumbler or other brown ale

1 quart stock, chicken or vegetable, preferably homemade

1 tablespoon rice flour (optional)

4 ounces butter, unsalted

4 ounces goat cheese or chèvre, crumbled

2 tablespoons Italian leaf parsley, chopped

1 tablespoon thyme leaves, fresh

kosher salt and freshly cracked pepper to taste

Variations:

To make this dish vegetarian, you can omit the bacon and substitute 4 tablespoons of unsalted butter for the bacon grease the onions and mushrooms are sautéed in.

Recipe courtesy of Sean Z. Paxton

Directions:

In a large Dutch oven, over medium heat, add the bacon lardons and render out the fat from the bacon. It will take 8-10 minutes, stirring frequently, to cook the bacon evenly on all sides. Once the bacon starts to become crispy, remove it from the pot using a slotted spoon and place in a bowl.

Add the onions (or shallots) and cook/stir for 4 minutes, just until they become translucent. Next add the chanterelle mushrooms and sauté for 8 minutes, until they start to turn brown around the cut edge. Add the garlic, thyme and rosemary to the mushrooms and sauté for another 3-4 minutes. Remove half of the mixture and add to the bowl with the rendered bacon. Add the pearl barley to the pot and toast the grain for 2-3 minutes, evenly coating with the bacon fat. Deglaze the pot with 12 ounces of brown ale, removing any of the fond (browned bits on the bottom of the pan) and then add the stock. Bring the mixture to a boil, then turn the heat down to medium low, cover and let cook until the pearl barley is tender, about 45-50 minutes. About 35 minutes in, add the remaining 12 ounces of brown ale (this keeps the beer flavor fresh and helps keep the bitterness level in check). Also check the consistency of the mixture; if it seems dry, add more stock, water or beer. If it is soupy, remove the lid and continue to cook.

Once the grain is fully cooked (test a few grains), add the rice flour and stir until the mixture becomes thick. The rice flour will combine with the remaining liquid to make a sauce that simulates the texture of risotto. Turn off the heat and stir the butter and goat cheese into the barley and let sit for a few minutes. Check the seasoning and add salt and freshly cracked pepper to taste. Toss the Italian leaf parsley and thyme in with the mushrooms and bacon and warm in a sauté pan for 1-2 minutes. Pour the pearl barley risotto onto a warmed serving platter and garnish with the warmed mushrooms and bacon mixture. Or mix the reserved mushrooms and bacon into the risotto and portion onto individual plates. Serve immediately.

REGION 3   EAST BAY

The East Bay region consists of Alameda and Contra Costa counties, i.e. the significant Wisconsin-shaped landmass separating San Francisco Bay from Central Valley. This is one of the beer hotspots of Northern California, with over a dozen Beer Destinations and more than fifty listings. While Berkeley and Oakland are as far away as many San Francisco-based beer lovers will typically venture, the public transportation extends well beyond those two cities, and the areas further east and south have plenty to offer as well.

Jack London Square and Berkeley's culinary scene (everything from roaming food trucks to the inspiring Chez Panisse) are two of the major draws in the region, and the Berkeley and Oakland craft beer scenes keep up accordingly, featuring brewpubs like Jupiter and Triple Rock Brewery & Alehouse in downtown Berkeley, plus Dying Vines Brewing and Linden Street Brewery, both of which are brewed at the latter's facilities near Oakland's Inner Harbor. Beer Revolution and The Trappist are within a short walk of each other (as well as Jack London Square, downtown Oakland, and Lake Merritt), and Berkeley Bowl's West Berkeley location and Ledger's Liquors offer great bottle shopping just a few minutes off the highway.

Further out, the brewers at Ale Industries in Concord produce some phenomenal lower-alcohol beers at their warehouse location next to MoreBeer!, while Drake's Brewing Company's Barrel House provides a prime opportunity to sample the brewery's standard lineup and delicious limited-release beers. Handles Gastropub in Pleasanton raises the bar for both food and beer menus in the region, while the upscale ØL Beercafe & Bottle Shop is Walnut Creek's answer to The Trappist. A stop at Perry's Liquor in Livermore is a great way to check off any lingering items on one's shopping list.

While the scenery beyond Berkeley and Oakland is mainly comprised of highways, quiet rolling hillsides, and shopping centers, the East Bay also has a wealth of regional and state parks. It's also the most accessible neighboring region (via public transportation) for folks staying in San Francisco.

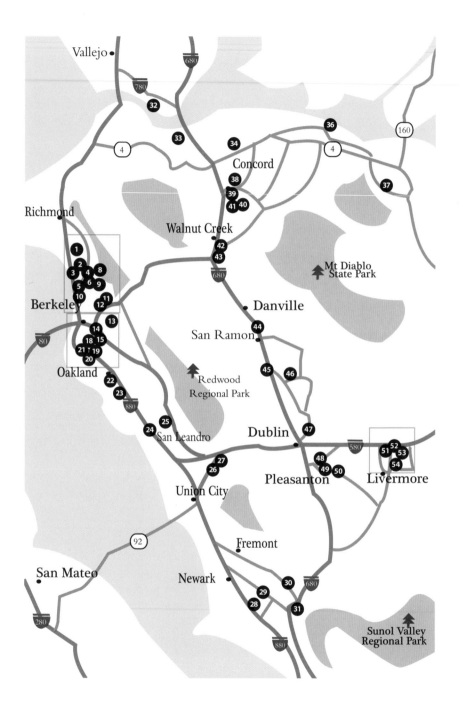

5 to try

Ale Industries Orange Shush Drake's Denogginizer Dying Vines Hop Candi
Linden Street Urban People's Common Lager Schooner's American Ale

① Elevation 66 Brewing Company – El Cerrito   Brewpub

② Pyramid Alehouse & Brewery – Berkeley   Brewpub

③ Trumer Brauerei – Berkeley   Brewery

④ Oak Barrel Winecraft – Berkeley   Homebrew Shop

⑤ Lanesplitter Pizza & Pub – West Berkeley   Restaurant/Beer Bar

⑥ Ledger's Liquors – Berkeley   Bottle Shop

⑦ Bison Brewing – Berkeley   Brewery

⑧ Triple Rock Brewery & Alehouse – Berkeley   Brewpub

⑨ Jupiter – Berkeley   Brewpub

⑩ Berkeley Bowl – West Berkeley   Grocery Store

⑪ Star Grocery – Berkeley   Grocery Store

⑫ Barclay's Restaurant & Pub – Oakland   Restaurant/Beer Bar

⑬ Cato's Ale House – Oakland   Beer Bar/Restaurant

⑭ CommonWealth Cafe & Public House – Oakland   Café/Beer Bar

95

uncharted territory

510 Brewing Company (Fremont) MacArthur Garage Brewery (Oakland) Faction Brewing (TBD)

15 Luka's Taproom & Lounge – Oakland   Restaurant

16 Dying Vines Brewing – Oakland   Brewery

17 Oakland Brewing Company – Oakland   Brewery

18 Pacific Coast Brewing Co. – Oakland   Brewpub

19 The Trappist – Oakland   Beer Bar

20 Beer Revolution – Oakland   Beer Bar

21 Linden Street Brewery – Oakland   Brewery

22 Lucky 13 – Alameda   Beer Bar

23 Encinal Market – Alameda   Grocery Store

24 Drake's Brewing Company – San Leandro   Brewery

25 The Englander Pub – San Leandro   Beer Bar/Restaurant

26 The Bistro – Hayward   Beer Bar

27 Buffalo Bill's Brewery – Hayward   Brewpub

28 Cork-n-Bottle Liquors – Fremont   Bottle Shop

29 Jack's Brewing Company – Fremont   Brewpub

30 Mission Liquors – Fremont   Bottle Shop

31 Mission Pizza & Pub – Fremont   Restaurant/Beer Bar

32 The Warehouse Cafe – Port Costa   Restaurant/Beer Bar

33 Creek Monkey Tap House – Martinez   Brewpub/Beer Bar

34 Black Diamond Brewing Company – Concord   Brewery

35 Heretic Brewing Company – Pittsburg   Brewery

36 E.J. Phair Brewing Company – Pittsburg   Brewpub

37 Schooner's Grille & Brewery – Antioch   Brewpub

38 E.J. Phair Brewing Company – Concord   Brewpub

39 Monument Wine & Spirits – Concord   Bottle Shop

40 Ale Industries – Concord   Brewery

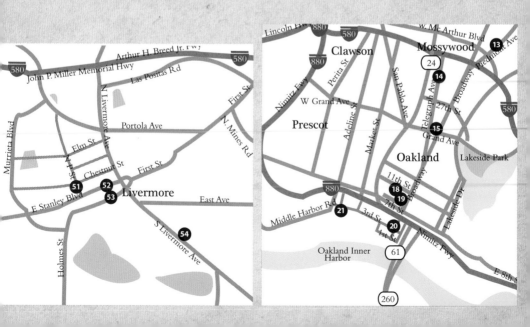

1 Elevation 66 Brewing Company
Brewpub

WWW.ELEVATION66.COM

10082 San Pablo Ave., El Cerrito, CA 94530, (510) 525-4800—Walking distance from the El Cerrito Plaza BART station. Just east of Hwy 580 and Hwy 80, between central Albany and central El Cerrito, directly off Hwy 123/San Pablo Ave.

OPEN M-W: 3 p.m.–11 p.m., Th: 11:30 a.m.–11 p.m., F-Sa: 11:30 a.m.–midnight, Su: 10 a.m.–11 p.m.

Elevation 66 is a recent (and welcome) addition to El Cerrito's beer scene, and their brews proved to be top-notch. Esther's Vanilla Stout, in particular, stole the show, showing softly integrated vanilla alongside plenty of chocolate and roasted-malt notes. Fully realized at an especially drinkable 3.5% ABV, one doesn't often find beers like this in Northern California. Their East Bay IPA was also exceptional, with lots of hop flavor and a hugely satisfying, grapefruit-centered bitterness. It's a stellar example of West Coast IPA.

In addition to their engaging beer list (which offered six guest beers, including frequent appearances from Linden Street and Sudwerk), our food was excellent and reasonably priced. When we last visited, the "grilled cheese spontanee" featured Pt. Reyes bleu, curry-pear chutney, arugula, and local herb focaccia bread.

> HEAD BREWER: David J. Goodstal
> ESTABLISHED: 2011
> BE SURE TO TRY: Esther's Vanilla Stout

2 Pyramid Alehouse & Brewery
Brewpub

WWW.PYRAMIDBREW.COM

901 Gilman St., Berkeley, CA 94710, (510) 528-9880—Northwest Berkeley, near the corner of Eighth St. and Gilman St.

OPEN Su-Th: 11:30 a.m.–10 p.m., F-Sa: 11:30 a.m.–11 p.m.

While this long-standing brewery got its start and maintains its main offices in Washington, the Berkeley location brews on site and also serves as a production facility (the Walnut Creek location does not). The standard lineup here (Hefeweizen, Apricot, and Thunderhead IPA) isn't worth going out of your way for, but their Snow Cap Winter Warmer is one of the longest-running seasonal beers in the country and worth a sample. They're currently developing some new brews (Helles Smokey, Red Wheat With Fig) for 2012.

> ESTABLISHED: 1984
> TOURS: One tour daily
> ELSEWHERE: Bottles, Draft

3 Trumer Brauerei
Brewery

WWW.TRUMERBRAUEREI.COM

1404 Fourth St., Berkeley, CA 94710, (510) 526-1160—Northwest Berkeley, near the corner of Camelia St. and Fourth St.

OPEN Only open for tours, offered M-F at 3:15 p.m. Reservations recommended.

Trumer's Berkeley location only makes one beer, but that single beer is a brilliant example of the Pilsner style (see sidebar). Trumer is generally only open for its scheduled weekday tours, but we've also ended up there for homebrew competitions and San Francisco Beer Week events that they've kindly hosted.

BREWMASTER: Lars Larson
ESTABLISHED: 2004 (Austria brewery est. 1601)
BE SURE TO TRY: Pils
TOURS: One tour daily on weekdays
ELSEWHERE: Bottles, Draft

④ Oak Barrel Winecraft
Homebrew Shop

(www)

WWW.OAKBARREL.COM

1443 San Pablo Ave., Berkeley, CA 94702, (510) 849-0400—Northwest Berkeley, near the corner of Page St. and San Pablo Ave.

OPEN M-F: 10 a.m.–6 p.m., Sa: 10 a.m.–5 p.m.

In business for over fifty years, Oak Barrel Winecraft caters to the makers of beer, wine, and vinegar.

STYLE:
PILSNER TRUMER PILS

The term Pilsner (or Pilsener) has come to represent lagers in general for many beer drinkers, due to the way in which pale lagers have been marketed. But this style category holds much more specific meaning in craft beer terms. Pilsner was first brewed in 1842 by Josef Groll at what would later become known as the Pilsner Urquell brewery in the town of Plzeň (or Pilsen) in the Czech Republic. The style quickly became (1) massively popular across the globe and (2) open to interpretation. The more specific (and tastier) classifications of Pilsner refer to a narrower subset of lagers: typically very clear, golden in color, with a significant hop presence. They're especially drinkable, refreshing beers, with the best having sufficient soft malts and hoppiness to satisfy.

Trumer Pils (when fresh—hugely important in styles like this) is one delicious example of a German-style Pilsner, with a crisp and clean lager feel, quietly toasty malts, and significant herbal and mineral-like hop contributions, giving the overall package a refreshing bitterness. North Coast Scrimshaw is another solid Pilsner, tending to have a slightly rounder body than Trumer. Moonlight's Reality Czeck-style Pils stands out as one of our personal favorites. Distinctions between American, Czech, and German-style versions can be somewhat fuzzy, with the key distinctions usually being that American styles often use adjuncts (corn, rice, sugar, etc.) to lighten the beer's body, and that Czech-style Pilsners often have a little bit more heft than their German counterparts. Still, all three are firmly hopped pale lagers.

The Northern California Craft Beer Guide

Lanesplitter Pizza & Pub
Restaurant/Beer Bar

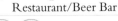

WWW.LANESPLITTERPIZZA.COM

2033 San Pablo Ave., Berkeley, CA 94702, (510) 845-1652—West Berkeley, near the corner of University Ave. and Hwy 123/San Pablo Ave.

OPEN Every day: 11 a.m.–midnight

This Lanesplitter location is the best of the bunch, with thirteen taps including two house beers (pale ale from Drake's and hefeweizen from Firestone Walker), a rotating seasonal offering from Drake's, and (at least when we stopped in) multiple taps from Moonlight and Ale Industries. Lagunitas seasonals in bottles as well. Apparently two of the other Lanesplitter locations, in Temescal and Emeryville, also serve beer.

 Ledger's Liquors
Bottle Shop

WWW.LEDGERSLIQUORS.COM

1399 University Ave., Berkeley, CA 94702, (510) 540-9243—A short walk from the North Berkeley BART station. West Berkeley, near the corner of Acton St. and University Ave.

OPEN Tu-Sa: 10 a.m.–8 p.m.

The complementary selection to Berkeley Bowl's seemingly endless, filled-out beer aisle. Ledger's Liquors is where one goes for harder-to-find beers in Berkeley, with hundreds of scattered bottles on the shelves, significant lineups from U.S. and international brewers, and a haphazard Northern California assortment that includes out-there breweries like Snowshoe, Half Moon Bay, Palo Alto Brewing, and even El Dorado Brewing Company. Ledger's is also a great place to pick up glassware and publications like Celebrator and Northwest Brewing News. A bit dusty, but there's stuff you won't find anywhere else.

Bison Brewing
Brewery

WWW.BISONBREW.COM

Berkeley, CA, (510) 697-1537

Dan's doing some excellent work in terms of both certified-organic beers and industry sustainability (see sidebar Organic Brewing on page 105). Our favorite from Bison's year-round lineup is their Organic IPA: an earthy, floral IPA that seemed more English-inspired than a citrusy, American-style IPA. Their Honey Basil Ale and Gingerbread Ale are both solid as well, with the latter hinting at gingerbread cookies and cocoa.

BREWMASTER: Daniel Del Grande
ESTABLISHED: 1989
BE SURE TO TRY: Organic IPA
SEASONALS: Honey Basil Ale (occasional), Gingerbread Ale (fall)
ELSEWHERE: Bottles, Draft

8 Triple Rock Brewery & Alehouse

Brewpub

WWW.TRIPLEROCK.COM

1920 Shattuck Ave., Berkeley, CA 94704, (510) 843-2739—A short walk from the Downtown Berkeley BART station. In downtown Berkeley, near the corner of Hearst Ave. and Shattuck Ave.

OPEN M–W: 11:30 a.m.–1 a.m., Th–Sa: 11:30 a.m.–2 a.m., Su: 11:30 a.m.– midnight

Triple Rock was one of the first craft brewpubs to open in the country, and— along with Jupiter—they've shaped downtown Berkeley into a top-tier scene for craft beer. We've enjoyed Rodger's brewing since he was back at Drake's, and the wide range of Triple Rock brews are generally excellent across the board. A major standout for us is the IPAX, which offered loads of grapefruit and zesty pine notes from Simcoe hop additions; it's a delicious, vibrant West Coast IPA. Similarly assertive is the Bug Juice, a floral, mineral-tinged golden ale with solid bitterness. The seasonals tend to be complex and well-handled, the Dragon's Milk Brown Ale being a standout. Triple Rock has one-gallon "Beer in a Box" growlers, Monkey Head Arboreal Ale on Thursdays (one-liter bottles, in-house only), and cask-conditioned ales each Friday. They usually have about a dozen house taps, plus a few guest taps to round out the board. If that proves insufficient somehow, Bobby G's Pizzeria (no listing), just over a block away on University Ave., offers some choice craft taps as well.

HEAD BREWER: Rodger Davis

ESTABLISHED: 1985

BE SURE TO TRY: IPAX

SEASONALS: Dragon's Milk Brown Ale (occasional)

ELSEWHERE: Draft

LAST-MINUTE UPDATE: Rodger Davis departing in early 2012 to start Faction Brewing.

9 Jupiter

Brewpub

WWW.JUPITERBEER.COM

2181 Shattuck Ave., Berkeley, CA 94704, (510) 843-8277—Directly across from the Downtown Berkeley BART station. In downtown Berkeley, near the corner of Allston Way and Shattuck Ave.

OPEN M-Th: 11:30 a.m.–1 a.m., F: 11:30 a.m.–1:30 a.m., Sa: noon–1:30 a.m.,

Su: noon–midnight

Owned by the same people who own Triple Rock and Drake's, Jupiter brews the least beer of the three. They maintain a small on-site brewing system (the one-off, Jupiter-brewed beers we've tried have been solid), and the remainder of their house taps are actually brewed by Sudwerk (the Hefeweizen and Pils) and Drake's (pretty much everything else)—which is great, because we love both of those breweries.

Jupiter also keeps ten guest taps, which included multiple beers from Moonlight and Drake's (specifically labeled as such instead of lumped into the house taps). All told, this is a reasonably confusing, delicious nexus of Drake's, Sudwerk, and Northern California specialty beers. Jupiter gets packed in the evenings.

BREWMASTER: Jeff Kimpe

ESTABLISHED: 1992

BE SURE TO TRY: The Jupiter-brewed beers

10 Berkeley Bowl

Grocery Store

WWW.BERKELEYBOWL.COM

920 Heinz Ave., Berkeley, CA 94710, (510) 898-9555—Southwest Berkeley, near the corner of Ninth St. and Heinz Ave.

OPEN M-Sa: 9 a.m.–8 p.m., Su: 10 a.m.–6 p.m.

In addition to magnificent vegetables, this Berkeley Bowl also has one of the more enormous beer aisles you'll see, as well as one of the most comprehensive. I was quoted something like five-hundred-plus bottles, but the fact that they stock relatively full lineups from the breweries they carry makes their selection seem more expansive than many of the San Francisco locations that carry a few hundred more. If you're looking for something specific and not super-rare, this is a good place to look. The other Berkeley Bowl (on Oregon Street; no listing) has a smaller selection.

 ## Star Grocery
Grocery Store

WWW.STARGROCERY.NET

3068 Claremont Ave., Berkeley, CA 94705, (510) 652-2490—Southeast Berkeley, near the corner of The Uplands and Claremont Ave.

OPEN M-Sa: 8 a.m.–7 p.m., Su: 10 a.m.–5 p.m.

Beer-geek eclecticism, with a selection of imports (De Molen, Struise, Mikkeller) and Northern California beers (Shmaltz, High Water, Ale Industries, and Iron Springs, to name a few). Not enormous, but the familiar lineup of empty rare bottles over their beer coolers emphasizes that someone here definitely knows what's up.

Barclay's Restaurant & Pub
Restaurant/Beer Bar

WWW.BARCLAYSPUB.COM

5940 College Ave., Oakland, CA 94618, (510) 654-1650—A short walk from Rockridge BART station. Northeast

Oakland/Southeast Berkeley area, near the corner of Harwood Ave. and College Ave.

OPEN M-F: 11 a.m.–midnight, Sa-Su: 10 a.m.–midnight

An older, well-worn Oakland bar with about thirty taps featuring plenty of Northern California staples. An excellent place for events during San Francisco Beer Week. The main highlight when we visited were the multiple taps from Oakland Brewing Company. Dartboards and a tucked-in outdoor seating section.

Cato's Ale House
Beer Bar/Restaurant

WWW.CATOSALEHOUSE.COM

3891 Piedmont Ave., Oakland, CA 94611, (510) 655-3349—Northeast Oakland, near the corner of Montell St. and Piedmont Ave.

OPEN M-Th: 11:30 a.m.–midnight, F: 11:30 a.m.–1 a.m., Sa: 11:30 a.m.–midnight, Su: 11:30 a.m.–10 p.m.

Reasonably priced pub fare (their smoked bacon and pancetta are made on site) and almost two dozen taps that featured some harder-to-find things like Linden Street, Heretic, Triple Voodoo, and High Water when we last stopped in. Their sister location is Ben & Nick's Bar & Grill (a few blocks south of Barclay's; no listing), which tends to have a slightly more modest craft beer selection than Cato's. Both are fun, quirky pubs.

Organic Brewing

Northern California is home to a handful of organic breweries, including the first organic brewery in the country (Eel River Brewing Company) and the first certified-organic brewpub (Ukiah Brewing Company).

Organic ingredients are those grown without harmful chemicals or pesticides—i.e., the same way food was grown throughout most of human history—and in the context of beer this applies more specifically to the cereal grains (barley, wheat, etc.) and generally anything else used that isn't water or yeast, both of which are exempt. The U.S. Department of Agriculture's National Organic Program regulates the ingredients included in organic requirements, and until 2010 had excluded hops because there wasn't a reliable supply of organic ones in the U.S. Starting in 2013 organic hops will be required as well, though many organic breweries have already switched over due to improvements in the organic hop supply.

While some breweries offer only one or two organic brews (or worse, a full lineup of lackluster quality), Bison Brewing's entire lineup is both certified organic and more adventurous than most; the Honey Basil Ale and Chocolate Stout are both exceptional. Bison is one of the most influential voices in the craft beer industry when it comes to organic brewing and sustainability. Along with buying carbon offsets and encouraging consumers to make environmentally conscious choices, brewmaster Daniel Del Grande has been involved in numerous other environmental sustainability initiatives within the industry. Check out Bison Brewing's Causes web site (www.bisonbrew.com/causes) for additional information.

Organic beers and organic ingredients have been steadily improving as of late, and Northern California remains at the forefront of things. Other assertive organic brews worth highlighting include Eel River Triple Exultation, Napa Smith Organic IPA, and anything from Uncommon Brewers. For anyone down near Santa Cruz, check out the selection of organic supplies at Seven Bridges Cooperative, almost certainly "the world's only cooperatively owned, certified organic homebrew supply store."

The Trappist

⑭ CommonWealth Cafe & Public House
Café/Beer Bar

🍴 🥛 🌐

WWW.CMONOAKLAND.COM

2882 Telegraph Ave., Oakland, CA 94609, (510) 663-3001—North-central Oakland, near the corner of 29th St. and Telegraph Ave.

OPEN M–Sa: 9 a.m.–10:30 p.m., Su: 9 a.m.–3:30 p.m.

Big dimpled mugs, dark wood, studious patrons, and a great local taplist. About fifteen taps, with lots of East Bay breweries featured, like Dying Vines, Drake's, Ale Industries, Linden Street, and Oakland Brewing Company. Themed flights and beermosas (orange juice plus Ale Industries Orange Shush). The imports are predominantly from the United Kingdom, including bottles from BrewDog. A stellar and comfortable neighborhood café with an excellent selection of über-local beer. They're planning to expand in 2012.

commonWealth Cafe

Su: 10:30 a.m.–midnight

Casual diner ambiance with sixteen taps dedicated to good Belgian and Northern California beers. The bottle menu expands into a wider selection of Trappist ales (eight different bottles when we stopped in) and a modest selection of English beers. About two dozen bottles total. Weekly brunches and oyster specials. Walking distance from Fox Theater, The Paramount Theatre, and Lake Merritt.

16 Dying Vines Brewing
Brewery

WWW.DYINGVINES.COM

Oakland, CA

The Dying Vines lineup is currently being brewed at Linden Street. Their year-round offerings consist of three English-inspired beers under 5%: Ol' Brick Bitter (4%), Hop Candi (4.8%), and Dee'z Mild (4%). It isn't often that one sees American breweries focusing on British beer styles, and it's even less often that one sees them doing it so well. Ol' Brick Bitter (served on nitrogen) showed soft biscuit and toffee notes with a pleasant perimeter of earthy bitterness, while the Dee'z Mild was a delicious English brown: light chocolate notes and brown sugar, medium-light bodied, with a perfect mouthfeel and nice toasty finish. Hop Candi was the most interesting of all. Despite the name, the actual hop bitterness in the beer is very low, and so much of the herbal and floral hop character comes from late hop additions and dry hopping (which, simply phrased,

15 Luka's Taproom & Lounge
Restaurant

WWW.LUKASOAKLAND.COM

2221 Broadway, Oakland, CA 94612, (510) 451-4677—A short walk from 19th St. Oakland BART station. Central Oakland, near the corner of Grand Ave. and Broadway.

OPEN M-W: 11:30 a.m.–midnight, Th-F: 11:30 a.m.–2 a.m., Sa: 5:30 p.m.–2 a.m.,

The Northern California Craft Beer Guide

contribute more flavor and aroma than bitterness). Candied sweetness without cloying sweetness, Hop Candi on cask at Oakland's CommonWealth Cafe was a revelatory experience.

FOUNDERS: Kel Alcala, Richard Greenawald
ESTABLISHED: 2010
BE SURE TO TRY: Hop Candi
ELSEWHERE: Draft

17 Oakland Brewing Company
Brewery

WWW.OAKLANDBREWING.COM

Oakland, CA

The OBC has a relatively new (and quiet) presence in Oakland, but their beers can occasionally be found on tap throughout Northern California, in San Francisco, Sacramento, Pleasanton, etc. Though we weren't overly impressed with the CME IPA (butterscotch and modest hopping), we're still curious to try some of their upcoming brews. The best place we've seen for tracking them down is Barclay's Restaurant & Pub.

MASTER BREWER: James Costa
ESTABLISHED: 2009
ELSEWHERE: Draft
LAST-MINUTE UPDATE: Their imperial stout was excellent.

18 Pacific Coast Brewing Co.
Brewpub

WWW.PACIFICCOASTBREWING.COM

906 Washington St., Oakland, CA 94607,

(510) 836-2739—A short walk from 12th St. Oakland City Center BART station. Downtown Oakland, near the corner of Ninth St. and Washington St.

OPEN M-Th: 11:30 a.m.–midnight, F-Sa: 11:30 a.m.–1 a.m., Su: 11:30 a.m.–11 p.m.

Pacific Coast Brewing has twenty-four taps and typically features at least four of their own house-brewed beers. The high-quality guest taps are the main draw here, focused on California brews and fun seasonals.

BREWMASTER: Don Gortemiller
ESTABLISHED: 1988

19 The Trappist
Beer Bar

WWW.THETRAPPIST.COM

460 Eighth St., Oakland, CA 94607, (510) 238-8900—A short walk from 12th St. Oakland City Center BART station. Downtown Oakland, near the corner of Eighth St. and Broadway.

OPEN Su-Th: noon–midnight, F-Sa: noon–1 a.m.

Let's start at the basics: The Trappist has nicer furniture than we do. Everything else falls into place from there—the Belgian-focused beer selection, the proper glassware, the Cicerone-certified Beer Servers, the iconic metal beer signage, the insane bottle list, etc. You aren't likely to find many of their top-shelf beer offerings anywhere else in the Bay Area. The Trappist opened in 2007, adding their back bar (and second

The Trappist

set of taps) a couple years later, and a back patio in 2011. The latter is a great addition to the place, with long picnic tables and some relative calm from the traffic and the frequent bustle inside. This is one of the most meticulously tuned craft beer bars we've ever been to, and a major Beer Destination in East Bay.

20 Beer Revolution ⭐
Beer Bar

🍴 🍺 🛢

WWW.BEER-REVOLUTION.COM

464 3rd St., Oakland, CA 94607 (510) 452-2337—Walking distance from 12th St. Oakland City Center BART station. South-central Oakland, near the corner of Broadway and 3rd St.

OPEN M-Th: noon-10 p.m., F-Sa: noon-11 p.m., Su: noon-9 p.m.

THE craft beer destination in East Bay. Forty-seven taps, three coolers packed full of higher-end craft beer, weekly brewery events, proper glassware, regular cask-ale offerings. Major supporters of California beer. While Rebecca and Fraggle's Beer Revolution is a relative newcomer (opening in 2010), it's already become the must-visit beer spot in this part of the Bay Area. A punk-inclined vibe, wooden barrels and leather stools, an outdoor patio with occasional on-site food and food trucks: this is where beer geeks wisely gravitate. The Trappist is a short walk away, and together they're unstoppable. You won't go thirsty in Oakland.

21 Linden Street Brewery ⭐
Brewery

WWW.LINDENBEER.COM

95 Linden St., Suite 7/8, Oakland, CA 94607, (510) 812-1264—Walking distance from the West Oakland BART station. West Oakland, near the corner of Third St. and Linden St.

OPEN Hours in flux. Check web site or call ahead.

While Anchor may have the phrasing "steam beer" trademarked, we haven't seen anyone working more with this traditional brewing style than Adam Lamoreaux at Linden Street. All of his brews are fermented with lager yeast at warmer-than-normal temperatures, which is one key element of the steam beer or California Common style of brewing. Another is the use of Northern Brewer hops, which Adam uses exclusively. Linden Street is based in an old Westinghouse factory near Oakland's Inner Harbor, and getting to talk to Adam about the industrial and brewing histories of the area is an experience in itself (he mentioned that their brewery is the first production brewing facility in Oakland since 1959). We sampled three different Linden Street beers while we were in the area, including their Urban People's Common Lager (a straight-up, delicious California Common), Burning Oak Black Lager (roasted malts, cocoa, and a light bitterness), and The 'Town Lager, named with an abbreviation of Oakland's nickname. The last of these is a delicious, crisp and toasty lager that gets delivered in kegs via bicycle only. Linden Street likes to keep things local.

BREWER: Adam Lamoreaux
ESTABLISHED: 2005 (began brewing in 2009)
BE SURE TO TRY: Urban People's Common Lager
SEASONALS: The 'Town Lager (occasional)
ELSEWHERE: Draft

22 Lucky 13
Beer Bar

WWW.LUCKY13ALAMEDA.COM

1301 Park St., Alameda, CA 94501, (510) 523-2118—Central Alameda, near the corner of Encinal Ave./Hwy 61 and Park St.

OPEN Every day: 11:30 a.m.–2 a.m.

Located near the western end of the main shopping/restaurant section of Alameda, Lucky 13 has a quality lineup of California and international beers (about twenty taps and forty bottles) and a low-key outdoor seating area.

23 Encinal Market
Grocery Store

3211 Encinal Ave. Alameda, CA 94501, (510) 522-7171—GOING S: 880 Exit 38 (High St./Alameda), R@ High St. L@ Fernside Blvd. (0.8), R@ Encinal Ave. GOING N: 880 Exit 38 (High St./Alameda), L@ Coliseum Way, L@ High St., L@ Fernside Blvd. (0.8), R@ Encinal Ave.

OPEN M-Sa: 8 a.m.–9 p.m., Su: 8 a.m.–7 p.m.

BLONDE/GOLDEN ALE DRAKE'S BLONDE ALE

While Kölsch-style beers and cream ales tend to be more narrowly defined, they both technically fall into the larger category of blonde and golden ales. This category is essentially the answer to the question, "What's paler than a pale ale?" These brews will generally be blonde/golden in color (or at least close) and fermented with ale yeast. For breweries that don't brew lagers, these will often be their lightest and most approachable offerings: more flavorful than a macro pale lager, while less assertively hopped than a standard pale ale.

This is actually a good place to look in terms of overall artistry, as brewers that can make an exceptional blonde ale are probably doing other things right, too. Drake's Blonde Ale, while listed as Kölsch-style on the label, fits most comfortably inside the broader blonde/golden ale category, showing assertive toasty malts and lightly honeyed sweetness, balanced by a zesty mineral-like hop character.

Examples will often strike similar balances to a pale ale, with everything turned down a notch or two; "extra pale ales" effectively serve as the boundary between blonde and pale ales. Russian River Aud Blonde is another great one, while Mad River Steelhead Extra Pale Ale is closer to the dividing line.

A couple hundred bottles with a decent mix of California, Pacific Northwest, Danish (loads of Mikkeller), and Belgian beers. Significant lineups from North Coast, Anderson Valley, Drake's, and 21st Amendment.

24 Drake's Brewing Company
Brewery

WWW.DRINKDRAKES.COM

1933 Davis St., Building 177, San Leandro, CA 94577, (510) 568-2739— GOING S: 880 Exit 34 (Davis St.), R@ Davis St., L@ Timothy Dr., around back of Walmart. GOING N: 880 Exit 34 (Davis St.), L@ Davis St., L@ Timothy Dr., around the back of Walmart.

OPEN W-Th: 3 p.m.–8 p.m., F-Sa: noon–8 p.m., Su: 1 p.m.–6 p.m. (closed first Friday of the month)

Is any brewery in East Bay doing more things right than Drake's? Even without the recent addition of the Barrel House, their standard draft and bottled lineup is delicious: Blonde Ale (see sidebar), Hefeweizen, 1500 Pale Ale, Amber Ale, IPA—each fine-tuned, stylistically on point, and still assertive and unique. Their seasonal releases are more adventurous but just as good. Aroma Coma (get it fresh to savor those hoppy aromatics) took second place and the People's Choice award at the Bistro's Annual IPA Festival in 2011. Hopocalypse and Denogginizer (recently moved into the year-round lineup) are both intensely bitter and tasty double IPAs. The 3.8% Alpha Session, a dry-hopped and lower-alcohol beer with plenty of hop character, is one of the finest brews we've had in the past year. Oh yeah—and the Barrel House. Drake's barrel-aging efforts have expanded significantly since they started back in 2007, and had grown to over 150 barrels when we last counted: Merlot barrels, Bourbon barrels, brandy barrels, and many more. While not every beer coming out of Drake's is barrel-aged perfection, they rotate their barrel-aged taps regularly, and these are some of the most intriguing beers you'll find anywhere in Northern California. It can be a little challenging to find, but this is truly a top-notch place for craft beer.

HEAD BREWER: Brian Thorson
ESTABLISHED: 1989
BE SURE TO TRY: 1500 Pale Ale
SEASONALS: Alpha Session (occasional), Expedition Ale (spring), Aroma Coma (summer), Jolly Rodger Ale (fall), Hopocalypse Ale (winter)
ELSEWHERE: Bottles, Draft

25 The Englander Pub
Beer Bar/Restaurant

WWW.ENGLANDERPUB.COM

101 Parrott St., San Leandro, CA 94577, (510) 357-3571—Central San Leandro, near the corner of Washington Ave. and Parrott St.

OPEN M-Th: 11 a.m.–11 p.m., F-Sa: 11 a.m.–midnight, Su: 11 a.m.–9:30 p.m.

This English-influenced pub stocks a somewhat haphazard mix of English and Irish-pub offerings, California-brewed hoppy beers, and a basic selection of Belgian bottles. Bonus: a variety of cask-conditioned ales.

26 The Bistro
Beer Bar

WWW.THE-BISTRO.COM

1001 B St., Hayward, CA 94541, (510) 886-8525—A short walk from the Hayward Station BART. In central Hayward, near the corner of Main St. and B St.

OPEN Every day: 10 a.m.–1 a.m.

About a block away from Buffalo Bill's, The Bistro is a comfortable bar in central Hayward with a dozen craft-focused taps and a Belgium-minded bottle list. They also have an outdoor patio and live music basically every night. A few weekends a year, The Bistro hosts some of the most awe-inspiring beer events in the Bay Area, including the annual West Coast Barrel Aged Beer Festival each November.

27 Buffalo Bill's Brewery
Brewpub

WWW.BUFFALOBILLSBREWERY.COM

1082 B St., Hayward, CA 94541, (510) 886-9823—A short walk from the Hayward Station BART. In central Hayward, near the corner of Hwy 238/ Foothill Blvd. and B St.

The Warehouse Cafe

OPEN M-Th: 11 a.m.–10:30 p.m., F-Sa: 11 a.m.–11 p.m., Su: 11 a.m.–10 p.m.

Started up by "Buffalo" Bill Owens (who also started Bison Brewing), Buffalo Bill's was one of the first brewpubs in America—probably third or fourth, though I'd hesitate to state either confidently. The most engaging beer in their lineup was the America's Original Pumpkin Ale, which was lightly spiced with soft cinnamon and clove notes. They also occasionally have their Imperial Pumpkin Ale on tap: twice as big, at 9.8%.

FOUNDER: Bill Owens
ESTABLISHED: 1983
SEASONALS: America's Original Pumpkin Ale (fall)

28 Cork-n-Bottle Liquors
Bottle Shop

WWW.CORKNBOTTLELIQUORS.COM

5200 Mowry Ave., Fremont, CA 94538, (510) 608-4300—GOING S: 880 Exit 17 (Mowry Ave./Central Fremont), L@ Mowry Ave. GOING N: 880 Exit 17 (Mowry Ave./Central Fremont), R@ Mowry Ave.

OPEN M-W: 9 a.m.–11 p.m., Th-Sa: 9 a.m.–midnight, Su: 9 a.m.–10 p.m.

Though it doesn't look like much more than a typical strip mall liquor store, Cork-n-Bottle had a couple hundred bottles, including substantial lineups from Midnight

Sun, Mikkeller, and Stone. Their Northern California selections included Uncommon Brewers, Buffalo Bill's, and Ale Industries.

29 Jack's Brewing Company
Brewpub

🍴 ⊙ 🥛 🍾 🛢

WWW.JACKSBREWINGCOMPANY.COM

39176 Argonaut Way, Fremont, CA 94536, (510) 796-2036—GOING S: 880 Exit 17 (Mowry Ave./Central Fremont), L@ Mowry Ave. (1.4), R@ Argonaut Way/Fremont Hub. GOING N: 880 Exit 17 (Mowry Ave./Central Fremont), R@ Mowry Ave. (1.2), R@ Argonaut Way/ Fremont Hub.

OPEN M-F: 11 a.m.–10 p.m., Sa-Su: 11 a.m.–11 p.m.

Jack's Brewing Company's two locations (Fremont and San Ramon) are tucked away from the main brewing hotbed of East Bay, and their beers are generally only available on site—such that they're usually not very well known elsewhere in the Bay Area. But they're crafting some excellent brews here, across almost their entire lineup. The Grid Iron Amber Ale (near the hoppier end of the spectrum), Penalty Shot Porter, and Hardwood Pale Ale were all well-made examples of their respective styles. Still, the Pumpkin seasonal stole the show, offering up layered nutmeg and cinnamon with sturdy carbonation and a creamy texture.

BREWMASTER: Will Erickson
ESTABLISHED: 1999
BE SURE TO TRY: Hardwood Pale Ale
SEASONALS: Pumpkin (fall)

30 Mission Liquors
Bottle Shop

WWW.MYSPACE.COM/MISSION_LIQUORS

39945 Mission Blvd., Fremont, CA 94539, (510) 651-2202—Northeast Fremont, Mission Valley Shopping Center, near the corner of Las Palmas Ave. and Hwy 238/Mission Blvd.

OPEN Su-Th: 9 a.m.–11 p.m., F-Sa: 9 a.m.–midnight

Mission Liquors stocks a couple hundred craft bottles, including larger selections from Allagash, Nøgne Ø, Lost Abbey, and Mikkeller. They host beer samplings about once a month in their back tasting room.

31 Mission Pizza & Pub
Restaurant/Beer Bar

🍴

WWW.MISSIONPIZZA.COM

1572 Washington Blvd., Fremont, CA 94539, (510) 651-6858—GOING S: 680 Exit 15 (Washington Blvd./Irvington District), L@ Washington Blvd. GOING N: 680 Exit 15 (Washington Blvd./Irvington District), L@ Washington Blvd.

OPEN M-Th: 11 a.m.–9:30 p.m., F: 11 a.m.–10 p.m., Sa: 11:30 a.m.–10 p.m., Su: 11:30 a.m.–9:30 p.m.

A highly endearing pizza joint with a beer-geek feel. Mission Pizza & Pub's thirty-five craft-focused taps included beers from Drake's, Trumer, Lost Coast, Napa Smith, and Sierra Nevada when we last stopped by, along with Mission-

branded beers made by Jack's Brewing. Their walls are lined with antique bottles and cans (look for the old stubby of Rodenbach), and there's a small stage area equipped for live music.

32 The Warehouse Cafe
Restaurant/Beer Bar

5 Canyon Lake Dr., Port Costa, CA 94569, (510) 787-1827—GOING E: 80 Exit 27 (Pomona St./Crockett) (0.5), L@ Pomona St. (1.3), L@ Carquinez Scenic Dr. (1.6), L@ Canyon Lake Dr. GOING W: 80 Exit 27 (Pomona St./Crockett), L@ Pomona St. (1.3), L@ Carquinez Scenic Dr. (1.6), L@ Canyon Lake Dr.

OPEN M-Th: 3 p.m.–closing, F: noon–2 a.m., Sa: 10 a.m.–2 a.m., Su: 10 a.m.–closing

Originally built for storing grain and other farm produce in the late 1800s, Port Costa's iconic Warehouse Cafe will be celebrating its fiftieth anniversary as a restaurant and bar in early 2012. The place seems closer to an antique shop than a typical beer bar, with its old ticket booth, faded cloth-covered chandeliers, and the gigantic lit-up polar bear in a glass case. A neat curiosity off the beaten path. Order a Sierra Nevada Pale Ale and peruse the restaurant's countless dusty nooks. Few taps, but nearly three hundred craft bottles.

33 Creek Monkey Tap House
Brewpub/Beer Bar

WWW.CREEKMONKEY.COM

611 Escobar St., Martinez, CA 94553, (925) 228-8787—Central Martinez, near the corner of Castro St. and Escobar St.

OPEN M–Th: 11 a.m.–9 p.m., F–Sa: 11 a.m.–10 p.m., Su: 10 a.m.–8 p.m.

Creek Monkey was more of a craft beer bar than an overt brewpub as of late 2011, but they're planning to expand their on-site tap selection to include at least two or three house-brewed beers. The Damned, a 4.3% dry stout and the only Creek Monkey beer available when we visited, offered cola and chocolate notes in a quiet package. The remainder of their twenty-three or so taps are for guest beers, many from highly regarded East Bay breweries (Ale Industries, Linden Street, Heretic, etc.). The location itself is essentially a multi-story house converted into a spotless bar and café environment, and the outdoor patio and beer garden in the back overlook the quiet creek nearby. Significant brewing changes are planned for 2012.

ESTABLISHED: 2011

34 Black Diamond Brewing Company
Brewery

WWW.BDBREWING.COM

2470 Bates Ave., Concord, CA 94520, (925) 356-0120—From Hwy 680: follow Hwy 4 E (2.0) toward Pittsburg/Antioch, Exit 15B (Port Chicago Hwy N, keep left) (1.5), L@ Bates Ave.

OPEN M–F: 3:30 p.m.–7:30 p.m.

Black Diamond's sampling bar is part of their larger brewing facility in northern Concord, and it's a great place to sample the brewery's full lineup. Black Diamond was originally a brewpub in Walnut Creek, and their name comes from the area's historic coal mining industry. Available either in six-packs or bombers, our favorite of the six-pack beers is the FreeStyle Belgian Blonde, a rounded blonde with a quiet Belgian yeast contribution. Their 22-ounce bottles are typically more assertive, including the Rampage IPA (juicy citrus, grapefruit), Peak XV Imperial Porter (cocoa, dark chocolate), and hoppy seasonal Wheat Wacker.

BREWMASTER: Derek Smith
ESTABLISHED: 1994
BE SURE TO TRY: Peak XV Imperial Porter
SEASONALS: Wheat Wacker (occasional)
ELSEWHERE: Bottles, Draft

35 Heretic Brewing Company
Brewery

WWW.HERETICBREWING.COM

Pittsburg, CA, (925) 526-6364

There haven't been many brewery openings more anticipated than Jamil Zainasheff's Heretic Brewing. Jamil is one of the most recognized figures in the homebrewing community: two-time recipient of the American Homebrewers Association's prestigious Ninkasi Award, co-author of two homebrewing books, and radio show host at The Brewing Network. We were able to track down two of Heretic's releases (Evil Twin and Evil Cousin) at Handles Gastropub in Pleasanton. Evil Twin was our favorite of the two, offering a potent mineral hop character melded to a rich malt core of cola, red fruits, and hints of creamy vanilla. Evil Cousin, approximating a West Coast imperial IPA, fittingly showed a surplus of citrusy hop character. It will be easier to track Heretic's brews in 2012, as they've started bottling Evil Twin, Evil Cousin, and Shallow Grave Porter. They've also got some intriguing sour and barrel-aged beers on the horizon.

BREWERS: Jamil Zainasheff, Chris Kennedy
ESTABLISHED: 2010
BE SURE TO TRY: Evil Twin
ELSEWHERE: Bottles, Draft

36 E.J. Phair Brewing Company
Brewpub

WWW.EJPHAIR.COM

200 East Third St., Pittsburg, CA 94565, (925) 252-9895—From Hwy 680: follow Hwy 4 E (10.2) toward Pittsburg/Antioch, Exit 23 (Railroad Ave.), L@ Railroad Ave. (1.2), R@ E 3rd St.

OPEN M-Th: 11 a.m.–9 p.m., F: 11 a.m.–10 p.m., Sa: 10 a.m.–10 p.m., Su: 10 a.m.–8 p.m.

Second location (for details, see main listing: E.J. Phair Brewing Company – Concord on facing page).

 37 Schooner's Grille & Brewery
Brewpub

WWW.SCHOONERSBREWERY.COM

4250 Lone Tree Way, Antioch, CA 94509, (925)-776-1800—Southern Antioch, directly off Lone Tree Way.

OPEN M-Th: 11 a.m.–10 p.m., F-Sa: 11 a.m.–12:30 a.m., Su: 10 a.m.–10 p.m.

The standout of Schooner's standard lineup is their American Ale (see sidebar), but Craig is brewing up some other tasty offerings as well, such as the creamy Oatmeal Stout and IPA (The latter took first place at The Bistro's Annual IPA Festival in 2011). Schooner's brewpub shares their parking lot with an AMC theater, so it's a good place to enjoy a couple of pints and then catch a movie. While much of Schooner's brewing has been focused on their main lineup as of late, we've had some of their delicious limited-released beers as well. If you see the tart, dark Vindication anywhere, don't pass up the chance to try it.

MASTER BREWER: Craig Cauwels
ESTABLISHED: 2001
BE SURE TO TRY: American Ale
ELSEWHERE: Draft

38 E.J. Phair Brewing Company
Brewpub

WWW.EJPHAIR.COM

2151 Salvio St., Ste L, Concord, CA 94520, (925) 691-4253—Walking distance from the Concord BART station. In

CREAM ALE SCHOONER'S AMERICAN ALE

Cream ales were much more common in the U.S. during pre-Prohibition times, when they were brewed (generally speaking) as a slightly bolder alternative to mass-produced pale lagers. Ale and/or lager yeasts were both reportedly used in the past, and today brewers can use either type, or both. Of greater import is that the final product has, at most, a very mild resultant fruitiness. Often referred to as "lawnmower beer," cream ales are meant to drink like a lager, with relatively high carbonation and not too much else to draw your attention away from mowing. (Disclaimer: This book does not condone drinking + lawnmower.)

Much like pale lagers, so much of what cream ales are lies in how it feels to drink one. Cream ales don't usually set one's heart aflame, so when one does it's worth singling it out. Schooner's American Ale uses both flaked corn (typical) and rolled oats (less so) to make a hugely drinkable version of the style: crisp and quiet aroma, effervescent carbon dioxide, and modest impacts of crackery malts and mineral bitterness balancing each other out. Another to search for is Anderson Valley's Summer Solstice (a.k.a. Cerveza Crema).

The Northern California Craft Beer Guide

The Brewing Network

The Brewing Network (www.thebrewingnetwork.com) started up in 2005 and has become the craft beer world's main source for beer radio content. Broadcasting out of Pacheco and headed by Justin Crossley, The Brewing Network hosts a number of different shows that feature cutting-edge brewers, craft beer personalities, and industry experts. While much of the content (available via online streaming, podcasts, or digital download) is particularly of interest to homebrewers, even those who can't tell their false bottom from a hole in the ground will find something both amusing and surreptitiously educational.

The Home Brewed Chef is a monthly program featuring Sean Z. Paxton, a.k.a The Homebrew Chef (see Cooking and Pairing with Beer sidebar on page 88), one of the key industry experts in cooking with craft beer and figuring out what beer to pair with the result. For anyone who got the false-bottom reference, programs like The Jamil Show and Brew Strong bring together homebrewing luminaries like Jamil Zainasheff (of East Bay's Heretic Brewing Company) and John Palmer (author of the tome How to Brew). To meet the BN brewcasters up close and personal, you can also check out their area craft beer events, including the annual Winter Brews Festival.

central Concord across from Todos Santos Plaza, near the corner of Grant St. and Salvio St.

OPEN M-F: 11 a.m.–11 p.m., Sa-Su: 10 a.m.–11 p.m.

While E.J. Phair produces their own house-brewed beers, their excellent guest taps tend to overshadow their own brews. Comprising about half of their fourteen taps, the guest beers generally include numerous top-shelf Northern California breweries (Russian River, Bear Republic, etc.). They also offer bottled Belgian beers. Kegs and growlers are only available through the Pittsburg location, but growlers can be refilled in Concord.

BREWER: J.J. Phair
ESTABLISHED: 2005
ELSEWHERE: Draft

39 Monument Wine & Spirits
Bottle Shop

2250 Monument Blvd., Concord, CA 94520, (925) 682-1514—GOING S: 680 Exit 49 (Monument Blvd.) (1.1), L@ Monument Blvd. (1.1). GOING N: 680 Exit 49B (Monument Blvd.), R@ Monument Blvd. (1.0).

OPEN M-Th: 9 a.m.–8 p.m., F-Sa: 9 a.m.–9 p.m., Su: 9 a.m.–7 p.m.

Excellent, scattered, occasionally dusty selection of craft beer. They had vintages of Russian River bottles that we couldn't find anymore, despite living six blocks from the brewery. Their selection places them in the same category as Perry's and Ledger's. Their markups can be pretty sizable for limited releases.

e Industries

40 ## Ale Industries
Brewery

WWW.ALEINDUSTRIES.COM

975 Detroit Ave., Unit E, Concord,
CA 94518, (925) 470-5280—GOING N:
680 Exit 49B (Monument Blvd.), R@
Monument Blvd. (1.7), R@ Detroit Ave.
(0.7). GOING S: 680 Exit 49 (Monument
Blvd.), L@ Monument Blvd. (1.7), R@
Detroit Ave. (0.7).

OPEN Th-F: 3 p.m.–7 p.m., Sa: noon–7
p.m.

This was one of our first official stops
for the guide, and four months and
several hundred samples later we still
consider this one of our favorites in all
of Northern California. Right next to
More Beer!, Ale Industries is tucked
around to the left, inside of a warehouse,
and the person pouring your beer is very
likely one of the people who brewed
it. The beers here are both stylistically
challenging and masterfully done. Their
Orange Shush (previously Orange
Kush) is witbier-like, but the addition
of chamomile brings along additional
tea-like floral and citrus notes that fit
perfectly with this beer's creamy, pillowy
texture.
Their 2012 Table Beer ("The Beer of
the Future"!) was a dark, yeast-driven
session ale with just 3.0% ABV and loads
of flavor for something this lean. So
much of the flavor and aroma in the 2012
arises from the blend of Chimay and La
Chouffe yeast strains used to ferment
it. Most impressive of all, though, was
the 24 East, perhaps the closest thing
to a "traditional" beer that we tried. It

ØL Beercafe

One of the most advanced homebrew shops out there. MoreBeer! not only stocks a phenomenal line of beer- and winemaking products and coffee-roasting supplies, they also have their own manufacturing warehouse, where they produce small-scale brewing systems and MoreBeer!-branded equipment. (It doesn't hurt that Ale Industries is right next door…) MoreBeer! has two other showrooms in California, in Los Altos and Riverside.

tasted like a beautifully crafted German Helles, emphasizing its toasty Pilsner malt character, though with a somewhat amped-up hop profile. We made sure to bring home a growler for our friends to try. We'd encourage others to do the same.

BREWERS: Morgan Cox, Steve Lopas
ESTABLISHED: 2009
BE SURE TO TRY: Orange Shush
SEASONALS: 24 East (occasional)
ELSEWHERE: Bottles, Draft

41 MoreBeer!
Homebrew Shop

(www)

WWW.MOREBEER.COM

995 Detroit Ave., Unit G, Concord, CA 94518, (925) 671-4958/(800) 600-0033—GOING N: 680 Exit 49B (Monument Blvd.), R@ Monument Blvd. (1.7), R@ Detroit Ave. (0.7). GOING S: 680 Exit 49 (Monument Blvd.) (1.1), L@ Monument Blvd. (1.7), R@ Detroit Ave. (0.7).

OPEN M-F: 9 a.m.–6 p.m., Sa-Su: 10 a.m.–5 p.m.

42 ØL Beercafe & Bottle Shop
Beer Bar/Bottle Shop

WWW.BEER-SHOP.ORG

1541 Giammona Dr., Walnut Creek, CA 94596, (925) 210-1147—A short walk from Walnut Creek BART station. In central Walnut Creek, near the corner of Locust St. and Giammona Dr.

OPEN Every day: noon–11 p.m.

Having recently opened in fall 2011, ØL Beercafe & Bottle Shop has already proven an ideal fit for Walnut Creek. Lots of rare draft offerings, meticulous beer service (plus proper glassware), and an enormous selection of bottles available both on site and to go. The beer menu is predominantly focused on top-tier imports, with excellent American beers rounding things out. The dark wooden tasting rooms are reminiscent of a wine-country bistro, and the upscale ambiance fits squarely into the overall Walnut Creek vibe.

Pyramid Alehouse
Brewpub

WWW.PYRAMIDBREW.COM

1410 Locust St., Walnut Creek, CA 94596, (925) 946-1520—Walking distance from Walnut Creek BART station. In central Walnut Creek, near the corner of Cypress St. and Locust St.

OPEN Su-Tu: 11:30 a.m.–10 p.m., W-Th: 11:30 a.m.–10:30 p.m., F-Sa: 11:30 a.m.– 11 p.m.

Chain location (for details, see main listing: Pyramid Alehouse & Brewery – Berkeley on page 98).

Pete's Brass Rail and Car Wash
Restaurant/Beer Bar

WWW.PETESBRASSRAIL.COM

201 Hartz Ave., Danville, CA 94526, (925) 820-8281—GOING S: 680 Exit 40 (El Cerro Blvd.), R@ El Cerro Blvd. L@ Danville Blvd. (0.5). GOING N: 680 Exit 38 (Sycamore Valley Rd.), L@ Sycamore Valley Rd. W, R@ San Ramon Valley Blvd. (0.5), L@ Hartz Ave.

OPEN M-Th: 11 a.m.–9:30 p.m.+, F-Sa: 11 a.m.–10 p.m.+, Su: 11 a.m.–8:30 p.m.+

While you won't really be able to get your car washed or check "brass rail" off your shopping list, Pete's does have an engaging selection of craft beer. This is a quirky, casual family restaurant with

twenty taps, including lesser-seen stuff from East Bay and beyond. They rotate through hundreds of different brews, so the tap list is constantly changing. We noticed selections from Ale Industries, Bison, and Dust Bowl last time we stopped in.

Jack's Brewing Company
Brewpub

WWW.JACKSBREWINGCOMPANY.COM

2410 San Ramon Valley Blvd., San Ramon, CA 94583, (925) 362-1059— GOING S: 680 Exit 36 (Crow Canyon Rd.), R@ Crow Canyon Rd., L@ San Ramon Valley Blvd. (0.3), U-turn. GOING N: 680 Exit 34 (Bollinger Canyon Rd.), L@ Bollinger Canyon Rd., R@ San Ramon Valley Blvd. (1.2).

OPEN Su-Th: 11 a.m.–10 p.m., F-Sa: 11 a.m.–midnight

Second location (for details, see main listing: Jack's Brewing Company – Fremont on page 115).

The Hop Yard
Restaurant/Beer Bar

WWW.HOPYARD.COM

470 Market Pl., San Ramon, CA 94583, (925) 277-9600—GOING S: 680 Exit 34 (Bollinger Canyon Rd.), L@ Bollinger Canyon Rd. (0.8), R@ Market Pl. GOING N: 680 Exit 34 (Bollinger Canyon Rd.), R@ Bollinger Canyon Rd. (0.6), R@ Market Pl.

OPEN Every day: 11 a.m.–10 p.m.+

Second location (for details, see main listing: The Hop Yard – Pleasanton below).

HopTech Homebrewing Supplies
Homebrew Shop

WWW.HOPTECH.COM

6398 Dougherty Rd., Ste 7, Dublin, CA 94568, (925) 875-0246/(800) 379-4677— In east Dublin, directly off Dougherty Rd.

OPEN M-Tu: 9:30 a.m.–6 p.m., Th-F: 9:30 a.m.– 6 p.m., Sa: 10 a.m.–4 p.m., Su: 10 a.m.–2 p.m.

Located near Dublin Public Storage, HopTech has been in business since 1983 and carries a wide range of products for both beginning and advanced homebrewers. They also offer occasional brewing classes.

The Hop Yard
Restaurant/Beer Bar

WWW.HOPYARD.COM

3015-H Hopyard Rd., Pleasanton, CA 94588, (925) 426-9600—Directly off Hopyard Rd. in northwest Pleasanton.

OPEN Every day: 11 a.m.–10 p.m.+

The Hop Yard has about thirty craft-focused tap handles and hosts regular brewery nights. Their house hefeweizen is produced off-site by Snowshoe Brewing Company (last time we checked) out in Arnold.

Handles Gastropub
Restaurant/Beer Bar

WWW.HANDLESGASTROPUB.COM

855 Main St., Pleasanton, CA 94566, (925) 399-6690—Directly off Main St. in central Pleasanton.

OPEN M-Th: 11:30 a.m.–10 p.m., F-Sa: 11:30 a.m.–1 a.m., Su: 9:30 a.m.–10 p.m.

Handles Gastropub just opened in 2011, and it's quickly become the most enticing craft beer destination in the area. Certified Cicerone Chad Moshier manages all things beer at Handles, including their thirty-eight taps, their well-chosen and affordable bottle list (Jolly Pumpkin, Pretty Things), and their two house beers: the Sun Bathed Blonde and Hop Shack Brown, which Chad brews specifically for Handles at Hermitage.

The tap selection at Handles is both locally and beer-geek-minded, featuring limited releases and lesser-seen East Bay breweries such as Dying Vines, Ale Industries, Heretic, and Oakland Brewing Company. In true Cicerone fashion, Handles offers beer and food pairings, featuring a rotating selection of three draft beers paired with food in their "Flight & Bites" pairings. The house-smoked meat and homemade sauces are a deserved point of pride, there's a huge beer garden open in warm weather, and they offer wines on tap.

That would be more than enough to

Handles Gastropub

make this place a Beer Destination. But the cherry-on-top part of Handles are those two house brews. Sun Bathed Blonde is a crisp, beautifully made Kölsch-style beer, while Hop Shack Brown (food-friendly and named after their in-house barbecue cooker) is truly one of the most delicious brown ales out there: layered milk chocolate, marshmallow, vanilla, and cola notes in a malty, masterfully done rendition. (Chad, if you could go ahead and start bottling those, please.)

50 Pleasanton Main Street Brewery
Brewpub

WWW.MAINSTBREWERY.COM

830 Main St., Pleasanton, CA 94566, (925) 462-8218—Directly off Main St. in central Pleasanton.

OPEN Tu-Th: 11:30 a.m.–10 p.m., F-Sa: 11:30 a.m.–midnight, Su: 11:30 a.m.–8 p.m.

Directly across the street from Handles Gastropub, Pleasanton Main Street

Brewery keeps a minimum of four house-brewed beers on tap, usually featuring their pale ale, IPA, hefeweizen, and something on the darker side. They also try to keep about a dozen guest taps available, and most Fridays and Saturdays feature live music. While not included in the symbols above, they occasionally have kegs available.

HEAD BREWER: Matt Billings
ESTABLISHED: 1996

51 Perry's Liquor
Bottle Shop

WWW.PERRYSLIQUOR.COM

1522 Railroad Ave., Livermore, CA 94550, (925) 443-0550—GOING E: 580 Exit 52B (N Livermore Ave.), R@ N Livermore Ave. (1.2), R@ Railroad Ave., keep left. GOING W: 580 Exit 52B (N Livermore Ave.), L@ N Livermore Ave. (1.3), R@ Railroad Ave., keep left.

OPEN M-F: 8 a.m.–midnight, Sa-Su: 8 a.m.–1 a.m.

Finest bottle selection in the area by far. This is beer-geek heaven, with beer lineups from Stillwater, The Bruery (including their Provision series), High Water, Mikkeller, Alpine, Fantôme, and plenty more when we last visited. The same folks opened up Livermore Saloon, which (not surprisingly) has a sweet tap list. While there are apparently a number of places called Perry's Liquor in the area, you want the one in Livermore.

52 Tap 25
Beer Bar

WWW.TAPTWENTYFIVE.COM

25 S Livermore Ave., Livermore, CA 94550, (925) 294-8970—GOING E: 580 Exit 52B (N Livermore Ave.), R@ N Livermore Ave. (1.3). GOING W: 580 Exit 52B (N Livermore Ave.), L@ N Livermore Ave. (1.3).

OPEN Th-Sa: noon–10 p.m., Su: noon–8 p.m.

Newly opened in 2011, Tap 25 is essentially a beer-tasting room covertly tucked into a courtyard of winetasting rooms. They feature twenty-five frequently rotating craft taps, with a huge Northern California focus and, when we last visited, a bunch of neat limited-release stuff from breweries in East Bay. The courtyard is a shared outdoor imbibing space, and tapas can be ordered nearby. Their web site maintains an updated tap list.

53 Livermore Saloon
Beer Bar

WWW.LIVERMORESALOON.COM

2223 First St., Livermore, CA 94550, (925) 454-1449—GOING E: 580 Exit 52B (N Livermore Ave.), R@ N Livermore Ave. (1.3), R@ 1st St. GOING W: 580 Exit 52B (N Livermore Ave.), L@ N Livermore Ave. (1.4), R@ 1st St.

OPEN M: 5 p.m.–2 a.m., Tu-Sa: 2 p.m.–2 a.m., Su: noon–2 a.m.

Having recently changed ownership, Livermore Saloon is now run by the same folks who operate Perry's Liquor (the Livermore store). A fun, dark and narrow dive bar with a younger crowd and geeked-out beer. Their twenty-two taps included local rarities from breweries such as Drake's, Heretic, and The Bruery – definitely leveraging Perry's beer-buying acumen. First Street Alehouse (no listing) nearby has a far more modest beer menu.

54 The Good Brewer
Homebrew Shop

(www)

WWW.GOODBREWER.COM

2960 Pacific Ave., Livermore, CA 94550, (925) 373-0333—GOING E: 580 Exit 52B (N Livermore Ave.), R@ N Livermore Ave. (1.6), L@ East Ave., R@ Dolores St., R@ Pacific Ave. GOING W: 580 Exit 52B (N Livermore Ave.), L@ N Livermore Ave. (1.6), L@ East Ave., R@ Dolores St., R@ Pacific Ave.

OPEN W: 10 a.m.–5:30 p.m., Th-Sa: 10 a.m.–6 p.m., Su: 11 a.m.–5 p.m.

About half a mile southeast of downtown Livermore, The Good Brewer offers homebrewing classes and carries ingredients and equipment for making beer, wine, cheese, and more.

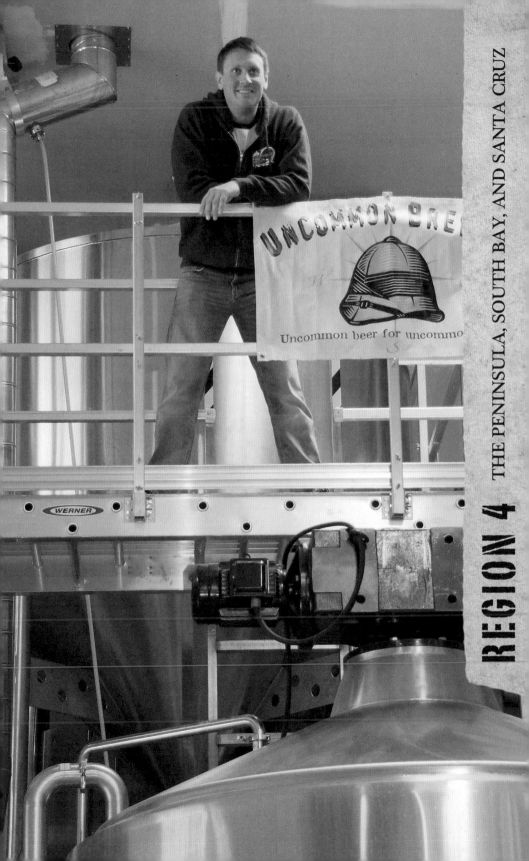

The Peninsula, South Bay, and Santa Cruz region includes the three counties south of San Francisco and East Bay: San Mateo, Santa Clara, and Santa Cruz. Much of this area was relatively new to us, and few of the breweries here distribute significantly outside the region (Uncommon Brewers and Gordon Biersch being two notable exceptions).

While the rest of the Bay Area has set the bar pretty high, the local beer scene to the south is on the upswing, and there's excellent beer to be found if you know where to look.

Though Silicon Valley is often the catch-all term for much of the region, the actual areas comprising the three counties vary enormously, and we often felt like we were somewhere else entirely. The beachside location of Half Moon Bay Brewing—on a warm day, at least—had us reminiscing about brewpub views heading north of San Diego (and Oregon's Pacific City). Los Gatos, to the southwest of San Jose, seemed like a toned-down, more endearing version of certain Marin shopping districts. Santa Cruz was like being in Davis— though a grittier rendering mixed with much of the North Coast mindset. Morgan Hill felt like a beer find in Central Valley. Some spots near San Jose just made us think we should care more about sports.

Numerous breweries are crafting great beer south of San Francisco, and we chose El Toro Brewing Co. and Steelhead Brewing Co. – Burlingame as our standout breweries in this region, both for offering a variety of well-crafted styles and for having great venues in which to sample them. burger. (with a small "b") in Santa Cruz has a draft list that sets it head and shoulders above everywhere else. And K&L, Bobby's Liquors, and The Willows Market have unique beer selections that put them on another level entirely. As in other regions, many local markets (Draeger's Markets, New Leaf, etc.) also provide a decent selection of craft beer in a pinch.

For keeping up with the ever-evolving craft beer scene in the greater South Bay region, Peter Estaniel (at www.betterbeerblog.com) provides excellent coverage on the latest in local events and beer news.

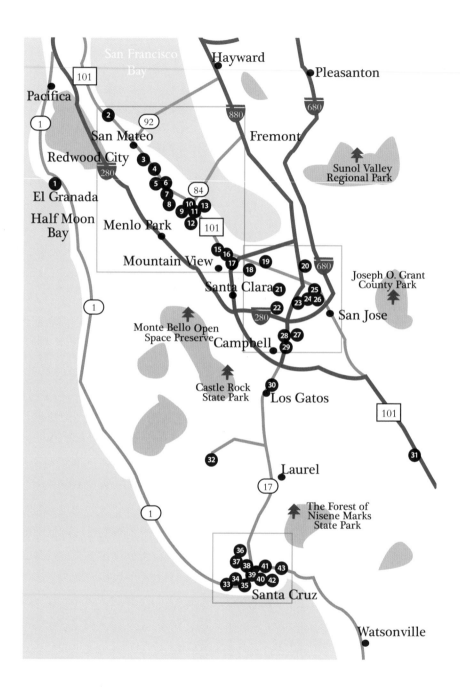

5 to try

El Toro Poppy Jasper Firehouse Hops on Rye Palo Alto Brewing Barely Legal Coconut Porter Steelhead Bombay Bomber IPA Uncommon Brewers Siamese Twin

1 Half Moon Bay Brewing Company – Half Moon Bay   Brewpub

2 Steelhead Brewing Co. – Burlingame   Brewpub

3 Devil's Canyon Brewing Company – Belmont   Brewery

4 The Refuge – San Carlos   Restaurant/Beer Bar

5 Gourmet Haus Staudt – Redwood City   Beer Bar/Bottle Shop

6 Martins West Gastropub – Redwood City   Restaurant

7 Angelica's Bistro – Redwood City   Restaurant

8 K&L Wine Merchants – Redwood City   Bottle Shop

9 British Bankers Club – Menlo Park   Restaurant/Beer Bar

10 The Willows Market – Menlo Park   Grocery Store/Bottle Shop

11 The Rose and Crown – Palo Alto   Beer Bar/Restaurant

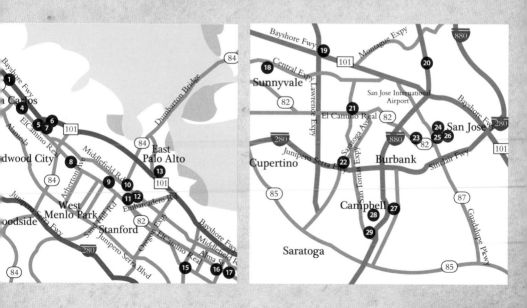

uncharted territory

12 Gordon Biersch – Palo Alto   Brewpub

13 Firehouse Brewery – East Palo Alto   Brewpub

14 Palo Alto Brewing Company – Palo Alto   Brewery

15 MoreBeer! – Los Altos   Homebrew Shop

16 Tied House Brewery & Café – Mountain View   Brewpub

17 Artisan Wine Depot – Mountain View   Bottle Shop

18 Firehouse Brewery – Sunnyvale   Brewpub

19 Faultline Brewing Company – Sunnyvale   Brewpub

20 Beer and Wine Makers of America – San Jose   Homebrew Shop

21 Bobby's Liquors – Santa Clara   Bottle Shop

22 Harry's Hofbrau – San Jose   Restaurant

23 Wine Affairs – San Jose   Beer Bar/Bottle Shop

24 Teske's Germania – San Jose   Restaurant

25 Los Gatos Brewing Co. – San Jose   Brewpub

26 Gordon Biersch – San Jose   Brewpub

27 Rock Bottom – Campbell   Brewpub

28 Campbell Brewing Company at Sonoma Chicken Coop – Campbell   Brewpub/Restaurant

29 Fermentation Solutions – Campbell   Homebrew Shop

30 Los Gatos Brewing Co. – Los Gatos   Brewpub

31 El Toro Brewing Co. – Morgan Hill   Brewpub

32 Boulder Creek Brewing Company – Boulder Creek   Brewpub

33 Santa Cruz Mountain Brewing – Santa Cruz   Brewery

34 Parish Publick House – Santa Cruz   Beer Bar/Restaurant

35 burger. – Santa Cruz   Restaurant/Beer Bar

36 Santa Cruz Ale Works – Santa Cruz   Brewery

37 Uncommon Brewers – Santa Cruz   Brewery

38 Seven Bridges Cooperative – Santa Cruz   Homebrew Shop

39 Red Restaurant & Bar – Santa Cruz   Restaurant/Beer Bar

40 99 Bottles of Beer on the Wall – Santa Cruz   Beer Bar/Restaurant

41 Surfrider Café – Santa Cruz   Restaurant

42 Seabright Brewery – Santa Cruz   Brewpub

43 41st Avenue Liquor – Capitola   Bottle Shop

① Half Moon Bay Brewing Company
Brewpub

WWW.HMBBREWINGCO.COM

390 Capistrano Rd., Half Moon Bay, CA 94019, (650) 728-2739—Northern edge of Half Moon Bay. GOING S: Hwy 1, R@ Capistrano Rd. (0.5). GOING N: Hwy 1, L@ Capistrano Rd.

OPEN M-Th: 11:30 a.m.–10 p.m., F: 11:30 a.m.–11 p.m., Sa: 11 a.m.–11 p.m., Su: 11 a.m.–10 p.m.

Definitely one of the more scenic brewpub locations you'll find, Half Moon Bay features a plush outdoor seating area looking over the water, plus live music on the weekends. While some of the beers tended toward the too-light side of things, it was nice to see a brewery focusing on beers under 5%. The Sandy Beach Blonde Hefeweizen was a solid hybrid of American and German interpretations, offering up soft cloves and pepper along with lemony notes and a husky wheat character. The Princeton-by-the-Sea IPA was also quite good: orange, lemon, and grapefruit hop flavors without an overbearing bitterness.

> BREWMASTER: Kirk Hillyard
> ESTABLISHED: 2000
> BE SURE TO TRY: Princeton-by-the-Sea IPA
> SEASONALS: Pumpkin (fall)
> ELSEWHERE: Bottles, Draft

Steelhead Brewi

② Steelhead Brewing Co. ⭐
Brewpub

WWW.STEELHEADBREWERY.COM

333 California Dr., Burlingame, CA 94010, (650) 344-6050—GOING S: 101 Exit 419B (Broadway), L@ California Dr. (1.1). GOING N: 101 Exit 417A (Dore Ave.), L@ N Bayshore Blvd. (0.6), L@ Peninsula Ave. (0.8), R@ California Dr.

OPEN Su-M: 11:30 a.m.–9 p.m.+, Tu-Th: 11:30 a.m.–10 p.m.+, F-Sa: 11:30 a.m.–11 p.m.+

Steelhead Brewing Co. has three different locations, including one in Irvine and the original brewpub in Eugene, Oregon,

eelhead Brewing

which opened in 1991. Each has their own brewer, and Emil Calvori's doing an impressive job at the Burlingame location. There were a total of eight or ten different beers on tap when we stopped in, including a number of tasty seasonals, but the real strength here was in the standard lineup: Hairy Weasel Hefeweizen, Broadway Blonde, Raging Rhino Red, and Bombay Bomber IPA. Their IPA was the most upfront of the group, a beautiful hybrid between an English IPA and an American one, showing lots of grapefruit and floral hoppiness with toasty, biscuit-like malts; the version served via cask (a regular feature at the brewery) showed more of its core toastiness. Those three others are ultimately quieter styles but beautifully done here: the Hefeweizen was a juicy, citrusy American wheat, and the Blonde (a cream ale) had effervescent, Champagne-like carbonation along with light fruitiness and a dry, cornflake-like finish. The layered maltiness of their Raging Rhino was masterfully handled. One additional feature of this brewpub is their cavernous billiards room at the back of the restaurant. It houses six regulation tables and a full second bar. Reservation details are available on their web site.

HEAD BREWER: Emil Calvori
ESTABLISHED: 1995
BE SURE TO TRY: Bombay Bomber IPA
SEASONALS: Pumpkin Pie Ale (fall), Double Play IPA (occasional)

❸ Devil's Canyon Brewing Company
Brewery

WWW.DEVILSCANYONBREWERY.COM

111 Industrial Rd. #7, Belmont, CA 94002, (650) 592-2739—GOING S: 101 Exit 412 (Ralston Ave./Notre Dame De Namur University), keep left (Harbor Blvd.) (0.6), L@ Industrial Rd. GOING N: 101 Exit 411 (Holly St.) (0.8), R@ Industrial Rd. (0.8).

OPEN Growler fills/keg pickups by appointment. Open once a month for Beer Friday.

While Devil's Canyon's open hours are typically limited to their monthly Beer Fridays (or by appointment for growler and keg pickups), you can find their bottles and draft accounts throughout the Bay Area. The most common is their popular Full Boar Scotch Ale, a solid example of the style showing a light smoked peatiness and notes of cola and brown sugar. Devil's Canyon also has the only currently operating Brew-on-Premise program we've seen in Northern California, which allows customers to brew their own small batches of beer on site, though as of late this program was limited to larger groups.

BREWMASTER: Chris Garrett
ESTABLISHED: 2001
BE SURE TO TRY: Full Boar Scotch Ale
ELSEWHERE: Bottles, Draft

❹ The Refuge
Restaurant/Beer Bar

WWW.REFUGESC.COM

963 Laurel St., San Carlos, CA 94070, (650) 598-9813—GOING S: 101 Exit 411 (Holly St., keep right) (0.8), L@ El Camino Real (0.5), R@ Arroyo Ave., L@ Laurel St. GOING N: 101 Exit 411 (Holly St., keep left) (1.1), L@ El Camino Real (0.5), R@ Arroyo Ave., L@ Laurel St.

OPEN Tu–Th: 11:30 a.m.–2:30 p.m., 5:30 p.m.–9 p.m., F: 11:30 a.m.–2:30 p.m., 5:30 p.m.–10 p.m., Sa: noon–10 p.m.

Hand-carved pastrami sandwiches with plenty of Belgian beer. The Refuge has about eighteen taps, with some fun deviations from the Belgian theme, as well as a pricey reserve bottle list (Mikkeller, Fantôme, and so on).

❺ Gourmet Haus Staudt
Beer Bar/Bottle Shop

WWW.GOURMETHAUSSTAUDT.COM

2615 Broadway, Redwood City, CA 94063, (650) 364-9232—GOING S: 101 Exit 409 (Whipple Ave.) (0.8), R@ Brewster Ave., L@ Perry St., R@ Broadway. GOING N: 101 Exit 408 (Hwy 84 W/Woodside Rd.) (0.5), R@ Veterans Blvd. (0.7), L@ Main St., R@ Broadway, L@ Broadway/Marshall St.

OPEN M: 10 a.m.–6 p.m., Tu–Sa: 10 a.m.–10 p.m.

Trouble Brewing

Sometimes beer can be taken a bit too seriously. It's a precarious balance, as craft beer lovers recognize both that malt- and hop-based beverages can be just as masterful and worthy of focused attention as grape-based ones, and that most of us have no interest in emulating the bad habits of the wine world. It can get weird. For those occasional moments of accidentally extended pinkies, there's Trouble Brewing.

Arne Frantzell, an artist (among other pursuits) based in Redwood City, has been creating the satirical series since spring of 2011. Whether it's the latest extreme brewing idea from Dogfish Head and The Bruery, the internal shenanigans at Stone and Lost Abbey, or simply the sometimes-a-little-too-familiar internal workings of the beer-geek couple, Arne's there to take the edge off. Currently you can see his work at The Full Pint (www.thefullpint.com) and Trouble Brewing's Facebook page. You may also stumble across examples of his artwork on recent collaborative labels he's done with Stone Brewing Co. and De Struise Brouwers.

I requested the adjacent cartoon from Arne for a couple reasons. For one, my fellow über-geeks will appreciate the White Birch reference. But secondly, and more importantly, everybody else won't get it, and I think that second reading of the strip is better aligned with one of the central underpinnings of this book. People inherently have different tastes and perception thresholds, one person's flaw is another person's feature, and your palate is your own. If we wanted to feel awkward about this, we could go drink wine.

Bierschnaps, Beer Whiskey

The initial steps to making beer and whiskey are quite similar, as they involve malted barley being fermented by yeast up to beer-like strengths. The overarching difference is that the "wash," as it's called for whiskey, is un-hopped and subsequently distilled. Northern California, perhaps not too surprisingly, is home to at least two distilleries that are bringing hops into the process.

Essential Spirits (www.essentialspirits.com) is a micro-distillery in Mountain View producing a small line of products that includes a Cabernet-based grappa, a pear brandy, and—most importantly—"Classick," or Bier-schnaps. Classick is a clear, Vodka-like product that's distilled from the company's microbrewed pale ale, featuring American hops and malt. K&L Wine Merchants is the easiest place to track it down.

Charbay Winery & Distillery (www.charbay.com) is owned and operated by the Karakasevic family out of Napa Valley. This award-winning business has been part of the artisanal distillery movement since 1983, and they currently offer two beer-based products. Doubled & Twisted was first distilled from a California IPA back in 2004, then aged for a very short time in mostly neutral barrels before being left to age in stainless steel. The IPA's hop flavors come through quite prominently, and Master Distiller Marko Karakasevic plans for subsequent batches to use Bear Republic Racer 5. Charbay's Whiskey, on the other hand, was distilled back in 1999 from Northern California Pilsner (I bet I can guess which one…), and releases occur as various barrels are deemed ready. Unlike Doubled & Twisted, this product has been aging for years in charred oak barrels, resulting in a complex whiskey that's most assuredly on the pricier side of things.

German specialty store with a beer garden pouring eleven excellent German taps, along with two guest taps (recently: limited-release beers from Midnight Sun and Ballast Point). A well-organized selection of bottles. Additionally, these folks tend to host some pretty interesting events during San Francisco Beer Week.

Martins West Gastropub
Restaurant

WWW.MARTINSWESTGP.COM

831 Main St., Redwood City, CA 94063, (650) 366-4366—GOING S: 101 Exit 409 (Whipple Ave.) (1.0), R@ Main St. GOING N: 101 Exit 408 (Hwy 84 W/Woodside Rd.) (0.5), R@ Veterans Blvd. (0.7), L@ Main St.

OPEN M: 3 p.m.–9 p.m., Tu: 3 p.m.– 10 p.m., W-F: 11:30 a.m.–10 p.m., Sa: noon–10 p.m.

Farm-to-table gastropub on the same block as Angelica's Bistro. A small number of choice taps with a wider-ranging bottle list. The latter featured everything from spiced beers and witbiers to a nice lineup of IPAs.

⑦ Angelica's Bistro
Restaurant

WWW.ANGELICASBISTRO.COM

863 Main St., Redwood City, CA 94063, (650) 365-3226—GOING S: 101 Exit 409 (Whipple Ave.) (1.0), R@ Main St. GOING

N: 101 Exit 408 (Hwy 84 W/Woodside Rd.) (0.5), R@ Veterans Blvd. (0.7), L@ Main St.

OPEN M-Th: 11 a.m.–9 p.m., F-Sa: 11 a.m.–midnight

Angelica's Bistro is on the same block as Martins West Gastropub. In addition to having their own theater and stage for live shows, there's a well-maintained beer and wine garden for enjoying their fifty-plus craft and international beers. They also recently featured Beer Crawl Tables and a Beer & Wine Club.

⑧ K&L Wine Merchants
Bottle Shop

WWW.KLWINES.COM

3005 El Camino Real, Redwood City, CA 94061, (877) 559-4637/(650) 364-8544—GOING S: 101 Exit 408 (Hwy 84 W/Woodside Rd.) (0.9), L@ Middlefield Rd. (1.0), R@ Fifth Ave., R@ El Camino Real. GOING N: 101 Exit 406 (Hwy 84 E/Marsh Rd.), L@ Hwy 84 W/Marsh Rd. (follow Marsh Rd.) (1.3), R@ Middlefield Rd., L@ Fair Oaks Ln. (0.6), R@ El Camino Real (0.7).

OPEN M-F: 10 a.m.–7 p.m., Sa: 9 a.m.– 7 p.m., Su: 10 a.m.–6 p.m.

Whereas Bobby's Liquors was singled out for its eclecticism and The Willows Market for its breadth, K&L Wine Merchants fills another niche: hundreds of highly regarded singles from big-name brewers from around the globe. Alesmith, De Struise Brouwers, Great Divide, Hair of the Dog, Jolly Pumpkin, Mikkeller,

Stone, etc. Their inventory is available online, and the selection is right up there with The Willows Market. (Skip K&L's San Francisco store, as almost all the beer is here.)

British Bankers Club
Restaurant/Beer Bar

WWW.BRITISHBANKERSCLUB.COM

1090 El Camino Real, Menlo Park, CA 94025, (650) 327-8769—GOING S: 101 Exit 406 (Hwy 84 E/Marsh Rd.), R@ Marsh Rd. (1.1), L@ Middlefield Rd. (1.1), R@ Ravenswood Ave. (0.6), R@ El Camino Real. GOING N: 101 Exit 404B (Willow Rd. W) (1.3), R@ Middlefield Rd. (0.7), L@ Ravenswood Ave. (0.6), R@ El Camino Real.

OPEN M-F: 10 a.m.–2 a.m., Sa-Su: 9 a.m.–2 a.m.

While craft beer isn't the focus here, this gastropub has a decent selection of twenty taps and a bottle menu that had plenty of Bear Republic and Flying Dog (the latter based in Maryland), plus an eclectic mix of international bottles. They offer a variety of draft pour sizes. Generally speaking, I'd advise against the 34-ounce ones.

 The Willows Market
Grocery Store/Bottle Shop

WWW.WILLOWSMARKET.COM

60 Middlefield Rd., Menlo Park, CA 94025, (650) 322-0743—GOING S: 101 Exit 404B (Willow Rd. W) (1.2), L@

Blackburn Ave. R@ Baywood Ave., R@ Woodland Ave., R@ Middlefield Rd. GOING N: 101 Exit 403 (University Ave.) (1.8), R@ Middlefield Rd. (0.5).

OPEN Every day: 6 a.m.–midnight

A low-key specialty grocery store with an absurd beer selection. Individual shelving units for Belgian and German beers, multiple shelving units for British beer, an entire section consisting solely of sour ales and gueuzes… I asked Ali to pinch me, but she was too busy beer shopping. A solid collection of regional beer as well: Almanac, Devil's Canyon, El Toro, High Water, Firehouse. At least a few hundred well-organized bottles, many with helpful Ratebeer.com shelf tags. They even had Stone Brewing BBQ and hot sauces. In the unlikely event you can't find something, Beltramo's (1540 El Camino Real; no listing) is less than two miles away.

The Rose and Crown
Beer Bar/Restaurant

WWW.ROSEANDCROWNPA.COM

547 Emerson Ave., Palo Alto, CA 94301, (650) 327-7673—GOING S: 101 Exit 403 (University Ave.), L@ University Ave. (1.7), L@ Emerson St. GOING N: 101 Exit 403 (University Ave.) (2.3), L@ Emerson St.

OPEN Every day: 11:30 a.m.–closing

Definitely more of a beer-geek focus than many of the beer bars in South Bay. This British-style pub has twenty-plus taps and

included highlights from Russian River, Firestone Walker, and Sierra Nevada when we dropped in. They also had a sweet bottle list and the widest selection I've seen of beers by the Palo Alto Brewing Company (same owner).

12 Gordon Biersch
Brewpub

WWW.GORDONBIERSCH.COM

640 Emerson St., Palo Alto, CA 94301, (650) 323-7723—GOING S: 101 Exit 404B (Willow Rd. W) (1.3), L@ Middlefield Rd. (0.5), R@ University Ave. (0.5), L@ Emerson St. GOING N: 101 Exit 403 (University Ave.) (2.3), L@ Emerson St.

OPEN Su-Th: 11:30 a.m.–11 p.m., F-Sa: 11:30 a.m.–1 a.m.

Chain location (for details, see main listing: Gordon Biersch – San Jose on page 147).

13 Firehouse Brewery
Brewpub

WWW.FIREHOUSEGRILL.COM

1765 E. Bayshore Rd., Ste A, East Palo Alto, CA 94303, (650) 326-9700—GOING S: 101 Exit 403 (University Ave.), R@ University Ave., R@ Donohoe St. GOING N: 101 Exit 403 (E Palo Alto), R@ Donohoe St.

OPEN M–W: 11 a.m.–9:30 p.m., Th–Sa: 11 a.m.–10 p.m., Su: 10 a.m.–9 p.m.

Second location (for details, see main listing: Firehouse Brewery – Sunnyvale on facing page).

⑭ Palo Alto Brewing Company
Brewery

WWW.PALOALTOBREWING.COM

Palo Alto, CA

While a relatively new addition to the region, Palo Alto Brewing Co. is already making highly regarded beers, including Hoppy Ending Pale Ale and Barely Legal Coconut Porter. Their Porter is delicious, offering silky layers of milk chocolate supported by some bitter roasted notes appearing mid-palate. One of the more ambitious, robust beers coming out of this region. While The Rose and Crown is your best bet for sampling Palo Alto Brewing, look for their bottles throughout the southern Bay Area.

BREWER: Kasim Syed
ESTABLISHED: Circa 2009
BE SURE TO TRY: Barely Legal Coconut Porter
ELSEWHERE: Bottles, Draft

⑮ MoreBeer!
Homebrew Shop

WWW.MOREBEER.COM

991 N. San Antonio Rd., Los Altos, CA 94022, (650) 949-2739/(800) 600-0033—GOING S: 101 Exit 400C (San Antonia Rd. S) (2.2), L@ W El Camino Real, R@

Sherwood Ave., R@ N San Antonio Rd. GOING N: 101 Exit 399B (Old Middlefield Way) (1.4), L@ San Antonio Rd. (1.2), L@ W El Camino Real, R@ Sherwood Ave., R@ N San Antonio Rd.

OPEN M–F: 10 a.m.–6 p.m., Sa–Su: 10 a.m.–5 p.m.

Chain location (for details, see main listing: MoreBeer! – Concord on page 122).

⑯ Tied House Brewery & Café
Brewpub

WWW.TIEDHOUSE.COM

954 Villa St., Mountain View, CA 94041, (650) 965-2739—GOING S: 101 Exit 399 (Shoreline Blvd.), R@ N Shoreline Blvd., L@ Villa St. GOING N: 101 Exit 398 (Moffett Blvd./Nasa Pkwy), L@ Moffett Blvd. (1.3), R@ Villa St.

OPEN M–Th: 11:30 a.m.–10 p.m., F: 11:30 a.m.–11 p.m., Sa: 11:30 a.m.–10 p.m., Su: 11:30 a.m.–9 p.m.

Tied House is connected to a variety of different brands and labels, including Hermitage and Coastal Fog. The actual brewpub offers a number of them via draft or in bottles, including Hermitage and their single hop series the last time we stopped by. Their best-selling amber, a fruity take on the style with mineral and earthy hops, is worth checking out. Note that their sampler options tend to be limited to just a few seasonals.

BREWMASTER: Ron Manabe
ESTABLISHED: 1988
ELSEWHERE: Bottles, Draft

Artisan Wine Depot
Bottle Shop

WWW.ARTISANWINEDEPOT.COM

400 A Villa St., Mountain View, CA
94041, (877) 946-3730/(650) 969-
3511—GOING S: 101 Exit 398B (Hwy 85
S/Santa Cruz/Cupertino) (1.2), Exit 23
(Central Expy), R@ Central Expy (0.5),
L@ Castro St., L@ Villa St. GOING N: 101
Exit 398 (Moffett Blvd./Nasa Pkwy), L@
Moffett Blvd. (1.3), L@ Villa St.

OPEN M-F: 10 a.m.–7:30 p.m., Sa: noon–
6 p.m., Su: noon–4 p.m.

Slightly disorganized selection of craft
beer, with a strong emphasis on well-
crafted imports (Belgian and German,
predominantly) and a decent lineup from
California, including Russian River and
Lost Abbey.

18 Firehouse Brewery
Brewpub

WWW.FIREHOUSEGRILL.COM

111 S. Murphy Ave., Sunnyvale, CA
94086, (408) 773-9500—GOING S: 101
Exit 396A (N Mathilda Ave./Sunnyvale)
(1.7), L@ W Washington Ave., L@ S
Murphy Ave. GOING N: 101 Exit 396B
(Mathilda Avenue S/Sunnyvale) (1.8), L@
W Washington Ave., L@ S Murphy Ave.

OPEN M-W: 11 a.m.–10:30 p.m., Th-Sa:
11 a.m.–11 p.m., Su: 9:30 a.m.–10 p.m.

Billed as a "neighborhood sports brewery,"
the main appeal here for us was their

hoppy seasonals. The Cluster Fuggles had
an assertive English-style hop character
(earthy, lightly citrusy), while their Hops
on Rye stole the show: soft and spicy rye
qualities, some crystalline sugars, and loads
of earthy bitterness.
BREW MASTER: Steve Donohue
ESTABLISHED: 2005
BE SURE TO TRY: Whatever's hoppy
ELSEWHERE: Bottles, Draft

19 Faultline Brewing Company
Brewpub

WWW.FAULTLINEBREWING.COM

1235 Oakmead Pkwy, Sunnyvale, CA
94085, (408) 736-2739—GOING S:
101 Exit 394 (Lawrence Expy), R@
Lawrence Expy. (0.6), L@ E Arques
Ave. (0.5), L@ Oakmead Pkwy (0.6).
GOING N: 101 Exit 392 (follow San Tomas
Expy.) (0.8), R@ Scott Blvd. (1.3), R@
Oakmead Pkwy (0.6).

OPEN M-Tu: 11 a.m.–10:30 p.m., W-F:
11:30 a.m.–10:30 p.m., Sa: 5 p.m.–10 p.m.

While there's a recurrent sports-bar feel
to much of San Jose, Faultline has more of
the crisp-tablecloth and attentive-service
atmosphere. Their cask-conditioned
Brown was the only mild disappointment
(the standard version was far better), and
while nothing particularly stood out,
their Kolsch, Pale Ale, Brown Ale, IPA,
and Hefeweizen were all well-handled.
The growler offerings consist of those
infrequently seen five-liter minikegs.
Faultline often hosts live music on the
weekend to accompany the dinner crowd.
BREWMASTER: Peter Catizone

Harry's Hofbrau

ESTABLISHED: 1994
BE SURE TO TRY: Your favorite style
SEASONALS: Holiday Strong (occasional)

20 Beer and Wine Makers of America
Homebrew Shop

WWW.BEERANDWINEMAKERS.COM

755 E. Brokaw Rd. San Jose, CA 95112, (408) 441-0880—GOING S: 880 Exit 5 (Brokaw Rd.), R@ E Brokaw Rd. GOING N: 880 Exit 5 (Brokaw Rd.), L@ E Brokaw Rd.

OPEN Tu-F: 11 a.m.–6 p.m., Sa-Su: 11 a.m.–3 p.m.

The closest homebrew shop to downtown San Jose, Beer and Wine Makers of America has been around since 1975 and sells equipment and supplies for making one's own beer, mead, cider, wine, soda, and more.

21 Bobby's Liquors ★
Bottle Shop

WWW.BOBBYSLIQUORS.COM

2327 El Camino Real, Santa Clara, CA 95050, (408) 984-1120—GOING S: 101 Exit 392 (San Tomas Expy) (2.4), L@ El Camino Real, U-turn@ Los Padres Blvd. GOING N: 101 Exit 392 (San Tomas Expy) (2.7), L@ El Camino Real, U-turn@ Los Padres Blvd.

OPEN Su-Th: 9 a.m.–1 a.m., F-Sa: 9 a.m.– 2 a.m.

It might not look like much from the outside, but the beer selection tucked away in the back corner here is jaw-dropping. Plenty of Northern California rarities (Triple Voodoo, Sonoma Springs, Ale Industries, El Toro), an exceptional lineup of top-tier American and import beers (including Midnight Sun, Lost Abbey, Pretty Things, and Mikkeller), and a number of über-large-format Belgian bottles that I haven't seen anywhere else. Magnum of Rochefort 8? Yes, please.

22 Harry's Hofbrau
Restaurant

WWW.HARRYSHOFBRAU.COM

390 Saratoga Ave. San Jose, CA 95129, (408) 243-0434—GOING S: 280 Exit 7 (Saratoga Ave./Saratoga), L@ Saratoga Ave. GOING N: 280 Exit 7 (Saratoga Ave.

N, keep right) (0.6).

OPEN Every day: 11 a.m.–11 p.m.

Something of an anomaly in the Harry's Hofbrau chain, the San Jose location recently upgraded its craft beer selection. Thirty-plus bottles and fourteen taps, eight of which were focused on fun, limited-release West Coast offerings when we came by. A cavernous, German-influenced restaurant with a lengthy bar and cafeteria-style ordering.

23 Wine Affairs
Beer Bar/Bottle Shop

WWW.THEWINEAFFAIRS.COM

1435 The Alameda, San Jose, CA 95126, (408) 977-0111—Just west of downtown San Jose, near the corner of Hester Ave. and The Alameda.

OPEN M: 4 p.m.–10 p.m., Tu: 2:30 p.m.–10 p.m., W-Th: 2:30 p.m.–11 p.m., F-Sa: 1 p.m.–midnight, Su: 2:30 p.m.–8 p.m.

Wine Affairs can perhaps best be understood as a beer bar trapped in a wine bar's body. They feature twelve rotating taps and a beer list offering about a hundred bottles, including Russian River, High Water, and The Bruery (the lattermost from Southern California). Also offers a tapas menu. A great spot to try some samples or converse over a pint.

24 Teske's Germania
Restaurant

WWW.TESKES-GERMANIA.COM

255 N. First St., San Jose, CA 95113, (408) 292-0291—Downtown San Jose, near the corner of Devine St. and N. First St.

OPEN Tu-F: 11 a.m.–2 p.m., 5 p.m.–9:30 p.m., Sa: 5 p.m.–9:30 p.m.

Family-owned German restaurant with a beer garden and a modest tap selection, in liters and half liters.

25 Los Gatos Brewing Co.
Brewpub

WWW.LGBREWINGCO.COM

163 W. Santa Clara St., San Jose, CA 95113, (408) 600-1181—Downtown San Jose, near the corner of San Pedro St. and W. Santa Clara St.

OPEN Su-Th: 11:30 a.m.–9 p.m.+, F-Sa: 11:30 a.m.–10 p.m.+

Second location (for details, see main listing: Los Gatos Brewing Co. – Los Gatos on page 150).

26 Gordon Biersch
Brewpub

WWW.GORDONBIERSCH.COM

33 E. San Fernando St., San Jose, CA 95113, (408) 294-6785—Downtown

STOUT
EL TORO NEGRO OATMEAL STOUT

In eighteenth-century England, the term "stout" served to designate stronger versions of a particular beer style, such as a "stout porter." Through a series of verbal slippages, slap fights, and so on (beer historians Martyn Cornell and Ron Pattinson are far more patient with this sort of thing), stouts and porters came to be recognized as semi-distinct styles, only to (ta-da!) later be crammed together stylistically in modern-day brewing.

Here's what's most important about stout, in all its manifestations (Irish dry, oatmeal, imperial, sweet, hoppy, etc.): they're dark ales, brewed with a noticeable amount of roasted specialty malts, and those specialty malts typically contribute chocolate- and coffee-like notes along with a bitterness that, in contrast to IPAs and similar brews, is malt-derived rather than hop-derived (though many have a healthy dose of hops as well). Dark color isn't any indication of strength, however, and most dry stouts are under 5%; nonetheless, they're much more flavorful than most macro pale lagers. In other words, Guinness is a "meal in a glass" only if you'd otherwise be eating carrot sticks and skim milk.

That said, those highly potent imperial stouts (see sidebar on page 171) should be considered a sometimes food.

El Toro Negro Oatmeal Stout is a perfect example of why a drink-based approach to learning beer styles is usually the most illuminative: cocoa notes, bittersweet chocolate, cola, and a creaminess (originating from the addition of rolled oats) that tempers that dark-malt bitterness perfectly. A delicious, medium-bodied oatmeal stout. (Stouts tend to be easier to delineate within the style's subcategories.) Other local renditions worth seeking out include Lost Coast's 8 Ball, Bear Republic Big Bear, North Coast Old No. 38, and Lagunitas Cappuccino Stout.

San Jose, near the corner of S. Second St. and E. San Fernando St.

OPEN Su-W: 11:30 a.m.–11 p.m., Th: 11:30 a.m.–midnight, F-Sa: 11:30 a.m.–1 a.m.

I chose the San Jose location of Gordon Biersch for their central listing simply because their Brewery and Bottling Facility is also located in San Jose. Here's the general layout of things: Gordon Biersch and Rock Bottom recently became subsidiaries of the same company (Craftworks), though their brands have been kept separate. Gordon Biersch, I was told, has individual on-site brewers for each of their restaurants, as well as a separate set of folks producing their bottles and off-site kegs out of the Brewery and Bottling Facility. So, every off-site experience should be relatively consistent, while the restaurants will vary a bit. They've got numerous locations throughout the U.S., and recently opened a few restaurants in Taiwan. I've enjoyed their Maibock on multiple occasions, though our travel budget disallowed us from checking consistency in the Taiwanese versions. At the San Jose location, the strongest renditions for us were the Golden Export and the Czech Pilsner. Gordon Biersch focuses on German-style offerings, and the Golden Export was a crisp, rounded lager with malty notes of cereal and toast, while the Czech Pilsner had a spicy noble-hop character with just a light touch of honeyed sweetness. Your mileage may vary elsewhere.

BREWER: Jeff Liles (San Jose brewpub)
ESTABLISHED: Circa 1990 (Palo Alto location in 1988)
BE SURE TO TRY: Golden Export
ELSEWHERE: Bottles, Draft

27 Rock Bottom
Brewpub

WWW.ROCKBOTTOM.COM

1875 South Bascom Ave., Unit 700, Campbell, CA 95008, (408) 377-0707—GOING S: 17 Exit 25 (Hamilton Ave.), L@ E Hamilton Ave., R@ S Bascom Ave. GOING N: 17 Exit 25 (Hamilton Ave.), R@ Creekside Way, L@ Campisi Way, R@ S Bascom Ave.

OPEN M-Th: 11 a.m.–10 p.m., F-Sa: 11 a.m.–closing, Su: 11 a.m.–10 p.m.

While the Rock Bottom chain has restaurants across the country, this is their only location in Northern California. They were pouring four standard Rock Bottom beers (Kölsch, White Ale, IPA, and Red Ale) and four specific to the brewery when we visited. The Kölsch and White Ale were the best of the group, although the sulfur characteristics of the Kölsch (though not atypical in the style) grew to be a bit much.

BREWMASTER: Scott Guckel
BE SURE TO TRY: White Ale

28 Campbell Brewing Company at Sonoma Chicken Coop
Brewpub/Restaurant

WWW.SONOMACHICKEN.COM

200 E. Campbell Ave., Campbell, CA 95008, (408) 866-2699—GOING S: 17 Exit 25 (Hamilton Ave., keep right), L@ N Central Ave., R@ Grant St., L@ N 2nd St., R@ E Campbell Ave. GOING N: 17 Exit 25 (Hamilton Ave.), L@ Creekside Way, L@ E Hamilton Ave., L@ N Central Ave., R@ Grant St., L@ N 2nd St., R@ E Campbell Ave.

OPEN M-Th: 11 a.m.–10 p.m., F: 11 a.m.–11 p.m., Sa: 9 a.m.–11 p.m., Su: 9 a.m.–10 p.m.

A hybrid arrangement connecting the Sonoma Chicken Coop chain's Campbell location with Campbell Brewing Company. Their lineup was quite good, particularly the lighter-bodied, peppery Hefeweizen and the ESB, which showed a rich biscuity maltiness. An atypical amalgam between a brewpub and a fast food chain.

BREWMASTER: Jim Turturici
ESTABLISHED: 2002
BE SURE TO TRY: ESB

29 Fermentation Solutions
Homebrew Shop

WWW.FERMENTATIONSOLUTIONS.COM

2507 Winchester Blvd., Campbell, CA 95008, (408) 871-1400—GOING S: 17 Exit 23 (San Tomas Expy), R@ San Tomas Expy, Exit@ Winchester Blvd. N. GOING

CAMPBELL

The Northern California Craft Beer Guide

149

El Toro Brewing

N: 17 Exit 23 (Camden Ave./San Tomas Expy), L@ White Oaks Rd., L@ Camden Ave., Exit@ Winchester Blvd. N.

OPEN M–F: 10 a.m.–6 p.m., Sa: 10 a.m.–5 p.m., Su: 11 a.m.–4 p.m.

One of at least two homebrew shops within a short drive of downtown San Jose, Fermentation Solutions has been around for more than twenty-five years and carries products for making beer, wine, mead, and more.

30 Los Gatos Brewing Co.
Brewpub

WWW.LGBREWINGCO.COM

130 N. Santa Cruz Ave., Los Gatos, CA 95030, (408) 395-9929—GOING S: 17 Exit 20B (Saratoga Los Gatos Rd./State Route 9 S/Los Gatos/Saratoga) (0.5), L@ N Santa Cruz Ave. GOING N: 17 Exit 19 (Santa Cruz Ave.), R@ Montebello

Way/S Santa Cruz Ave. (0.4).

OPEN M–F: 11:30 a.m.–closing, Sa-Su: 10 a.m.–closing

Los Gatos has one of the more consistent beer lineups in the greater San Jose area. Their Lexington Lager, Dog Tale Pale, and Harry Porter (!) were all enjoyable, as was their cask beer (Mama Cask Elliot). They're one of the few places we've been that usually has something on cask year-round. Their Hue Hefe was the highlight: aromatic, effervescent, well-balanced between banana and clove components. One of the more precise hefeweizens we've sampled in Northern California. Bonus: a classily appointed place.

BREWMASTER: Kent Wheat
ESTABLISHED: 1991
BE SURE TO TRY: Hue Hefe

31 El Toro Brewing Co. ⭐
Brewpub

WWW.ELTOROBREWING.COM

17605 Monterey Rd., Morgan Hill, CA 95037, (408) 782-2739—GOING S: 101 Exit 367 (Cochrane Rd.), R@ Cochrane Rd. (0.8), L@ Monterey Rd. (1.2). GOING N: 101 Exit 366 (E Dunne Ave.), L@ E Dunne Ave. (1.1), R@ Monterey Rd. (0.6), U-turn@ E Central Ave.

OPEN Tu–Th: 11:30 a.m.–midnight, F-Sa: 11:30 a.m.–1 a.m., Su: 11:30 a.m.–midnight

I was pretty excited about going here originally, as Ali hadn't yet tried their Poppy Jasper—the delicious amber ale

they're known for around the Bay Area, which they've been quietly making since back in the mid-90s. It's a perfect amber for me: cereal toastiness and light caramelization at the center, with a mineral and citrus hop presence that's both satisfying and stays out of the way of the malt contributions. I was hoping they'd have it on tap so she could check it out. They had five different versions. Perhaps I wasn't mentally prepared. Normally when I go to a brewery's web site and see twenty-plus beers listed on their "Beer" page, this means that they're listing all of the beers they make throughout the year. "Silly man," said El Toro (figuratively, as brewpubs don't talk). "That's only part of our current beer list." Everything we sampled from their lineup of twenty-five-plus house-brewed beers was excellent. Three different dry-hopped versions of Poppy Jasper (using Columbus, Summit, and Willamette hops), plus the special cask version, plus the original version. I've spoken highly of their oatmeal stout (see sidebar on page 148). We went home with six-packs of the double IPA. The William Jones Wheat beer is one of the more flavorful American wheats I've tried lately. A braver person would have sampled their Ghost Chili Golden Ale (we needed our taste buds). While you're here, check out their bar—particularly its colorful inlay of a local, semiprecious quartz called poppy jasper.

BREWMASTER: Geno Acevedo
ESTABLISHED: 1994 (brewpub opened in 2006)
BE SURE TO TRY: Poppy Jasper(s)
ELSEWHERE: Bottles, Draft

32 Boulder Creek Brewing Company
Brewpub

WWW.BOULDERCREEKBREWERY.NET

13040 Highway 9, Boulder Creek, CA 95006, (831) 338-7882—Central Boulder Creek, directly off Central Ave./Hwy 9.

OPEN Su-Th: 11:30 a.m.–10 p.m., F-Sa: 11:30 a.m.–10:30 p.m.

Definitely off the beaten path, Boulder Creek Brewing Co. is a long, windy drive from San Jose. This is a pretty old and weathered brewpub with a well-brewed lineup of nonchalant beers. Their ESB was our favorite of the group, offering light touches of butterscotch alongside a balancing earthy bitterness. Boulder Creek also makes the Santa Cruz Brewery brand of beers (they're brewing on the original Santa Cruz Brewery's equipment); perhaps the most convenient place to try both lineups is at Surfrider Café in Santa Cruz.

HEAD BREWER: Michael Demers
ESTABLISHED: 1989
ELSEWHERE: Draft

33 Santa Cruz Mountain Brewing
Brewery

WWW.SANTACRUZMOUNTAINBREWING.COM

402 Ingalls St., Suite 27, Santa Cruz, CA 95060, (831) 425-4900—Western Santa Cruz. GOING E: Hwy 1 S, R@ Swift St. GOING W: Hwy 1 N, L@ Swift St.

An attractive tasting room (the bronze tree with hanging mugs is a nice touch) nestled next to a number of winery tasting rooms. The beers are of variable quality, with the Peoples Porter being our favorite.

ESTABLISHED: 2005
BE SURE TO TRY: Peoples Porter
SEASONALS: Thy Twisted Sister (occasional)
ELSEWHERE: Bottles, Draft

34 Parish Publick House
Beer Bar/Restaurant

WWW.PARISHPUBLICKHOUSE.COM

841 Almar Ave., Santa Cruz, CA 95067, (831) 421-0507—Western Santa Cruz. GOING E: Hwy 1 S, R@ Almar Ave. GOING W: Hwy 1 N, L@ Almar Ave.

Bacon. In a culture of internet memes and foodie inclinations, is there any more powerful opening sentence?

We'll get to the bacon beer, no worries. But throughout their entire main lineup, Uncommon Brewers in Santa Cruz has quietly proven itself to be one of the most adventurous breweries in the country, utilizing non-traditional spices and ingredients that go far beyond malts, hops, yeast, and water. Their Golden State Ale includes toasted poppy seeds (from California's state flower), while the Baltic Porter incorporates a rich presence of star anise and licorice root. Siamese Twin, our favorite of the mainstays, is their Belgian-style dubbel, with coriander, Thai spices, and kaffir lime leaves. In each example, these odd additions are seamlessly integrated into the base beer, and Head Brewer Alec Stefansky is constantly tweaking the recipes between batches. As he summarized their approach: "We're not trying to do flavored beer. It's beer with flavor."

The latest batches from Uncommon have been notably more precise than I remember from a year or two back—Siamese Twin will be making regular appearances in our fridge—and that's especially true with the latest version of their Bacon Brown Ale. Made with bacon-cured pork added directly to the boil, the final product is a lightly smoky brown ale, with touches of maple syrup alongside a mild saltiness and toasty finish. I've suffered through some pretty terrible bacon beers, but this one's masterfully brewed, and a reminder of how much America's craft beer scene is built upon both experimentation and persistence.

Other upcoming releases from Uncommon include the return of their Rubidus Red Ale (brewed with maple syrup and candy cap mushrooms) and their new American Special Bitter: a smooth, 14.5% monster aged on redwood. Alec has a number of other things on the horizon in terms of both beer releases and added brewery features, so stay tuned. Other Northern California examples exploring less-charted territories include Moonlight's gruits (herbs, spices, redwood tips) and selections from Shmaltz's HE'BREW line.

OPEN Every day: 11 a.m.–2 a.m.

One of the better craft beer locations in Santa Cruz, Parish Publick House is a few blocks from Santa Cruz Mountain Brewing. It's a familiar setting: a dark, worn-in tavern serving pub food. About fifteen taps, half of them focused on Northern California, plus an impressive six-page bottle list organized by style (including a "Shit Beer" section offering $2 Hamm's—just in case). Uncommon and Santa Cruz Ale Works were well represented, and the pub even had two-ounce pours of Sam Adams Utopias (27% ABV) on the menu when we stopped in.

35 burger. ⭐
Restaurant/Beer Bar

WWW.BURGERSANTACRUZ.COM

1520 Mission St., Santa Cruz, CA 95060, (831) 425-5300—Western Santa Cruz, directly off Hwy 1/Mission St.

OPEN Su-Th: 11 a.m.–10 p.m., F-Sa: 11 a.m.–11 p.m.

If you want to know what's happening in the Santa Cruz craft beer scene, the answer is burger. A recent addition, burger. specializes in two things: burgers and beer. You should not be the least bit surprised by this.
Their enormous burger menu features Humboldt grass-fed beef (free-range,

organic, and pesticide-free) and local and organic produce as much as possible. They're also 100% wind-powered. Their beer menu is the most geek-friendly you'll find in Santa Cruz, featuring about forty-seven taps and, when we last stopped in, beers from Moonlight, High Water, and Uncommon, along with difficult-to-find styles like Belgian lambic and Flanders Red. Huge beer list. Huge burger list. This place tends to get pretty busy.

36 Santa Cruz Ale Works
Brewery

WWW.SANTACRUZALEWORKS.COM

150 Dubois St., Ste E, Santa Cruz, CA 95060, (831) 425-1182—Northern Santa Cruz. GOING E: Hwy 1 S, L@ River St., L@ Encinal St. (0.5), L@ Dubois St. GOING W: Hwy 1 N, R@ River St., L@ Encinal St. (0.5), L@ Dubois St.

OPEN Tasting room open by appointment only.

As Uncommon Brewers provides Santa Cruz with locally produced experimental brews, Santa Cruz Ale Works provides the locally produced American standards. Marc Rosenblum has professional

brewing experience to spare, including stints at Lagunitas, Pyramid, and about eight years as head brewer at Seabright, and one can immediately tell that this is not timid brewing. The Hefeweizen is chewy and citrusy, with a juicy central orange note, and the IPA shows plenty of American-style hop flavor and bitterness. On the other side of the spectrum, both the Dark Knight Oatmeal Stout (cocoa and dark fruits) and the Cruz Control Red (red fruit and caramel) exhibited loads of rich maltiness. Note that Santa Cruz Ale Works, like Uncommon Brewers, is only open by appointment, so be sure to call ahead.

> HEAD BREWER: Marc Rosenblum
> ESTABLISHED: 2007 (started selling beer in 2008)
> BE SURE TO TRY: IPA
> SEASONALS: Cruz Control Red (occasional)
> ELSEWHERE: Bottles, Draft

37 Uncommon Brewers
Brewery

WWW.UNCOMMONBREWERS.COM

303 Potrero St., Ste 40-H, Santa Cruz, CA 95060, (831) 621-6270—Northern Santa Cruz. Going E: Hwy 1 S, R@ River St.,

The Northern California Craft Beer Guide

R@ Potrero St. Going W: Hwy 1 N, L@ River St., R@ Potrero St.

OPEN By appointment only.

This was our favorite brewery stop in Santa Cruz, situated in the warehouse section off of Potrero Street. Look for the signage near the railroad tracks. The brewery smelled softly of star anise when we stopped in, like holiday cookies (at least where I come from), and while Alec Stefansky didn't have a formal tasting bar or growler filling station, he's got some out-there amenities coming up that I can't even talk about yet. From someone whose brewery is based squarely on odd ingredients (see sidebar on page 153), would you expect anything less? This place is well on its way to Beer Destination status. When you visit, definitely check out the tall shelves of environmentally minded KeyKegs. Hint: they're spherical.

HEAD BREWER: Alec Stefansky
ESTABLISHED: 2007
BE SURE TO TRY: Siamese Twin
SEASONALS: Bacon Brown Ale (occasional), American Special Bitter (occasional)
ELSEWHERE: Bottles, Draft

38 Seven Bridges Cooperative
Homebrew Shop

WWW.BREWORGANIC.COM

325A River St., Santa Cruz, CA 95060, (831) 454-9665/(800) 768-4409— Northern Santa Cruz. GOING E: Hwy 1 S, R@ River St. GOING W: Hwy 1 N, L@ River St.

OPEN M-Sa: 10 a.m.–6 p.m., Su: noon–4 p.m.

While we refrained from singling out any homebrew shops with a Beer Destination marker (since they're geared toward a subgroup of the book's readership), Seven Bridges Cooperative would very likely warrant one. This well-organized, comparably tidy homebrew shop may very well be the world's only all-organic one: organic malts, organic hops, organic adjuncts, organic brewing kits (including a clone of Bison Chocolate Stout, with the recipe provided by the brewer himself). They even had organic green coffee beans.

39 Red Restaurant & Bar
Restaurant/Beer Bar

WWW.REDSANTACRUZ.COM

200 Locust St., Santa Cruz, CA 95060, (831) 425-1913—Downtown Santa Cruz. GOING E: Hwy 1 S, R@ Laurel St. (0.5), L@ Chestnut St., R@ Locust St. GOING W: Hwy 1 N, slight L@ Chestnut St. Extension, L@ Locust St.

OPEN Every day: 3 p.m.–2 a.m.

Red lights, red furniture, red menus. This comfortable lounge is your best bet for craft beer in downtown Santa Cruz, with about thirty taps and a rotating selection of California beer and imports. Nothing especially hard to find, but a good place for Moonlight and Belgian beers. They even had aged magnums of Anchor Christmas Ale.

Campbell Brewing

99 Bottles of Beer on the Wall
Beer Bar/Restaurant

WWW.99BOTTLES.COM

110 Walnut Ave., Santa Cruz, CA 95060,
(831) 459-9999—Downtown Santa Cruz.
GOING E: Hwy 1 S, R@ Walnut Ave. (0.6),
L@ Pacific Ave., L@ Walnut Ave. GOING
W: Hwy 1 N, slight L@ Chestnut St.
Extension, L@ Lincoln St., L@ Pacific
Ave., L@ Walnut Ave.

OPEN M-Th: noon–1 a.m., F: noon–
1:30 a.m., Sa: 11:30 a.m.–1:30 a.m., Su:
11:30 a.m.–midnight

99 Bottles has a somewhat similar
selection to Red Restaurant & Bar,
albeit with more macro beers and less
ambiance. Between bottles and draft,

they offer about ninety-nine different
brews, plus sampler trays of either three
or five draft beers. They tend to have
multiple taps from Uncommon and
Santa Cruz Ale Works.

41 Surfrider Café
Restaurant

WWW.SURFRIDERCAFE.NET

429 Front St., Santa Cruz, CA 95060,
(831) 713-5258—Downtown Santa Cruz.
GOING E: Hwy 1 S, R@ Laurel St. (0.8),
L@ Front St. GOING W: Hwy 1 N, slight
L@ Chestnut St. Extension (0.6), L@
Laurel St., L@ Front St.

OPEN Su-Th: 11:30 a.m.–10 p.m., F-Sa:
11:30 a.m.–11 p.m.

Apparently these folks are closely related to Boulder Creek Brewery, and their seven taps focused on the Boulder Creek beers as well as their Santa Cruz Brewery brand. They sell samples individually, and this is a convenient option for sampling these beers without traveling the windy roads out to Boulder Creek.

㊷ Seabright Brewery
Brewpub

WWW.SEABRIGHTBREWERY.COM

519 Seabright Ave., Santa Cruz, CA 95062, (831) 426-2739—East of Santa Cruz Beach Boardwalk, near the corner of Murray St. and Seabright Ave.

OPEN Every day: 11:30 a.m.–11:30 p.m.

Seabright offers particularly big "sample" pours, something like six ounces when we visited. Their Recluse Brown was their most consistently good beer beyond frigid temperatures, showing cola, chocolate, light nuttiness, and a touch of vanilla. Other engaging beers included The Blur (7.4% IPA), Oatmeal Stout, and Sacrilicious (6.8% red ale), although each of these slowly gravitated toward the too-sweet side of things as they warmed.

BREWER: Jason Chavez
ESTABLISHED: 1988
BE SURE TO TRY: Recluse Brown

㊸ 41st Avenue Liquor
Bottle Shop

2155 41st Ave., Capitola, CA 95010, (831) 475-5117—East of Santa Cruz. GOING E: Hwy 1 S Exit 438 (41st Ave.), R@ 41st Ave. GOING W: Hwy 1 N Exit 438 (41st Ave./Capitola), L@ 41st Ave.

OPEN M-Th: 10 a.m.–9 p.m., F: 10 a.m.–10 p.m., Sa: 10 a.m.–9 p.m., Su: 10 a.m.–8 p.m.

Your best bet for a bottle shop in the Santa Cruz area. Hundreds of bottles, including plenty of California, German, and Belgian beers (multiple gueuzes and krieks available). Well-rotated, well-chosen selection.

Half Moon Bay Brewing

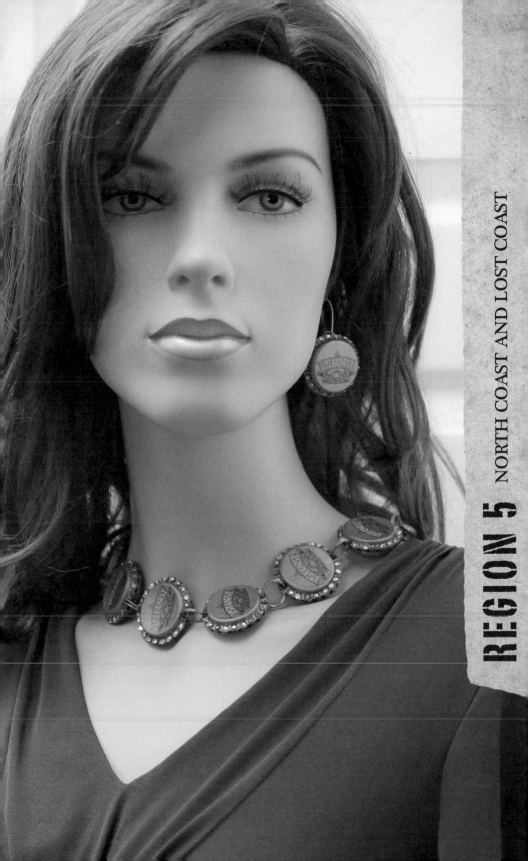

THE HOPLAND BREWERY

Mendocino Brewing

CURTAIN COMPANY

ARCATA, CALIFORNIA

20z Pint ... $5⁰⁰
12oz Glass ... $3⁷⁵
3oz Sample ... $1²⁵

GROWLERS
NEW   REFILL
* $23⁰⁰   * $11⁰⁰
* $27⁰⁰   * $18⁰⁰

$5⁰⁰ /item
on Credit Trans

BEERS ON TAP   ABV IBU
* India Pale Ale   6.4 50

* Give us each ons our Daily
  Belgian Died
  Some ads guy

BEERS ON TAP   ADV IBU
BELGIAN PALE ALE   6.7 35
* IMPERIAL GOLDEN ALE 6.8 35
INDIAN RED   5.3 35

FEVER

The North Coast and Lost Coast region encompasses beer spots in Northern California north of Sonoma and Napa counties and west of the long series of national forests cordoning it off from Region 6. For us, researching this region was an opportunity to revisit many of the places we'd seen back in 2008 during a month-long road trip down the coastline—slowly snaking our way from Seattle to San Diego in search of a place to call home. Since we took that trip, the region's craft beer scene has expanded with some excellent new spots.

While Southern California offers warm beaches and developed waterfront, Northern California is a masterpiece of winding scenic drives, craggy overlooks, and barely touched coast.

It's a wonderful area both for exploring and finding some peace and quiet, whether you're following the curves of Highway 1 or heading up north to wander through the redwoods. Many of the region's beer stops are near town centers, and campgrounds are plentiful.

We've singled out four Beer Destinations in this chapter that are particularly excellent. Two of them—Anderson Valley Brewing Company and North Coast Brewing Co.—will be celebrating twenty-five years in the craft beer business in 2012, and their stellar lineups are tasty evidence of why they've managed to flourish for so long. Our other two Beer Destinations are relative newcomers. Redwood Curtain Brewing is creating some excellent Belgian styles in Arcata, while the bottle selection at Blondies Food and Drink is what we wish the interior of our fridge looked like.

Note that this chapter and those that follow represent a marked departure from those covering the Bay Area, and public transportation options are immensely reduced. Be safe and plan ahead—all the cool kids are doing it.

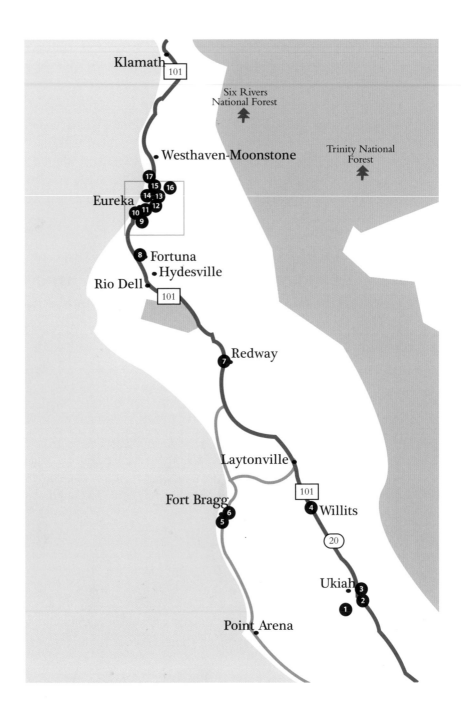

Klamath
101

Six Rivers
National Forest

Trinity National
Forest

• Westhaven-Moonstone

17
15 16
14 13
Eureka 11 12
10 9

8 • Fortuna
• Hydesville
Rio Dell
101

Redway 7

Laytonville •

Fort Bragg 6
5

101
4 Willits

20

Ukiah 3
2
1

Point Arena •

5 to try

Anderson Valley Poleeko Pale Ale Eel River Triple Exultation North Coast Old Stock Ale
Redwood Curtain India Pale Ale Six Rivers Paradise Moon Coffee Porter

1 Anderson Valley Brewing Company – Boonville Brewery

2 Mendocino Brewing Company – Ukiah Brewery

3 Ukiah Brewing Company – Ukiah Brewpub

4 Shanachie Pub – Willits Beer Bar

5 Piaci Pub & Pizzeria – Fort Bragg Restaurant

6 North Coast Brewing Co. – Fort Bragg Brewpub

7 Redway Liquor & Deli – Redway Convenience Store

8 Eel River Brewing Co. – Fortuna Brewpub

9 Brick & Fire Bistro – Eureka Restaurant

10 North Coast Co-op – Eureka Grocery Store

11 Lost Coast Brewery – Eureka Brewpub

12 Redwood Curtain Brewing Company – Arcata Brewery

13 North Coast Co-op – Arcata Grocery Store/Homebrew Shop

14 Humboldt Brews – Arcata Beer Bar/Restaurant

15 Blondies Food and Drink – Arcata Restaurant/Bottle Shop

16 Mad River Brewing Company – Blue Lake Brewery/Homebrew Shop

17 Six Rivers Brewery – McKinleyville Brewpub

AMBER ALE ANDERSON VALLEY BOONT AMBER ALE

Predominantly a U.S. phenomenon, amber ales fit snugly between American pale ales and brown ales, and the best of them take advantage of amped-up maltiness compared to the former (instead of just being hop-forward pale ales that happen to be red). Caramel and/or crystal malts are typically added, giving amber ales a rich caramel or toffee character along with, usually, citrusy American hops. The balance of malt versus hop varies, but I think the style tends to be most expressive when its central maltiness isn't overshadowed by the hops. Roasted and chocolate malt notes are typically avoided.

Anderson Valley Boont Amber Ale is a perfect example of what amber ales bring to the glass: restrained caramel sweetness, a vibrant red fruit character, and enough zesty hop bitterness to steer things. Other delicious local ambers include Speakeasy Prohibition Ale, Drake's Amber Ale, and El Toro Poppy Jasper.

① Anderson Valley Brewing Company
Brewery

WWW.AVBC.COM

17700 Hwy 253, Boonville, CA 95415, (707) 895-2337—Near the intersection of Hwy 128 and Hwy 253 in Boonville.

OPEN M–Th: 11 a.m.–6 p.m., F: 11 a.m.–7 p.m., Sa–Su: 11 a.m.–6 p.m.

It's hard to decide where to begin with Anderson Valley Brewing. There's the beer, most certainly. There's their environmental program, evidenced in everything from their waste-reduction awards to their significant solar panel array situated to the right of the front gate (offsetting 40% of their electricity use). There's the eighteen-hole disc golf course. There's the tasting bar, the gift shop, the pet-friendly beer garden. There's the Boontling.

The beer is delicious across the board, from the lighter-bodied Poleeko Pale Ale (which, poured fresh, is almost like a well-hopped lager) to the heftier specialty beers offered only at the brewery. Boont Amber (see sidebar) would be perfect for a game of disc golf, while the Barney Flats Oatmeal Stout is creamy, very lightly smoky, and includes layers of velvety chocolate notes. The Brother David's Double received a gold medal at the Great American Beer Festival in 2011. Their Fresh Hop Pale showcases citrusy hops grown on site.

Perhaps the most intriguing part for us, though, was the Boont culture and native folk language, Boontling, which originated more than a century ago, back when this area was a major hop-producing region. You can see traces of it throughout the tasting room itself, from the "Boont Steinber = Bahl Hornin'" note on the chalkboard (Boonville Beer = Good Drinking!) to the subtle uses of it in many of their beer names. Should you happen to meet some friendly locals or get tickets to the hugely popular Legendary Boonville Beer Festival (see sidebar Beer Festivals on page 169), someone may even teach you a bit of Boontling's more colorful vocabulary, such as "burlapping."

BREWMASTER: Fal Allen
ESTABLISHED: 1987
BE SURE TO TRY: Poleeko Pale Ale
SEASONALS: Summer Solstice (summer), Fresh Hop Ale (fall), Winter Solstice (winter)
TOURS: Two tours daily. See web site for details about attire.
ELSEWHERE: Bottles, Draft

② Mendocino Brewing Company
Brewery

WWW.MENDOBREW.COM

1252 Airport Park Blvd., Ukiah, CA 95482, (707) 467-2337—GOING N: 101 Exit 548A (Talmage), L@ Talmage Rd., L@ Airport Park Blvd. (0.5). GOING S: 101 Exit 548A (Talmage Rd., keep right), L@ Airport Park Blvd.

OPEN M-Th: 11 a.m.–10 p.m., F-Sa: 11 a.m.–11 p.m., Su: 11 a.m.–8 p.m.

Mendocino Brewing originated as The Hopland Brewery back in 1983, the second brewpub in the U.S. (and the first

3 Ukiah Brewing Company
Brewpub

WWW.UKIAHBREWINGCO.COM

102 S. State St., Ukiah, CA 95482, (707) 468-5898—GOING N: 101 Exit 549 (Central Ukiah), L@ E PerkinSt./Vichy Springs Rd. (0.7), L@ State St. GOING S: 101 Exit 549 (PerkinsSt./Vichy Springs Rd.), R@ E Perkins St.(0.5), L@ S State St.

OPEN M-Th: 11 a.m.–11 p.m., F-Su: 11 a.m.–1 a.m.

While Mendocino Brewing is located somewhat near the outskirts of town, Ukiah Brewing is right downtown. They became the first certified-organic brewpub (and second certified-organic restaurant) in the U.S. back in 2001. There are typically a few house-brewed beers on tap, including the basic lemony and mineral Pilsner Ukiah, which can also be found locally in cans, and the lightly caramelized Point Arena Pale.

BREWERS: Bret Cooperrider (Brewmaster), Mitch Parent (Head Brewer)
ESTABLISHED: 2000
ELSEWHERE: Bottles

4 Shanachie Pub
Beer Bar

50-B S. Main St., Willits, CA 95490, (707) 459-9194—Directly off S. Main St./Hwy 101 in Willits.

OPEN M-Sa: 3 p.m.–closing (open on Sunday seasonally)

in California) to open since Prohibition. Today, Mendocino has numerous brands in its portfolio, including Butte Creek, Carmel, and Kingfisher. While the latter two did nothing for us, the Mendocino and organic Butte Creek beers tended to be pretty decent, and the tasting room's Black Eye Ale (a 50/50 blend of Eye of the Hawk and Black Hawk Stout) combined the rich chocolatey flavors of the stout with the assertive bitterness of Eye of the Hawk. The Butte Creek lineup is also worth checking out.

BREWERS: Don Tubbs (Brewing Manager), Jason Schrider (Brew Supervisor)
ESTABLISHED: 1983
BE SURE TO TRY: Black Eye Ale
ELSEWHERE: Bottles, Draft

Friendly community feel, comfortable shaded outdoor area, and about twenty taps mixing Northern California brews with those you'd typically find in an Irish pub. While Shanachie Pub doesn't have a kitchen on site, it's right in central Willits and the restaurants nearby will generally deliver. They also have occasional barbeques in the garden. An inviting place for a pint. Live music and open mic nights. Cash only.

⑤ Piaci Pub & Pizzeria
Restaurant

WWW.PIACIPIZZA.COM

120 W. Redwood Ave., Fort Bragg, CA 95437, (707) 961-1133—Just off N. Main St./Hwy 1 in Fort Bragg. GOING N: L@ W Redwood Ave. GOING S: R@ W Redwood Ave.

OPEN M-Th: 11 a.m.–9 p.m., F: 11 a.m.–10 p.m., Sa: 4 p.m.–10 p.m., Su: 4 p.m.–9 p.m.

Piaci is an intimate pizzeria just a couple blocks down from North Coast Brewing Co. (see below). In addition to a solid bottle selection and their "Beer of the Moment" menu of rotating taps, Piaci had nine standard taps that would have kept us content for a long time: Trumer Pils, North Coast Old Rasputin, Moonlight Death & Taxes, El Toro Poppy Jasper… They also listed the head brewer for each beer—an endearing touch.

Beer Festivals

While beer samples at a brewpub can give you a glimpse into a brewer's soul (give or take), festivals give you a wide-angled peek into the region's beer culture. They can also incorporate a three-day music festival, a World War II supply ship, and pretzel necklaces beyond your wildest dreams.

A list of the major Northern California beer festivals and events is provided starting on page 261, and focuses on those festivities that are typically large and have been ongoing for a number of years. Dates will vary, details will vary, but all of them bring multiple breweries together to sample in one place. Festival locations also frequently afford a variety of nearby accommodations, and staying locally is strongly encouraged.

Choosing a favorite beer event is sort of like choosing a favorite child, in the sense that you have one but you still have to be diplomatic about the whole thing. (This may also be a good indication of why we don't have children yet.) Every event has its own appeal. San Francisco Beer Week and Sacramento Beer Week both include a ton of events spread out in numerous locations over these epic "weeks" (San Francisco's lasts for ten days; see sidebar on page 37). Brews on the Bay, sponsored by the San Francisco Brewers Guild, features the brewers of the city and takes places on the historic S.S. Jeremiah O'Brien in San Francisco Bay. The Mammoth Festival of Beers and Bluesapalooza, a huge blues and country music event in Mammoth Lakes, brings together over sixty breweries for an extended weekend.

If we were allowed to be slightly less diplomatic, however, two events that are always on our calendar are the West Coast Barrel Aged Beer Festival in Hayward (held around November and featuring a number of beers brewed specially for the event) and the Legendary Boonville Beer Festival, presented by Anderson Valley Brewing Company. For the latter, remember to pack your tent. Pretzels and string are optional.

BARLEY WINE/OLD ALE/STOCK ALE NORTH COAST OLD STOCK ALE

These three styles trace their roots back to England, and like many styles, their precise parameters and characteristics have changed and intermingled over the years. American craft interpretations began with Anchor Brewing Company's Old Foghorn barley wine in 1975, followed by Sierra Nevada Bigfoot in the 1980s. Today California is renowned for producing some of the world's finest strong ales; other excellent examples include hefty interpretations from Marin, Schooner's, Eel River, and Lagunitas.

While hoppiness can vary widely across these styles, some commonalities include rich maltiness, higher alcohol, full body, and (often) suitability for aging. North Coast Old Stock Ale is one of my personal favorites, showing fruit leather, caramel, a bit of vinous alcohol warmth, and a prominent hop bitterness that doesn't overshadow that delicious malt complexity. These styles are often cellared for years before consumption (vertical tastings with multiple vintages of Bigfoot or Old Foghorn are particularly popular among collectors), and aged beers will gradually see diminished hop character over time, while picking up sherry-like and dry caramel notes due to oxidative processes in the bottle. Don't wait too long, though, or oxidation will spoil the party.

6 North Coast Brewing Co.
Brewpub

WWW.NORTHCOASTBREWING.COM

444 N. Main St., Fort Bragg, CA 95437, (707) 964-3400—Directly off N. Main St./Hwy 1 in Fort Bragg.

OPEN Su–Th: 11:30 a.m.–9:30 p.m., F–Sa: 11:30 a.m.–10 p.m.

North Coast Brewing Co. is one of the most recognized American craft breweries out there, offering an award-winning lineup that includes everything from the stellar 4.4% Scrimshaw Pilsner to the far heftier Old Stock Ale (see sidebar Style: Barley Wine/Old Ale/Stock Ale) and Old Rasputin Imperial Stout (see sidebar Style: Imperial Stout). While many craft beer lovers will be pretty familiar with North Coast products, visiting the brewery itself was an opportunity to revisit some of their lesser-known brands, including the refreshing and slightly husky Blue Star American wheat and the floral Acme IPA, of which Ali and I shared a pitcher over the course of dinner. (In related news: We can wholeheartedly recommend the Country Inn Bed & Breakfast a couple blocks down the street.)

Of particular interest are Old Rasputin and Old No. 38 Stout, both of which are served via nitrogen at the brewpub, as opposed to traditional carbon dioxide. The latter is an especially appropriate one for those new to craft beer, offering a more flavorful, vanilla–tinged alternative to Guinness, which is also typically served via nitrogen. The brewery itself is directly across the street from the North Coast Taproom & Grill, while the Brewery

Shop (which sells kegs; open M–Sa: 10 a.m.–5 p.m.) sits on the opposite street corner.

BREWMASTER: Mark Ruedrich
ESTABLISHED: 1987
BE SURE TO TRY: Old No. 38 Stout or Old Rasputin (nitro)
SEASONALS: Bourbon-Barrel-Aged Old Rasputin (occasional), Bourbon-Barrel-Aged Old Stock (occasional)
ELSEWHERE: Bottles, Draft

⑦ Redway Liquor & Deli
Convenience Store

3362 Redwood Dr., Redway, CA 95560, (707) 923-3913—GOING N: 101 Exit 639B (Redway), L@ Redwood Dr. (2.4). GOING S: 101 Exit 642 (Redwood Dr./Redway) (2.1).

OPEN Every day: 9 a.m.–10:30 p.m.

The only craft beer stop between Willits and Fortuna, Redway Liquor & Deli provides a modest selection of Northern California beers, with an emphasis on the larger-format Sierra Nevada releases and a mildly disheveled selection of six-packs. One rare thing of note, however: a cooler dedicated to organic beers.

⑧ Eel River Brewing Company
Brewpub

WWW.EELRIVERBREWING.COM

1777 Alamar Way, Fortuna, CA 95540, (707) 725-2739—GOING N: 101 Exit 687 (Kenmar Rd.), L@ Kenmar Rd., R@ Alamar Way. GOING S: 101 Exit 688

STYLE: IMPERIAL STOUT NORTH COAST OLD RASPUTIN RUSSIAN IMPERIAL STOUT

Imperial stouts came into being around the late eighteenth century in London, when they were produced as an extra-strong version of conventional porter for export to Russia and the Baltic region (hence the ornery-looking Russian mystic on the North Coast bottle). These beers are typically much higher in alcohol than standard stouts, frequently pushing 10% ABV or well beyond that, and showcasing the potent flavors of the darker specialty malts: licorice, bitter chocolate, cocoa, roasted malts, coffee, etc. They tend to be served at slightly warmer temperatures than other beer, and they're especially popular during the winter months for pretty obvious reasons.

While American brewers have truly taken to this style—there are countless barrel-aged, coffee-added, chocolate-infused versions out there right now—the imperial stout style has no inherent need for all the bells and whistles. North Coast's Old Rasputin is a perfect example of an expressive imperial stout that doesn't overdo things, offering milk chocolate, roasted marshmallow, and licorice notes at an especially affordable price (one doesn't often see imperial stout in four-packs). It's a beautifully done beer that gains much of its bitterness from specialty malts. Another Northern California rendition doing everything right is FiftyFifty's Totality Imperial Stout.

Bottle Cap Art

Jack Van Stone's initial foray into his current artistic pursuits began back in 2006, right around the same time that he became the Bay Area Sales Manager for Lost Coast Brewery. Jack's a fun and creative dude by nature (I'll get to the costumes), and he was searching for inexpensive marketing approaches to promoting Lost Coast's lineup. He began with traditional bottle cap magnets, but soon expanded to include bottle cap earrings after he discovered examples made from used caps online. He started customizing things, looking for unused caps (which were less fragile to work with) and adding personalized touches, including applying glitter mixed with sand from beaches on the actual Lost Coast.

The earrings were a hit. Jack manufactured a number at once and handed them out at beer festivals, and it soon got to the point that people were looking forward to them specifically. He started adding small artistic flourishes (rhinestones, back-of-the-cap inlays) and branching out into more intricate pieces, including necklaces, pendants, rings, and clip-on earrings—many at the request of beer enthusiasts who appreciated his early work. While both labor- and time-intensive, it was a hobby that gradually grew into something else.

How does one find Jack at a festival within the craze of pretzel-festooned festivalgoers, one might ask? In our experience, it's not very hard. If you see a gentleman dressed up like a knight with a goblet and twelve pounds of bottle cap chainmail, that will be Jack. If you see someone wearing Flavor Flav-inspired attire consisting of a bottle cap necklace (attached to a Lagunitas wall clock) and a brewery coaster-lined blue jacket, that will be Jack. And if you see anyone adorned with bright yellow dreads constructed from the previous version of Drake's bottle caps, tell Jack we say hi.

Jack's work has recently appeared at the 2010 Design, Drink and Be Merry event in Redding, Pennsylvania, an art show at Jimmie Art Gallery in Berkeley, and at The Art of Beer celebration during Sacramento Beer Week 2012. His web site (www.jackscaps.com) provides details for ordering custom pieces, as well as participating in his Caps for a Cause fundraising projects.

(Riverwalk Dr./12thSt.), L@ Riverwalk Dr., L@ Alamar Way.

OPEN Every day: 11 a.m.–11 p.m.

Eel River laid claim to the title of the first certified-organic brewery in the country back in 1999, and later became the country's first biomass-powered brewery. The pub offers a spacious, well-landscaped beer garden with plenty of picnic tables, a horseshoe court, and even a gigantic fish. While some of the lighter beers were on the sweeter side, their Triple Exultation should not be missed, as it offers delicious layers of caramel, red fruits, and a touch of warming alcohol. The 2004 vintage of Triple Exultation won a bronze medal at the 2011 Great American Beer Festival in the Aged Beer category, so don't be afraid to tuck a couple bottles away.

> BREWMEISTER: Mike Smith
> ESTABLISHED: 1995
> BE SURE TO TRY: Triple Exultation
> ELSEWHERE: Bottles, Draft

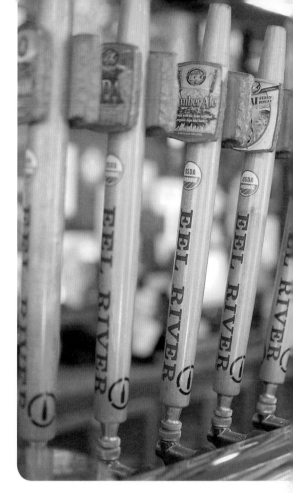

9 Brick & Fire Bistro
Restaurant

WWW.BRICKANDFIREBISTRO.COM

1630 E St., Eureka, CA 95501, (707) 268-8959—Off Hwy 101 in central Eureka. GOING N: R@ W 14th St.(0.6), R@ E St. GOING S: L@ H St. (0.6), R@ 15th St., L@ E St.

OPEN M, W–Th: 11:30 a.m.–8:30 p.m., F: 11:30 a.m.–9 p.m., Sa: 5 p.m.–9 p.m., Su: 5 p.m.–8:30 p.m.

Besides the brewery itself, this is the best place around to enjoy Redwood Curtain brews on tap. (They also offer a few regional bottles.) Our food was delicious here, particularly the roasted oysters, and the bar looks directly into the bistro's glowing brick oven. Cozy, so reservations are generally encouraged.

10 North Coast Co-op
Grocery Store

WWW.NORTHCOASTCO-OP.COM

25 Fourth St., Eureka, CA 95501, (707) 443-6027—Right off Hwy 101 in central Eureka. GOING N: L@ BSt., L@ 4th St.

GOING S: Directly off Hwy 101/4th St.

OPEN Every day: 6 a.m.–9 p.m.

One of two North Coast Co-ops (the other is in Arcata), this Whole Foods–like market included filled-out lineups of refrigerated six-packs from Lost Coast, Eel River, Mendocino, Anderson Valley, Mad River, and more, as well as a well-chosen import selection featuring Orval, Girardin Gueuze, and Unibroue beers.

⑪ Lost Coast Brewery
Brewpub

WWW.LOSTCOAST.COM

617 Fourth St., Eureka, CA 95501, (707) 445-4480—Right off Hwy 101 in central Eureka. GOING N: L@ ISt., L@ 4th St. GOING S: Directly off Hwy 101/4th St.

OPEN Su-Th: 11 a.m.–10 p.m., F-Sa: 11 a.m.–11 p.m.

Located in Central Eureka (six blocks from the city's North Coast Co-op), Lost Coast is one of the highest-production craft breweries in Northern California, with an especially popular lineup of beer that includes Alleycat Amber, Great White, and Indica IPA. Two of my favorites on tap at the café were the Downtown Brown and 8 Ball Stout, the latter being a sweeter stout offering plenty of cola and chocolate. They have limited-release beers pouring as well (we sampled a keg-conditioned IPA dry-hopped with Calypso hops, which was fantastic), plus discounted cases that, for whatever reason—dented box, crooked label, etc.— didn't make it out into distribution. Heck, even their bottle caps can become works of art (see sidebar on page 172).

HEAD BREWER: Matt Walsh
ESTABLISHED: 1990
BE SURE TO TRY: 8 Ball Stout
ELSEWHERE: Bottles, Draft

Redwood Curtain Brewing

12 Redwood Curtain Brewing Company

Brewery

WWW.REDWOODCURTAINBREWING.COM

550 S. G St. #6, Arcata, CA 95521, (707) 826-7222—GOING N: 101 Exit 713 (Hwy 255/Samoa Blvd./Arcata) (0.9), L@ S G St. (0.6). GOING S: 101 Exit 712 (S G St.) (0.7).

OPEN M-Th: 4 p.m.–10 p.m., F: 4 p.m.–11 p.m., Sa: noon–11 p.m., Su: noon–6 p.m.

Redwood Curtain is a rarity in Northern California, focusing almost entirely on Belgian-style brews. Their industrial setting just south of central Arcata is the epitome of a brewery visit: plenty of beers to sample, an assertive house character, and friendly brewery employees eager to chat about craft beer. Plus, their renditions of Belgian styles are some of the best you'll find in Northern California, although this may depend on your opinion of the Belgian yeast strain they're using. The Belgian Pale Ale, Belgian Red, and Dubbel were quite similar in this regard: chewy, with peppery notes and a soft, rounded ester profile from the yeast. We actually thought the Belgian Porter was the most assertive of the bunch, mixing that yeast character (vanilla, white pepper) with a chocolatey and biscuit core. Their India Pale Ale was a whole different beast, and a pretty kickass divergence from West Coast IPAs in general, showing chewy Maris Otter and Munich maltiness (i.e., charismatic European malts, instead of the crystal malts more frequently used in U.S. IPA brewing), plus a potent amalgam of citrusy American hops.

BREWMASTER: Eli Larue
ESTABLISHED: 2010
BE SURE TO TRY: Belgian Porter
ELSEWHERE: Draft

13 North Coast Co-op
Grocery Store/Homebrew Shop

WWW.NORTHCOASTCO-OP.COM

881 I St., Arcata, CA 95521, (707) 822-5947—GOING N: 101 Exit 714A (14th St./Humboldt State Univ), L@ 14th St., L@ I St.(traffic circle). GOING S: 101 Exit 713 (Hwy 255 S/Samoa Blvd./Samoa) (0.6), R@ I St.

OPEN Every day: 6 a.m.–9 p.m.

This North Coast Co-op has slightly more selection than the Eureka store, particularly in terms of larger-format bottles. It also offers a tiny homebrewing section with basic ingredients, equipment, and books.

14 Humboldt Brews
Beer Bar/Restaurant

WWW.HUMBREWS.COM

856 10th St., Arcata, CA 95521, (707) 826-2739—GOING N: 101 Exit 714A (14th St./Humboldt State Univ), L@ 14th St., L@ H St., R@ 10th St. GOING S: 101 Exit 714 (Sunset Ave./Humboldt State Univ) (0.9), R@ 10th St.

OPEN Every day: noon–11 p.m.

Just a block north of Arcata's North Coast Co-op, Humboldt Brews is somewhere between a college bar (a pool table, huge bar, macro bottles, plenty of live music) and a craft-centric café. The atmosphere

ad River Brewing

partly depends on what time you show up. The twenty taps focus on popular Northern California beers. Ten years ago, this was the home of Humboldt Brewing Company, though those beers are now brewed by Firestone Walker Brewing Company in Paso Robles. Their Red Nectar and Hemp Ale are both excellent and tend to be on tap here.

Blondies is a café and bottle shop (plus nine taps) right near Humboldt State University. Hugely impressed by the selection here: Hair of the Dog (from Portland), Jolly Pumpkin (Michigan), Mikkeller (Denmark), Pretty Things (Massachusetts)...bottles you probably won't find elsewhere in this region.

15 Blondies Food and Drink ⭐
Restaurant/Bottle Shop

WWW.BLONDIESFOODANDDRINK.COM

420 E. California Ave., Arcata, CA 95521, (707) 822-3453—GOING N: 101 Exit 714B (Sunset Ave.), R@ Sunset Ave., L@ L K Wood Blvd., R@ California Ave. GOING S: 101 Exit 714 (Sunset Ave./Humbolt State Univ), L@ Sunset Ave., L@ L K Wood Blvd., R@ California Ave.

OPEN M-Th: 10 a.m.–10 p.m., F-Sa: 10 a.m.–midnight, Su: 10 a.m.–8 p.m.

Best bottle selection around by far.

16 Mad River Brewing Company
Brewery/Homebrew Shop

WWW.MADRIVERBREWING.COM

101 Taylor Way, Blue Lake, CA 95525, (707) 668-4151 x106—GOING N OR S: Hwy 101 Exit 716A (Hwy 299 E) (5.5), Exit 5 (Blue Lake), R@ Chartin Rd., L@ S Railroad Ave. (0.7).

OPEN M-F: 1 p.m.–9 p.m., Sa: noon–9 p.m., Su: noon–7 p.m.

Mad River's Brew Master and Founder Bob Smith found inspiration in Ken Grossman's Homebrew Shop out in

Chico in the 1970s. When Grossman's Sierra Nevada Brewing Company had outgrown its original brewery by the late '80s, Smith and his investors purchased it, and Mad River Brewing Company was born. Today Dylan Schatz and the brewers of Mad River are making an impressive lineup of beers, from the spicy-hopped Steelhead Extra Pale Ale and Jamaica Red Ale (the latter was awarded a silver medal at the 2011 Great American Beer Festival) to the hugely floral Jamaica Sunset IPA, with its soft, tea-like center.

Visiting the brewery itself allows one to sample their limited-release seasonal specialties, which are brewed in smaller quantities on their pilot system and are typically some pretty out-there beers. Our last visit included samples of Rorschach III (an 8% Wee Heavy Scottish Ale), Super Chili Madness (an extra pale ale with five local pepper varieties), and John Barleycorn Barleywine from 2007 (offering loads of dry caramel while still holding up well). Mad River had significantly expanded its original tasting room since our last visit, and now includes a spacious beer garden. They also sell a limited selection of homebrew supplies.

HEAD BREWER: Dylan Schatz
ESTABLISHED: 1989
BE SURE TO TRY: Seasonal Specialties
SEASONALS: John Barleycorn Barleywine (fall)
TOURS: Available daily
ELSEWHERE: Bottles, Draft

17 Six Rivers Brewery
Brewpub

WWW.SIXRIVERSBREWERY.COM

1300 Central Ave., McKinleyville, CA 95519, (707) 839-7580—GOING N: 101 Exit 718 (Central Ave./McKinleyville, keep left) (0.8). GOING S: 101 Exit 718 (N Bank Rd., keep right onto Central Ave.), L@ Central Ave.

OPEN M: 4 p.m.–closing, Tu-Su: 11:30 a.m.–closing

Six Rivers Brewery is the northernmost beer stop in the section; Flatfender Brewing Co. (no listing), the homebrew shop up in Crescent City, was in questionable flux the last time we checked. About ten minutes north of central Arcata, Six Rivers can get pretty busy in the evening, particularly when there's live music. They've got a pretty nice lineup of beers here, from their Weatherman Wheat (more potent than most American wheats) to their Chili Pepper Ale, which was even spicier than the chili beer we tried at Mad River. Their Paradise Moon Coffee Porter is particularly good. It's their standard Moonstone Porter with 100% Kona coffee added, and trying the two beers side by side shows just how perfect that coffee addition is.

BREWMASTER: Carlos Sanchez
ESTABLISHED: 1996
BE SURE TO TRY: Paradise Moon Coffee Porter
SEASONALS: Pigskin Pumpkin Ale (fall)
ELSEWHERE: Bottles, Draft

American barley and wheat malts are
with a blend of noble hops to create this
refreshing beer. Blue Star is unfiltered
a complex note to the flavor profile

BLUE STAR®
WHEAT BEER

12 FL. OZ.

BREWED IN FORT BRAGG, CALIFORNIA

The Interstate-5 corridor heading north toward Oregon is bordered on both sides by mountainous terrain after Sacramento and Woodland. To the west, one passes Mendocino, Trinity, Six Rivers, and Klamath National Forests before reaching the border, and this scenic section affords a natural separation between this region and the North Coast/Lost Coast destinations in Region 5. Looking in the other direction toward northern Nevada are Plumas, Lassen, Shasta, and Modoc National Forests, as well as Lassen Volcanic National Park. Further east beyond these are untold mythical creatures, the edges of the charted world, and Ali's mom, who lives out in the wilderness past Alturas (hi, Diana!). In any case, little in the way of craft beer.

While the Oregonian beer landscape is of course outside the bounds of this book, Lisa Morrison's Craft Beers of the Pacific Northwest is an excellent, thoroughly researched guide for those continuing north.

Following Highway 99 north from Sacramento takes one past most of the breweries in the southern half of the region, from the stellar Sutter Buttes to the pilgrimage-worthy Sierra Nevada—an absolute must-stop for any beer lover traveling through the area. After rejoining Interstate 5, nearly all of the other craft beer stops (aside from a half-hour diversion out to Etna) are a short distance off the interstate.

While we spent much of our time in the Mount Shasta region—including hiking to the top of Black Butte (where overly friendly ground squirrels awaited us) and a bit of spelunking in Lake Shasta Caverns—this entire area is chock-full of scenic daytrips and small towns catering to nature-minded travelers. The State of Jefferson region up north has a secessionist history and culture unto itself, and numerous beer-centric festivals are held annually in craft-beer locales like Yuba City, Mt. Shasta, Oroville, and Chico.

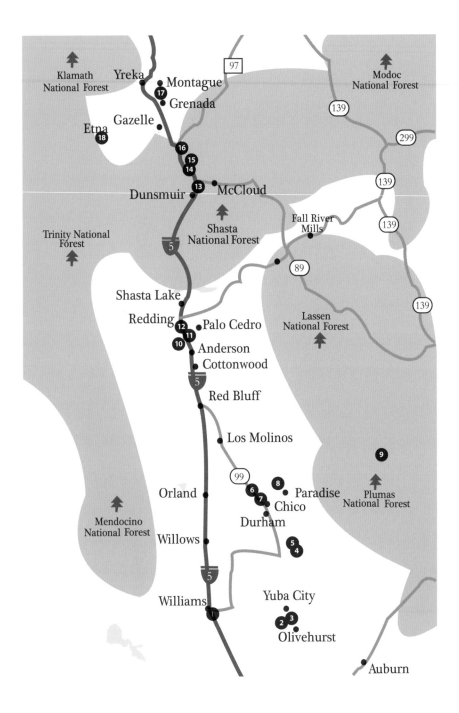

5 to try

1. Granzella's Deli – Williams   Bottle Shop/Beer Bar/Restaurant
2. Sutter Buttes Brewing – Yuba City   Brewpub
3. The Happy Viking – Yuba City   Beer Bar/Restaurant
4. Feather Falls Casino Brewing Co. – Oroville   Brewpub
5. Western Pacific Brewing & Dining – Oroville   Brewpub
6. Chico Home Brew Shop – Chico   Homebrew Shop
7. Sierra Nevada Brewing Co. – Chico   Brewpub
8. Feather River Brewing Co. – Magalia   Brewery
9. Pangaea Café & Pub – Quincy   Restaurant
10. Liquor Barn – Redding   Bottle Shop
11. The Alehouse Pub – Redding   Beer Bar
12. NorCal Brewing Solutions – Redding   Homebrew Shop
13. Dunsmuir Brewery Works – Dunsmuir   Brewpub
14. Berryvale Grocery – Mount Shasta   Grocery Store
15. The Goat Tavern – Mount Shasta   Beer Bar/Restaurant
16. Mt. Shasta Brewing Co. – Weed   Brewpub
17. Liquor Expo – Grenada   Bottle Shop
18. Etna Brewing Co. – Etna   Brewpub

uncharted territory

California Brewing Company (Anderson)

Granzella's Deli

① Granzella's Deli
Bottle Shop/Beer Bar/Restaurant

WWW.GRANZELLAS.COM

451 Sixth St., Williams, CA 95987, (530) 473-5583—GOING N: 5 Exit 577 (Williams), L@ E St./Hwy 20 Bus W, R@ 6th St. GOING S: 5 Exit 577 (Williams), R@ E St./Hwy 20 Bus W, R@ 6th St.

OPEN Every day: 6 a.m.–11 p.m.

Granzella's is your best bet for bottles before Redding, and it's only a few blocks off Interstate 5. Though the whole establishment is spread out over multiple buildings and entrance points, including Granzella's Gift Shop across the street, the Delicatessen area offers a large import selection (we saw Samichlaus, as one highlight) and a significant craft beer selection that included High Water, Mammoth, Caldera's great Oregon offerings, and Pennsylvania-based Victory the last time we were there. Around the back to the left (like, all the way around that gigantic building) is a spacious cocktail lounge pouring about half a dozen craft taps, including a few contract brews from Black Diamond. It's also something of a taxidermal wonderland.

② Sutter Buttes Brewing ⭐
Brewpub

🍴 🥛 🍾 🗄

WWW.SUTTERBUTTESBREWING.COM

421 Center St., Yuba City, CA 95991, (530) 790-7999—Off Hwy 99 in Yuba City. GOING N: Hwy 99, R@ Bridge St. (1.1), L@ Plumas St., R@ Center St. GOING S: Hwy 99, L@ Hwy 20 E/Colusa Ave. (1.0), R@ Shasta St., R@ Center St.

OPEN M: 11 a.m.–4 p.m., Tu–F: 11 a.m.–10 p.m., Sa: noon–11 p.m.

I still feel pretty bad that Ali missed this one; she was stuck at a work conference the afternoon I visited. An hour north of Sacramento, Sutter Buttes is on the pleasantly casual side. A row of ten stainless-steel serving tanks behind the bar is a good sign, as is the copy of Randy Mosher's Tasting Beer by the register. Away from Ali's protective presence, I had to keep reminding myself that "buttes" and "butts" are pronounced differently.

The lineup that Mark Martin and

company are making here is excellent, and further emphasized my sense of loss at not having my often-designated driver in tow. The Kolsch is one of the best examples I've seen of this difficult-to-brew style in Northern California, showing crisp cereal grains and a very light honeyed sweetness.

The Extra Pale Ale was my favorite of the lineup, though, pouring a bright golden color with an especially dry and citrus-forward focus, significantly drier and crisper than your average Pale Ale but weighing in at only 4.5%. The Franklin IPA, while on the sweeter side, still showed assertive citrusy and floral hop bitterness. On the malty end, the Annie Brown has lots of flavor going on for such a low ABV. Somehow, I ended up with the season's first pour of their Sutterfest, and I can only wish others the same luck.

> BREWER: Mark Martin
> ESTABLISHED: 2010
> BE SURE TO TRY: Extra Pale Ale
> SEASONALS: Sutterfest (fall)
> ELSEWHERE: Draft

❸ The Happy Viking
Beer Bar/Restaurant

WWW.THEHAPPYVIKING.COM

741 Plumas St., Yuba City, CA 95991,
(530) 671-7492—Off Hwy 99 in Yuba
City. GOING N: Hwy 99, R@ Bridge St.
(1.1), L@ Plumas St. GOING S: Hwy 99,
L@ Hwy 20 E/Colusa Ave. (0.9), R@
Plumas St.

OPEN M–W: 11 a.m.–10 p.m., Th:
11 a.m.–midnight, F-Sa: 11 a.m.–2 a.m.,
Su: 10 a.m.–10 p.m.

Less than two blocks down the street
from Sutter Buttes, The Happy Viking
is a family-friendly sports bar and
restaurant with fifty-five taps. Plenty of
craft offerings; about seven of the taps are
allocated to Sierra Nevada, including a
number of their rare, draft-only releases
(Chico's only about an hour further
north).

❹ Feather Falls Casino Brewing Co.
Brewpub

WWW.FEATHERFALLSCASINO.COM

#3 Alverda Dr., Oroville, CA 95966, (530)
533-3885—Plan ahead or GPS (1 hour
off Hwy 5).

OPEN M–Th: 10 a.m.–11 p.m., F:
10 a.m.–1 a.m., Sa: 7 a.m.–1 a.m., Su:
7 a.m.–11 p.m.

For how pristine the new brewing
equipment looks—lit up in bright orange
behind the bar—the overall quality
was lacking across the board, with the
Dancing Trees Hefeweizen being probably
their strongest showing. Even that suffered
as it was allowed to warm. Drink fast. For
what it's worth, they just opened in 2011,
and hopefully the brews will improve as
they get more familiar with their system.
BREWMASTER: Roland Allen
ESTABLISHED: 2011

❺ Western Pacific Brewing & Dining
Brewpub

WWW.DININGANDBREWING.COM

2191 High St., Oroville, CA 95965, (530)
534-9101—Off Hwy 99 in Oroville.
Head E on Hwy 162/Oroville Dam Blvd.
W (6.2), L@ Hwy 70 N (0.5), Exit 47
(Montgomery St.), R@ Montgomery St.
(1.1), R@ Oliver St.

OPEN M–Tu: 11:30 a.m.–8 p.m., W–Th:
11:30 a.m.–11 p.m., F-Sa: 11:30 a.m.–
closing

While Western Pacific doesn't necessarily
have the same beer-centric feel as a lot
of these destinations (and their brewing
system itself is a relatively recent addition
and a bit cramped), they're pouring some
pretty impressive brews here. Western
Pacific was once a train station, as
evidenced by the recurrent railroad theme
in the beer names and the occasional
trains rolling by.
Everything's good: the "DD" Blond, the
Keddie Red Ale, the "844" Oatmeal Stout.
Their bestsellers are the Belden Golden

Ale and the Chilcoot IPA, which reflects well on the local palate. The Belden is a pale-straw, hugely drinkable golden ale showing a nice balance of honeyed malts and a very modest mineral bitterness. The toasty finish hints at butterless popcorn. The Chilcoot IPA is exactly where it should be: focusing on juicy orange and grapefruit-laden hops, from the aroma to the flavor to the lingering bitterness. Their seasonal specials seem very promising as well, and we were lucky enough to be passing through at just the right time to sample their 100th Anniversary Zeus Ale, commemorating their one-hundredth batch of beer.

BREWER: Andy Klein
ESTABLISHED: 2009
BE SURE TO TRY: Chilcoot IPA
ELSEWHERE: Draft

⑥ Chico Home Brew Shop
Homebrew Shop

WWW.CHICOHOMEBREWSHOP.COM

1570 Nord Ave., Chico, CA 95926, (530) 342-3768—About 25 minutes off Hwy 5 (Exit 619). Head E on Hwy 32 (18.1).

OPEN Tu-Th: 10 a.m.–5 p.m., F: 10 a.m.– 6 p.m., Sa: 10 a.m.–5 p.m.

Originally founded by Ken Grossman in 1976 (a few years before he went on to establish Sierra Nevada), Chico Home Brew Shop has served as a do-it-yourself launching pad for countless brewers and vintners in Northern California. Twenty-five years in, it still supplies a very active local homebrewing community.

PALE ALE SIERRA NEVADA PALE ALE

Perhaps nothing is more iconic of American pale ale than Sierra Nevada's hugely popular flagship beer. First brewed back in 1980, Sierra Nevada Pale Ale uses whole-cone Cascade hops to provide that zesty, citrusy hop character that embodies American-style hoppy beers: lemon, grapefruit, even a bit of grassiness. A pale ale will generally be more balanced and lower in alcohol than an IPA, but it should still have a vibrant hop bitterness and flavor. A sweet, malty American pale ale probably isn't one.

English-style pale ales can be a bit more charismatic in the malt category (caramel, biscuity notes) and have more of an earthy, floral hop character, but most of the examples you'll find in Northern California fall on the citrusy side of things. Drake's 1500 is another pitch-perfect pale, showing off the orangey Amarillo hop variety, while Sutter Buttes Extra Pale Ale is a delicious example of the style's palest side.

YUBA CITY-OROVILLE-CHICO

The Northern California Craft Beer Guide

HEFEWEIZEN / WHEAT ALE SIERRA NEVADA KELLERWEIS HEFEWEIZEN

Wheat additions to a beer will typically add a vibrant wheat flavor and help create a sturdy, long-lasting head, and the presence of wheat is a defining characteristic of certain styles. Perhaps none is more familiar (or delicious) than German-style hefeweizen, and there's probably no better archetype for this style in Northern California than Sierra Nevada's Kellerweis. A relatively recent addition to their standard line of year-round beers, the Kellerweis pours quite-hazy and generates a thick, rocky head: clear signs one is in wheat beer territory. But the cornerstone of German-style hefeweizen is the yeast, particularly those clove- and banana-laden notes it provides, showcased clearly in this effervescent, hugely drinkable style.

Mammoth Floating Rock Hefeweizen is another excellent version of the German-influenced side, while Snowshoe Snoweizen Wheat and The Brewery at Lake Tahoe's Washoe Wheat Ale are clear examples of American wheats, which trade in that clove and banana character for husky wheat and a lemony acidity. The latter pairs nicely with slices of lemon or orange (with which they're often served), though German-style hefeweizens tend to fare pretty well all by themselves.

7 Sierra Nevada Brewing Co.

Brewpub

WWW.SIERRANEVADA.COM

1075 East 20th St., Chico, CA 95928, (530) 345-2739—About 35 minutes off Hwy 5 (Exit 619). Head E on Hwy 32/ Newville Rd. (17.4), L@ W East Ave. (1.9), R@ Hwy 99 S (3.2), Exit 384 (East 20th St.), R@ East 20th St.

OPEN Su–Th: 11 a.m.–9 p.m., F–Sa: 11 a.m.–10 p.m.

Few people have been as influential in the American craft beer movement as Sierra Nevada's owner and founder, Ken Grossman. Ever since their first batch of Sierra Nevada Pale Ale (see sidebar Style: Pale Ale) was brewed back in the fall of 1980, this company has inspired and supported multiple generations of craft brewers. They've become the second-largest craft brewery in the country behind Boston Beer Co./Samuel Adams, and their continued dedication to both quality and sustainable growth (see sidebar Environment and Sustainability) embodies artisanal brewing.

For how ubiquitous Sierra Nevada brews are in the craft beer world, nothing substitutes for a visit to the actual brewery. As their sustainability coordinator, Cheri Chastain, commented (in reference to all their different employees, including an on-staff painter): "Ken has created a little mini city here."

Their taproom and restaurant focus on locally sourced ingredients, and this is often the only place one can sample some of their limited-release offerings,

⚛ Environment and Sustainability

It isn't immediately obvious from looking at the label of a bottle of Sierra Nevada (the sustainability and marketing folks don't really hang out much), but Ken Grossman's brewery is quietly one of the country's greenest and most sustainably minded. Their carport and rooftops are covered by 2 megawatts of photovoltaic solar panels, which, combined with their enormous hydrogen fuel cell installations, provide more than half of their total electricity usage. Company cars include Toyota Priuses, Chevrolet Volts, and Nissan Leafs, and brewery visitors driving electric vehicles are able to recharge theirs on site for free. A full-time sustainability coordinator, Cheri Chastain, and full-time assistant help support these and other on-site programs, including carbon-dioxide recovery, water treatment, energy monitoring, composting, and organic recycling. Their thirty-page sustainability report, completed in 2010, is an environmental tome.

The big = bad mantra deflates pretty quickly in Chico, and when Cheri was asked why more craft brewers aren't implementing sustainability measures to this degree, she replied, "It's difficult unless you're as big as we are." Capital costs can be enormous for these projects, and many aren't financially viable at much-reduced scales. While smaller craft breweries tend to be pretty environmentally conscious anyway, there's always room for improvement. Ken Grossman, along with like-minded companies including New Belgium in Colorado and Great Lakes Brewing in Ohio, continue to push the industry in that direction.

including many Beer Camp-created beers and brews made with up-and-coming experimental hop varieties (Sierra Nevada is the largest buyer of whole-cone hops in the world). Tours of their three different on-site brew houses are offered multiple times daily including on the weekends, but be sure to arrive early to reserve a spot, and check their online tour policy beforehand.

HEAD BREWER: Steve Dresler
ESTABLISHED: 1980
BE SURE TO TRY: Pale Ale (bottled version on draft)
SEASONALS: Ruthless Rye IPA (spring), Summerfest (summer), Tumbler (fall), Celebration (winter), Bigfoot (winter)
TOURS: Guided tours held daily
ELSEWHERE: Bottles, Draft

8 Feather River Brewing Co.
Brewery

WWW.FEATHERRIVERBREWING.COM

Magalia, CA, (530) 873-0734

The best places to find Feather River brews are select bottle shops in the Chico/Mt. Shasta region. While we managed to track down their Honey Ale and Raging Rapids Ale in Redding, these beautifully pouring beers didn't have quite enough flavor to them. The seasonal Dark Canyon Ale sounded more complete.

MASTERBREWER: Roger Preecs
ESTABLISHED: 2000
ELSEWHERE: Bottles, Draft

9 Pangaea Café & Pub
Restaurant

WWW.PANGAEAPUB.COM

461 Main St., Quincy, CA 95971, (530) 283-0426—Directly off Hwy 70/Hwy 89/E. Main St. in Quincy.

OPEN M-F: 11 a.m.–9 p.m.

Pangaea Café & Pub (not to be confused with Pangaea Two Brews Café in Sacramento—very far away!) is about two hours' drive from Chico and is the easternmost destination in this section. The community-oriented café offers a Mug Club, organic menu options, and a nice selection of Northern California taps.

Western Pacific Brewing

 10 Liquor Barn
Bottle Shop

WWW.LIQUORBARNCA.COM

2627 Bechelli Ln., Redding, CA 96002, (530) 223-0452—GOING N: 5 Exit 677 (Cypress Ave.), L@ E Cypress Ave., L@ Bechelli Ln. GOING S: 5 Exit 677 (Cypress Ave.), R@ E Cypress Ave., L@ Bechelli Ln.

OPEN M-Th: 8 a.m.–9 p.m., F-Sa: 8 a.m.–10 p.m., Su: 9 a.m.–8 p.m.

The best-stocked bottle shop in the region. Knowledgeable staff and possibly the most comprehensive selection of Northern California beer you'll find anywhere—from Mammoth to High Water to Etna to Eel River. Plenty of glassware, plus an enormous liquor selection, should you somehow get bored of beer.

11 The Alehouse Pub
Beer Bar

WWW.REDDINGALEHOUSE.COM

2181 Hilltop Dr., Redding, CA 96002, (530) 221-7990—GOING N: 5 Exit 677 (Cypress Ave.), R@ E Cypress Ave., L@ Hilltop Dr. GOING S: 5 Exit 678A (Hwy 44 E/Lassen National Park) (0.5), Exit 2C (Hilltop Dr.), L@ Hilltop Dr. (0.6).

OPEN M-Th: 3 p.m.–midnight, F-Sa: 3 p.m.–1:30 a.m.

A great recent addition to Redding's craft beer scene, The Alehouse has the best

selection in the region: twenty-plus taps, one hundred-plus bottles, monthly cask events featuring Firestone Walker, and rarities from breweries like Stone and The Bruery in Southern California that you aren't going to find anywhere else nearby. They host an IPA festival each July, as well as an Oktoberfest event, and we counted about 273 billion hotels within walking distance.

12 NorCal Brewing Solutions
Homebrew Shop

WWW.NORCALBREWINGSOLUTIONS.COM

1101 Parkview Ave., Redding, CA 96001, (530) 243-2337—GOING N: 5 Exit 677 (Cypress Ave.), L@ E Cypress Ave. (0.9), L@ Parkview Ave. (0.6). GOING S: 5 Exit 677 (Cypress Ave.), R@ E Cypress Ave. (0.8), L@ Parkview Ave. (0.6).

OPEN Tu-F: 10 a.m.–5:30 p.m., Sa: 10 a.m.–4 p.m.

Excellent selection of homebrewing and winemaking supplies, available in-house and online. The shop's closely tied to the local beer community, and it's the last homebrew stop heading north until Medford, Oregon.

13 Dunsmuir Brewery Works
Brewpub

WWW.DUNSMUIRBREWERYWORKS.INFO

5701 Dunsmuir Ave., Dunsmuir, CA 96025, (530) 235-1900—GOING N: 5

Exit 730 (Central Dunsmuir), R@ Dunsmuir Ave. GOING S: 5 Exit 730 (Central Dunsmuir), L@ Dunsmuir Ave. (0.8).

OPEN Tu–Su: 11 a.m.–9 p.m.+

Dunsmuir Brewery Works is a recent and welcome addition to the small, historic town of Dunsmuir (see Beer Communities sidebar on page 199), about ten minutes south of Mount Shasta. Having previously worked at Third Street Aleworks in Santa Rosa and Mt. Shasta Brewing Co., Brewmaster Aaron Greener currently offers between two and six house-brewed beers, in addition to the brewpub's guest tap selection. Their flagship beer is the Rusty Spike Imperial Red (appropriately named for a town rich in railroad culture), while Blood, Sweat & Tears IPA is their best seller. All of their beers are unfiltered—a good thing—and a product of the much-prized local water. We got to sample their tasty ESB and Porter when we visited, the former a chewy, orange-laden version of the style. The Porter showed milk and dark chocolate mingling with vinous fruitiness.

BREWMASTER: Aaron T. Greener
ESTABLISHED: 2009
BE SURE TO TRY: Porter

⑭ Berryvale Grocery
Grocery Store

WWW.BERRYVALE.COM

305 S. Mt. Shasta Blvd., Mount Shasta, CA 96067, (530) 926-1576—

Dunsmuir Brewery Works

GOING N: 5 Exit 738 (Central Mt. Shasta), Merge @ W Lake St., R@ N Mt. Shasta Blvd. GOING S: 5 Exit 738 (Central Mt. Shasta), L@ W Lake St. (0.6), R@ N Mt. Shasta Blvd.

OPEN M–Sa: 8:30 a.m.–7:30 p.m., Su: 10 a.m.–6 p.m.

We stopped here for sandwiches before a hike, which turned into Ali shopping for sandwiches and me descending into a catatonic state in front of their beer cooler. While not an enormous selection, this natural-foods grocery store stocks only craft beer: Mad River, Butte Creek, Bear Republic, North Coast, High Water, and bottles from many other local breweries. The best Northern California beer selection in the area.

15 The Goat Tavern
Beer Bar/Restaurant

WWW.THEGOATMOUNTSHASTA.COM

107 Chestnut St., Mount Shasta, CA 96067, (530) 926-0209—GOING N: 5 Exit 738 (Central Mt. Shasta), Merge@ W Lake St., R@ Chestnut St. GOING S: 5 Exit 738 (Central Mt. Shasta), L@ W Lake St. (0.7), R@ Chestnut St.

OPEN Every day: 11 a.m.–9 p.m.

Right in downtown Mount Shasta, The Goat Tavern is perched on the triangular corner of Chestnut and Mt. Shasta Boulevard. Lots of patio seating, outdoor music as often as they can schedule it (including the neighborhood keyboard prodigy), and twelve craft-centric drafts

The Goat Tavern

PORTER MT. SHASTA SHASTAFARIAN PORTER

I've avoided diving into the historical backgrounds of the various styles for any number of reasons, not the least of which is that so much of the focused research into them has been either (1) patchy at best or (2) kind of like arguing about minutiae in a Star Wars film. Perhaps the most interesting historical tidbit here that one feels fully confident sharing is that porters were named after London's human porters, the couriers and laborers who played a vital and somewhat overlooked role in the commerce of London. It's a beer robust and satisfying enough for hard workers.

Clear historical distinctions between the broader porter and stout style categories (such as the use of roasted barley) have become less accurate over time, to say nothing of how these styles have consequently been reinterpreted by American brewers. Generally speaking, porters tend to be more on the creamy, fruity, caramel side (such as Baltic porters), while stouts will often veer toward a drier and more bitter presentation (such as dry stouts and imperial stouts). My head already kind of hurts.

Mt. Shasta Shastafarian Porter is our favorite offering from that brewery, partly because it shows off the rich caramel and nougat maltiness of the most impressive so-called porters. Some poorer renderings are just cola notes, which would probably feel even more disappointing if I had been lugging heavy cargo around a dock all day. The focus here is on the contributions of the dark specialty malts: roasted notes, smooth milk and dark chocolate; even, in the case of the Shastafarian, some hints of toasted marshmallow.

that they'll usually cycle through on a daily basis. The ceiling is loaded with their previous tap handles, and the locals love this place. We did, too.

16 Mt. Shasta Brewing Co.
Brewpub

WWW.WEEDALES.COM

360 College Ave., Weed, CA 96094, (530) 938-2394—GOING N: 5 Exit 747 (Hwy 97/Cent. Weed/Klam. Falls), L@ Hwy 97 S/S Weed Blvd., R@ College Ave. GOING S: 5 Exit 747 (Central Weed/College of Siskiyous), R@ S Weed Blvd., R@ College Ave.

OPEN Every day: noon–closing

Despite its name, Mt. Shasta Brewing is actually located about fifteen minutes north of Mount Shasta in the town of Weed. Originating from founder Abner Weed, who later became a California senator, the town's name became a point of contention when the brewery attempted to use it on their bottle caps. A 2008 tussle with the federal Alcohol and Tobacco Tax and Trade Bureau (TTB) ended up concluding in Mt. Shasta's favor—deservedly, considering the company's overall focus on beer names and labels that reflect their local

Mt. Shasta Brewing

community. Since then their bottle caps have proudly read, "Try Legal Weed." Considering the quality of their beer, it's good advice.

While I'll refrain from waxing poetic here about the Shastafarian Porter (see sidebar on page 196), it's one of very few beers that is almost constantly present in our fridge. The Weed Golden Ale and Lemurian Lager are both soft, toasty golden brews with a mineral hop character, while the Mountain High IPA showed a focused grapefruit hoppiness with a crystalline-sugar backdrop. The State of Jefferson Stout (making an

occasional appearance on tap) showed delicious, layered chocolates and a pear-like fruitiness. Yum.

The open-air feel, simple menu (brats, hot dogs, paninis), and eclectic décor, including a penny-farthing bicycle on the wall, make this an ideal spot to sample. Their brewer position was in flux last time we checked.

ESTABLISHED: 2003

BE SURE TO TRY: Shastafarian Porter

ELSEWHERE: Bottles, Draft

17 Liquor Expo
Bottle Shop

9320 Old Hwy 99, Grenada, CA 96038, (530) 436-0182—GOING N: 5 Exit 766 (Montague/Grenada), L@ County Rd. a-12, R@ Old Hwy 99 S. GOING S: 5 Exit 766 (Grenada/Gazelle), R@ County Rd. a-12, R@ Old Hwy 99 S.

OPEN M-Sa: 8 a.m.–8 p.m., Su: 9 a.m.– 8 p.m.

Liquor Expo is a large, warehouse-like liquor store visible from Highway 5. A filled-out selection of imports (Orval, Ayinger, and Traquair are excellent choices), plus nearly a full aisle of craft singles and six-packs.

18 Etna Brewing Co.
Brewpub

WWW.ETNABREW.NET

131 Callahan St., Etna, CA 96027, (530) 467-5277—From Hwy 5: follow Hwy 3 W (26.9) into downtown Etna, L@ Main St., R@ Callahan St.

Tu: 11:30 a.m.–4 p.m., W–Th: 11:30 a.m.–8 p.m., F–Sa: 11:30 a.m.– 9 p.m., Su: 11:30 a.m.–7 p.m.

Like many early American breweries (of which few remain; see introduction), Etna Brewing traces its lineage back to the nineteenth century and a German-born brewer. Alsace-born Charles Kappler founded the original Etna Brewing back in 1872, and the company successfully brewed beer (also like many early American breweries) until the onset of Prohibition in 1920. The brand was reborn seventy years later, on the site of the original bottling works, and the current brewpub showcases plenty of historical mementos and photographs.

The Etna lineup is quite solid in general, with their Old Grind Porter being my favorite of the ones regularly found in bottles: cola notes, light roast, some fruitiness, albeit on the quiet side. Many of their brews are both fine-tuned and restrained, including the Phoenix Red and draft-only seasonal Holy Hefeweizen. Slightly more forceful, their Mossback IPA offered up an expressive earthy and citrus hop character, with enough crystalline sweetness to make this seem more like a chewy Midwest version of the style. The Kappler Imperial Stout showed plenty of cola and red fruits, while their house-made root beer was a standout, showing a spicy, Sarsaparilla character one rarely sees in commercial soft drinks. Their tri-tip dinner (of mammoth proportions) was the perfect reward after an afternoon hiking Black Butte.

BREWMASTER: Bill Behm
ESTABLISHED: 1872 (current operations begun circa 1990)
BE SURE TO TRY: Mossback IPA
ELSEWHERE: Bottles, Draft

Beer Communities

As you travel around to all of these different breweries, you get a sense of the variety of different ways in which these places bring people together and establish themselves as a fundamental part of their communities. Anyone familiar with England's pub culture may more immediately appreciate this concept. But even at the upper limits of enormity (say, Sierra Nevada or Lagunitas, for instance) those elements are still apparent: families enjoying meals together, locals meeting up after work by the bar, employees whose livelihoods are closely commingled with the production and success of craft beer.

But it's easiest to notice at places like Dunsmuir Brewery Works. The town of Dunsmuir, rich in railroad heritage and "Home of the Best Water on Earth," is also home to about 1,800 residents. It gets a modest amount of tourism, encouraged by its trout fishing and scenic placement in the Shasta Cascades.

Dunsmuir Brewery's co-owners, Aaron Greener and Dave Clarno, opened the brewpub back in 2009, in a converted gas station across the street from the Dunsmuir Library and Ted Fay Fly Shop. While the beer Aaron makes is tasty in its own right, it was the sense of community that struck us most. A chef was grilling out front on the main patio, while open-mic participants played covers from David Bowie and The Black Keys. Ali and I were the only people who didn't know most everyone filling that patio, and yet it was evident that visitors were more than welcome. Aaron took us on a tour of the brewery and commented, in passing, on the fly-fishing tackle boxes and equipment on top of their main fridge—essentially home base for a fishing cooperative a few local customers have. We'd see similar situations time and again, whether we were in a spotless pub or a makeshift warehouse. As we passed through the quiet downtown section of Dunsmuir on our way back to our campsite, it became even more evident that we had just left the community's main meeting place.

RYE

This region is one of the book's largest, following Interstate 80 from the Bay Area to the Nevada border, through Sacramento, and Highway 50 from Sacramento to South Lake Tahoe. Beer places to the north were typically put into the preceding chapter, while those farther south ended up in the following one.

The Sacramento, Folsom, and Lake Tahoe regions offer a ton of good craft-beer opportunities, so many that there wasn't space to reasonably include everything. Places with more modest selections were removed in favor of more worthwhile stops—or, whenever possible, simply mentioned in a nearby listing. Nugget Markets, as one example, is a chain of grocery stores with solid craft-beer aisles located in the greater Sacramento area. There just wasn't sufficient room or reason to list them all individually.

The region itself is as diverse as the best Beer Destinations within it.

Sudwerk Restaurant & Brewery in Davis maintains a German theme in both brewing and décor. Auburn Alehouse is basically an archetype of the American brewpub. Loomis Basin Brewing offers an industrial warehouse location (with popcorn, mind you), while Jack Russell Brewing Company couldn't seem more removed from the bustle of a city. The lodge-like feel of FiftyFifty Brewing Co. in Truckee matches perfectly with its proximity to ski resorts and the surplus of outdoor activities surrounding the marvelously blue waters of Lake Tahoe.

Other Beer Destinations include the relatively recent additions of The Davis Beer Shoppe, Pangaea Two Brews Café near downtown Sacramento, and Samuel Horne's Tavern out in Folsom. As the lengthy list of up-and-coming breweries in the Uncharted Territory section suggests, change is afoot. Explore safely, stay locally, and savor the Destinations of one of Northern California's most rapidly evolving beer regions.

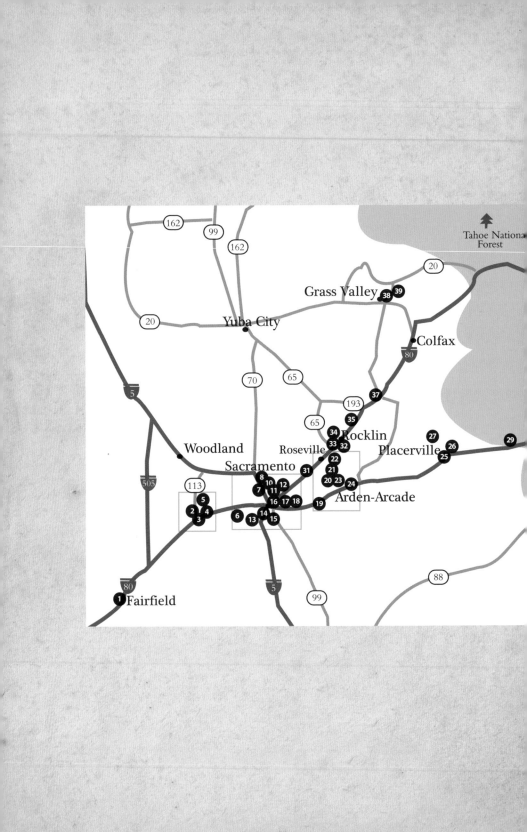

5 to try

FiftyFifty Totality Imperial Stout Loomis Basin Vindicator IPA Rubicon
Monkey Knife Fight Ruhstaller 1881 Sudwerk Pilsner

Truckee

80
40

ith Lake Tahoe 44
43
41
42

lorado
nal Forest 88

1	Blue Frog Grog & Grill – Fairfield Brewpub
2	The Davis Graduate – Davis Beer Bar/Restaurant
3	The Davis Beer Shoppe – Davis Bottle Shop/Beer Bar
4	Davis Food Co-op – Davis Grocery Store
5	Sudwerk Restaurant & Brewery – Davis Brewpub
6	RoCo Wine & Spirits – West Sacramento Bottle Shop
7	Ten22 – Sacramento Restaurant
8	River City Brewing Company – Sacramento Brewpub
9	Ruhstaller – Sacramento Brewery
10	Pyramid Alehouse – Sacramento Brewpub
11	Rubicon Brewing Company – Sacramento Brewpub
12	River Rock Tap House – Sacramento Beer Bar/Restaurant
13	Taylor's Market – Sacramento Grocery Store
14	Pangaea Two Brews Café – Sacramento Restaurant/Beer Bar
15	Brew Ferment Distill – Sacramento Homebrew Shop
16	The Shack – Sacramento Restaurant
17	Corti Brothers – Sacramento Grocery Store
18	Hoppy Brewing Company – Sacramento Brewpub

uncharted territory

American River Brewing Co. (Rancho Cordova) Berryessa Brewing Co. (Winters) Black Dragon
New Helvetia Brewing Company (Sacramento) ol' Republic Brewery (Nevada City)

19 Lockdown Brewing Co. – Rancho Cordova   Brewery

20 The Brewmeister – Folsom   Homebrew Shop

21 Samuel Horne's Tavern – Folsom   Beer Bar

22 Sudwerk Restaurant & Brewery (Riverside) – Folsom   Brewpub

23 Manderes – Folsom   Restaurant

24 The Tap Room at Whole Foods Market – Folsom   Beer Bar/Grocery Store

25 Placerville Brewing Company – Placerville   Brewpub

26 Brick Oven Pub – Placerville   Restaurant

27 Gold Hill Brewery and Vineyard – Placerville   Brewery

28 Old Hangtown Beer Works – Placerville   Nanobrewery

29 Jack Russell Brewing Co. – Camino   Brewery

30 El Dorado Brewing Company – Camino   Brewery

31 The Original Home Brew Outlet, Inc. – Sacramento   Homebrew Shop

32 Gordon Biersch – Roseville   Brewpub

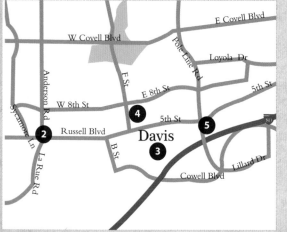

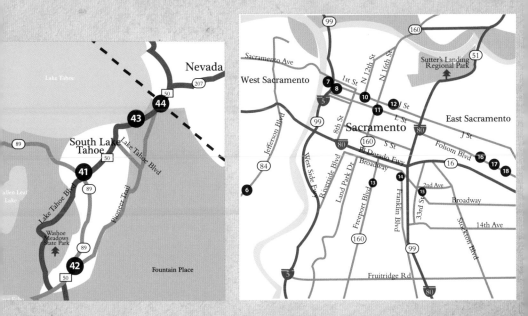

① Blue Frog Grog & Grill
Brewpub

WWW.BIGBLUEFROG.COM

1740 Travis Blvd., Fairfield, CA 94533, (707) 429-2337—GOING E: 80 Exit 45 (Travis Blvd.), R@ Travis Blvd. GOING W: 80 Exit 45 (Travis Blvd.), L@ Travis Blvd.

OPEN M-Th: 11:30 a.m.–10 p.m., F-Sa: 11:30 a.m.–11 p.m., Su: 11:30 a.m.–9 p.m.

Blue Frog is the main place to stop for beer between East Bay and Davis, heading east on Interstate-80: a family restaurant with a modest lineup of house-brewed beer. The Hefe, showing plenty of banana with toned-down pepper and clove notes, and the grapefruit-driven Indian Pale Ale were the most precise.

BREWMASTER: Nick Campbell
ESTABLISHED: 1999
BE SURE TO TRY: Indian Pale Ale
ELSEWHERE: Bottles, Draft

② The Davis Graduate
Beer Bar/Restaurant

WWW.DAVISGRAD.COM

805 Russell Blvd., Davis, CA 95616, (530) 758-4723—From Hwy 80 in Davis, Exit 70 (Hwy 113 N/Woodland) (1.9), Exit 28 (Russell Blvd./Davis), R@ Russell Blvd. (0.5).

OPEN M-F: 10:30 a.m.–midnight+, Sa-Su: 9 a.m.–midnight+

Though this establishment is located in a mall, you won't notice once you're inside. The Davis Graduate may best be described as a combination of college bar and craft-beer bar. University students, bench-style seating, an outdoor patio, and plenty of special events—live bands, televised rugby, UFC/MMA, etc.— many of which charge a cover, so plan ahead. Plus, an entire wall of craft beer that included Anderson Valley, Sudwerk, Moylan's, and Russian River the last time we visited. The sort of college bar you wish you'd had.

③ The Davis Beer Shoppe
Bottle Shop/Beer Bar

211 G St., Davis, CA 95616, (530) 756-5212—GOING E: 80 Exit 72 (Richards Blvd./Downtown), R@ Richards Blvd., R@ 1st St. GOING W: 80 Exit 72B (Richards Blvd. N/Downtown) (0.5), R@ 1st St.

OPEN M-W: 10 a.m.–10 p.m., Th: 10 a.m.–11 p.m., F: 10 a.m.–midnight, Sa: 9 a.m.–midnight, Su: 11 a.m.–7 p.m.

A relatively new addition to the Davis beer scene (it opened in 2011), The Davis Beer Shoppe is your best bet for rare and limited-release beers in the area. The shop itself is subtly partitioned into two separate areas due to two separate licenses—so while you can bring over any bottle to consume in-house in the beer-bar section, you can't peruse the bottle selection while consuming. That's my only complaint. While there were only eight taps the last time we checked, they rotate daily and

The Davis Graduate

④ Davis Food Co-op
Grocery Store

WWW.DAVISCOOP.COM

620 G St., Davis, CA 95616, (530) 758-2667—GOING E: 80 Exit 72 (Richards Blvd./Downtown), R@ Richards Blvd., R@ 1st St. (0.6). GOING W: 80 Exit 72B (Richards Blvd. N/Downtown) (0.5), R@ 1st St. (0.6).

OPEN Every day: 7 a.m.–10 p.m.

the sample lineup changes accordingly, typically to feature a number of different beers of the same style or from the same brewery. Yes, please. The bottle selection—from the latest barrel-aged stouts coming out of Denmark to the saison-centric lineup of Stillwater Artisanal Ales in Maryland—is one of the very best in the region.

While The Davis Beer Shoppe is the place to go for rare and limited-release brews in town, the Co-op has a great lineup of local and further-flung beers. The best part? You can buy single bottles of everything.

The Northern California Craft Beer Guide

Sudwerk Brewery

⑤ Sudwerk ⭐
Restaurant & Brewery
Brewpub

🍴 🥛 🍶 🍾 🛢️

WWW.SUDWERK.COM

2001 Second St., Davis, CA 95618, (530) 758-8700—GOING E: 80 Exit 72 (Richards Blvd./ Downtown), L@ Richards Blvd. (0.6), L@ Pole Line Rd. GOING W: 80 Exit 72A (Richards Blvd. S) (0.9), L@ Pole Line Rd.

OPEN Su–Tu: 11:30 a.m.–9:30 p.m., W–Th: 11:30 a.m.–9 p.m., F–Sa: 11:30 a.m.–10:30 p.m.

Sudwerk keeps close ties with UC Davis' professional brewing programs (see sidebar Beer Education on page 215), so perhaps it's no surprise that the German-style brews in Sudwerk's main lineup are both flawless and some of the best examples of these styles in the region. The helles-style Lager is a great example of a flavorful pale lager (see sidebar), while the crisp Pilsner kicks it up a notch with its firm mineral and herbal bitterness. Both are textbook, and similar comments could be made about the Marzen and Hefeweizen. The expansive beer garden, plus the high ceilings and bright copper kettles inside, add to the overall German theme.

One of the coolest parts of Sudwerk, though, is the relatively recent addition of the Dock

STYLE:

PALE LAGER SUDWERK LAGER

The pale lager classification is a fuzzy one (the beer itself should not be fuzzy) and encompasses a wide range of styles that typically have the following in common: (1) they're relatively pale in color, from light straw to a deep gold, and (2) they're made with lager yeast and fermented for extended periods of time at cooler temperatures. The latter tends to give these beers a crisp, clean flavor with minimal fruitiness.

Many lagers that satisfy the points above still end up in another category, such as Pilsners, which usually have a more significant core bitterness and hop character, or things like the pale bock styles, which tend to have a lot more oomph alcohol-wise. Beers that actually end up called pale lagers or lagers are most often those on the lightly hopped and less oomphy side of things. Mass-produced lite lagers (hereafter referred to as "water" or in less flattering terms) have falsely promoted the impression that any lager that's also pale is flavorless.

While one could seriously write a book on all the nuanced distinctions between the various types of pale lagers, it's easier to just drink one. Well-crafted pale lagers can be both hugely refreshing and miles from flavorless. Sudwerk Lager, crafted in the style of a German helles, shows that rich and toasty Pilsner malt contribution throughout, with a sprinkling of spicy noble-hop character. It's significantly less bitter than the Sudwerk Pilsner, but just as delicious. Auburn Export Lager is another expressive local example.

Store, which is located around the side of the restaurant and opens only for limited hours each week. Call ahead for the schedule. You can sample limited-release offerings, plus occasionally rub elbows with brewers-to-be.

BREWMEISTER: Jay Prahl
ESTABLISHED: 1990
BE SURE TO TRY: Pilsner
ELSEWHERE: Bottles, Draft

RoCo Wine & Spirits
Bottle Shop

WWW.ROCOSPIRITS.COM

2220 Lake Washington Blvd. #120, West Sacramento, CA 95691, (916) 760-8135—GOING E: 50/80-Bus Exit 1 (Harbor Blvd S) (0.5), L@ Industrial Blvd. (1.5). GOING W: 50/80-Bus Exit 1B (Harbor Blvd.), L@ Harbor Blvd. (0.5), L@ Industrial Blvd. (1.5).

OPEN Su-Th: 8 a.m.–1 a.m., F-Sa: 8 a.m.–2 a.m.

RoCo is quietly tucked into a shopping plaza near Lowe's Home Improvement, southwest of downtown Sacramento. The small, well-chosen beer aisle featured Lost Abbey, Allagash, Rodenbach, and Malheur.

Ten22
Restaurant

WWW.TEN22OLDSAC.COM

1022 Second St., Sacramento, CA 95814, (916) 441-2211—Right in Old Sacramento Historic District, near the corner of K St. and Second St.

OPEN Su-Th: 11:30 a.m.–11 p.m., F-Sa: 11:30 a.m.–midnight

Ten22 is a recent addition to the area's craft beer scene, and was named Best New Restaurant for 2010 by Sacramento Magazine. Solid selection of California beers and occasional events with local brewers.

 River City Brewing Company
Brewpub

WWW.RIVERCITYBREWING.NET

545 Downtown Plaza, Ste 1115, Sacramento, CA 95814, (916) 447-2739—Downtown Sacramento, inside Westfield Downtown Plaza near the corner of L St. and Fourth St.

OPEN M-Th: 11:30 a.m.–9:30 p.m., F-Sa: 11:30 a.m.–10:30 p.m., Su: 11:30 a.m.–8:30 p.m.

While the standard lineup here—including a Kölsch-style beer, a Vienna, and a big oak-aged amber—tends toward the adventurous, the execution was frequently off-base. The under-5% Cap City Pale was what we went back to: a lighter-bodied, more earthy and floral presence than typically found in pale ales on the West Coast. Their River City "growlers" are actually five-liter minikegs.

BREWMASTER: Brian Cofresi
ESTABLISHED: 1993
BE SURE TO TRY: Cap City Pale
ELSEWHERE: Draft

Ruhstaller
Brewery

WWW.RUHSTALLERBEER.COM

Sacramento, CA, (916) 919-5691

Anything Peter Hoey creates in the
brewhouse is something I want to track
down and drink. Ali and I would typically
stop at Sacramento Brewing Company
(one of Peter's previous employments,
now kaput) when traveling to visit family
in Nevada; I've driven out to Sacramento
solely to sample his sour beers debuting
from Odonata Beer Co. (also kaput), and
my server at Sutter Buttes, where Peter
most recently worked as a brewer, spoke
fondly of him as she poured me more of
their spot-on beer. It's exciting for us to
see Peter concocting his own recipes again,
and his partnership with proprietor J-E
Paino has already resulted in a couple of
phenomenal beers. I haven't gotten around
to trying the bottled versions yet, as they
just recently started appearing on shelves.
Brewery turnover in Sacramento has been
rough lately, in what was previously one of
the major beer-producing regions in the
country. The name Ruhstaller is actually
a nod to Captain Frank Ruhstaller, one
of the foremost brewing entrepreneurs
in Sacramento in his time (back in the
late 1800s, before Prohibition). The
1881 is a tribute to Sacramento's rich
beer history, and it's a hugely drinkable
amber ale with spicy and earthy hop
aroma and a tempered caramel and nutty
maltiness. Delicious, deftly brewed stuff.
Look for Ruhstaller brews on tap and in
bottles at craft beer locations throughout
Sacramento, Folsom, and Davis.

CONSULTANT: Peter Hoey
ESTABLISHED: 2011

BE SURE TO TRY: 1881
SEASONALS: Hop Sac (fall)
ELSEWHERE: Bottles, Draft

⑩ Pyramid Alehouse
Brewpub

WWW.PYRAMIDBREW.COM

1029 K St., Sacramento, CA 95814,
(916) 498-9800—Right in downtown
Sacramento, near the corner of 10th St.
and K St.

OPEN M-Th: 11:30 a.m.–9 p.m., F:
11:30 a.m.–11 p.m., Sa: noon–10 p.m., Su:
10 a.m.–7 p.m.

Chain location (for details, see main listing:
Pyramid Alehouse & Brewery - Berkeley
on page 98).

⑪ Rubicon Brewing Company
Brewpub

WWW.RUBICONBREWING.COM

2004 Capitol Ave., Sacramento, CA 95814,
(916) 448-7032—Right in downtown
Sacramento, near the corner of Capitol
Ave. and 20th St.

OPEN M-Th: 11 a.m.–11:30 p.m., F-Sa:
11 a.m.–12:30 a.m., Su: 11 a.m.–10 p.m.

Rubicon is part of the heart and soul of
the craft beer scene in Sacramento (the
first time I visited was to sample a release
from the since-defunct Odonata Beer
Co., which was debuting its beer there).
Normally, I'll get strange looks when I

ask for a monkey knife fight, but not here. Rubicon's Monkey Knife Fight is their delicious pale ale, with loads of orangey hop flavor and a modest bitterness. It's lighter-bodied than many pale ales, and the most fun thing on the menu to order. The India Pale Ale is a bulkier, hopped-up version, while the seasonal Winter Wheatwine weighs in around 10% and shows layers of mouth-coating raisins, red fruits, and caramelization. It's won multiple medals at the Great American Beer Festival.

HEAD BREWER: Scott Cramlet
ESTABLISHED: 1987
BE SURE TO TRY: Monkey Knife Fight
SEASONALS: Winter Wheatwine (fall-winter)
ELSEWHERE: Bottles, Draft

12 River Rock Tap House
Beer Bar/Restaurant

WWW.RIVERROCKTAPHOUSE.COM

2326 J St., Sacramento, CA 95816, (916) 273-4930—Right in downtown Sacramento, near the corner of J St. and 24th St.

OPEN M-F: 3 p.m.–midnight, Sa-Su: 11 a.m.–midnight

River Rock tends to have more of a nightlife feel in the evenings than a beer-geek crowd, though last call can be somewhat earlier than their posted hours suggest—plan ahead. About twenty-five taps, craft-beer focused, plus specialty blends including the aptly named "Dr. Kevorkian" (Guinness plus North Coast Old Stock Ale).

Beer Education

In case Northern California's lofty position in the craft beer world isn't already apparent, the region also happens to be home to one of the most highly regarded professional brewing schools in existence. The University of California, Davis has offered brewing science classes since the 1950s, and today their eighteen-week Master Brewers Program is one of a small handful of intensive U.S. brewing programs. (Other top-tier schools include the American Brewers Guild in Vermont and Siebel Institute in Chicago). It's also the only school in the country accredited by London's esteemed Institute of Brewing and Distilling. UC Davis professors Michael Lewis and Charles Bamforth each have more than thirty years' experience in brewing science education, and many of the world's top brewers have a UC Davis diploma hanging on their wall.

The program currently maintains close ties with Sudwerk Brewery in Davis, and classes are actually held in a UC Davis Extension classroom at the brewery (the magical "University Extension Master Brewers Program" door is adjacent to Sudwerk's Dock Store). Students get hands-on access to the two brewing systems on site, which are overseen by Sudwerk Brewmeister Jay Prahl, a UC Davis alumnus himself.

In addition to the Master Brewers Program, UC Davis offers numerous other brewing science programs. The university itself serves as home to a $1 million, 1.5-barrel brewery, which Dr. Bamforth uses to teach the undergraduate and graduate curricula. UC Davis also houses an extensive research program, exploring everything from the science of barley to how beer interacts with the human body.

⑬ Taylor's Market
Grocery Store

WWW.TAYLORSMARKET.COM

2900 Freeport Blvd., Sacramento, CA 95818, (916) 443-6881—GOING E: 50/80-Bus Exit 5 (15th St.), R@ 15th St., L@ Broadway, R@ Freeport Blvd. (0.6). GOING W: 50/80-Bus Exit 6A (26th St.) (0.6), L@ Hwy 160 S (0.8), R@ Freeport Blvd.

OPEN M-Sa: 9 a.m.–7 p.m., Su: 9 a.m.–6 p.m.

Taylor's Market is a specialty grocery store carrying a modest selection of larger-format California and European beers, including harder-to-find deliciousness like Fantôme and 3 Monts. As one employee put it, "We stock what we like to drink." They host occasional artisan beer-and-cheese pairings throughout the year.

⑭ Pangaea Two Brews Café ⭐
Restaurant/Beer Bar

WWW.PANGAEATWOBREWS.COM

2743 Franklin Blvd., Sacramento, CA 95818, (916) 454-4942—GOING E: 50/80-Bus Exit 5 (15th St.), L@ X St. (1.0), R@ 28th St., L@ Broadway, R@ Franklin Blvd. GOING W: 50 Exit 6A (26th St.), L@ 26th St., L@ Broadway, R@ Franklin Blvd.

OPEN Tu-Sa: 10 a.m.–10 p.m., Su: 11 a.m.–6 p.m.

Pangaea Two Brews has both a café section, with seventeen Belgian-centric taps, and a bottle-shop room. The latter is a relatively recent addition to the café, but it's already perhaps the best place to go for sour and Belgian-style beers in the area. The abundance of delicious sour beers is remarkable. Though the prices are a bit steep on some things, the selection from a few much-loved breweries like Jolly Pumpkin, Mikkeller, and Alpine is basically unmatched. Sundays here focus on sampling and beer education.

⑮ Brew Ferment Distill
Homebrew Shop

WWW.BREWFERMENTDISTILL.COM

3527 Broadway, Ste A, Sacramento, CA 95817, (916) 476-5034—GOING E: 50 Exit 7 (34th St.), R@ 34th St. (0.5), L@ 2nd Ave. R@ 36th St. R@ Broadway. GOING W: 50 Exit 8 (65th St.), L@ 65th St., R@ Broadway (2.3).

OPEN M: noon–7 p.m., W-F: noon–7 p.m., Sa-Su: 10 a.m.–5 p.m.

The closest homebrew shop to downtown Sacramento, Brew Ferment Distill is just a few minutes off Highway 50 and Interstate 80-Business. Within walking distance of Pangaea Two Brews Café (see above).

16 The Shack
Restaurant

WWW.EASTSACSHACK.COM

5201 Folsom Blvd., Sacramento, CA 95819, (916) 457-5997—GOING E: 50 Exit 8A (59th St.) (0.5), L@ 59th St., L@ Folsom Blvd. GOING W: 50 Exit 8 (65th St.) (0.8), R@ 59th St., L@ Folsom Blvd.

OPEN M: 11 a.m.–3 p.m., Tu–F: 11 a.m.–8 p.m., Sa–Su: 8 a.m.–3 p.m. (seasonal)

Down the street from Corti Brothers and Hoppy Brewing Company (see below), The Shack is a brunch-and-sandwich destination offering nearly a hundred different craft beers: saisons, sour beers, Trappist ales, ciders, etc. We've never had trouble finding something to sip out on their patio. Beer tastings are usually offered on a weekly basis.

17 Corti Brothers
Grocery Store

WWW.CORTIBROS.BIZ

5810 Folsom Blvd., Sacramento, CA 95819, (916) 736-3803—GOING E: 50 Exit 8A (59th St.) (0.5), L@ 59th St., L@ Folsom Blvd. GOING W: 50 Exit 8 (65th St.), R@ 65th St., L@ Folsom Blvd. (0.5).

OPEN M–Sa: 9 a.m.–7 p.m., Su: 10 a.m.–6 p.m.

Specialty foods shop focusing somewhat more on wine, but their refrigerated beer aisle stocks plenty of international beers one won't find elsewhere. Walking distance from The Shack and Hoppy Brewing.

18 Hoppy Brewing Company
Brewpub

WWW.HOPPY.COM

6300 Folsom Blvd., Sacramento, CA 95819, (916) 451-4677—GOING E: 50 Exit 8A (59th St.) (0.5), L@ 59th St., R@ Folsom Blvd. GOING W: 50 Exit 8 (65th St.) (0.8), R@ 59th St., R@ Folsom Blvd.

OPEN M–W: 11 a.m.–midnight, Th–F: 11 a.m.–1 a.m., Sa: 10 a.m.–1 a.m., Su: 10 a.m.–midnight

Southeast of downtown Sacramento, Hoppy Brewing has a very strong central lineup of brews, in addition to their one-off brewer's specials. Their Golden Nugget Cream Ale is a crisp, slightly fruity version of the style, while both the Liquid Sunshine Blonde Ale and Hoppy Face Amber showcase a zesty citrus hop character. A popular blend to order is the "Ramber," which combines their Stony Face Red and Hoppy Face Amber. The Burnt Sienna Ale, though, is the rare treat: brewed with smoked malt, it's a non-traditional chewy and hoppy beer with an inky smokiness. While not overwhelming, the smoke's not timid either, and Burnt Sienna is a nice stepping stone into the more assertive German rauchbiers (smoke beers).

BREWERS: Ed Kopta (Brewing Operations Manager), Troy Paski (President)
ESTABLISHED: 1994
BE SURE TO TRY: Burnt Sienna Ale
ELSEWHERE: Bottles, Draft

Samuel Horne's Tavern

The last time we stopped in, the Lockdown beers were being contract-brewed at St. Stan's in Modesto; that's subject to change, of course. Lockdown's limited hours and warehouse locale give it a fun after-work vibe, but their Stony Bar Scotch Ale was the lone highlight within a generally lackluster lineup.

ESTABLISHED: 2004
ELSEWHERE: Bottles, Draft

20 The Brewmeister
Homebrew Shop

WWW.FOLSOMBREWMEISTER.COM

802 A Reading St., Folsom, CA 95630, (888) 423-3730/(916) 985-7299—GOING E: 50 Exit 23 (Folsom Blvd.), L@ Folsom Blvd. (2.5), R@ Bidwell St., R@ Reading St. GOING W: 50 Exit 23 (Folsom Blvd.), L@ Folsom Blvd. (2.3), R@ Bidwell St., R@ Reading St.

OPEN M-F: noon–6 p.m., Sa-Su: 10 a.m.–4 p.m.

Homebrewing and winemaking shop serving the Folsom area. The Brewmeister offers online sales and is a short walk from Samuel Horne's, which occasionally runs promotions for Brewmeister customers.

19 Lockdown Brewing Co.
Brewery

WWW.LOCKDOWNBREWINGCOMPANY.COM

11327 Trade Center Dr. #350, Rancho Cordova, CA 95742, (916) 835-7416—GOING E: 50 Exit 18 (Sunrise Blvd.), R@ Co Rd. E2/Sunrise Blvd., L@ Trade Center Dr. GOING W: 50 Exit 18 (Sunrise Blvd.), L@ Co Rd. E2/Sunrise Blvd. (0.5), L@ Trade Center Dr.

OPEN W-F: 4 p.m.–8 p.m.

21 Samuel Horne's Tavern ★
Beer Bar

WWW.SAMUELHORNESTAVERN.COM

719 Sutter St., Folsom, CA 95630, (916) 293-8207—GOING E: 50 Exit 23 (Folsom

amuel Horne's Tavern

Blvd.), L@ Folsom Blvd. (2.7), R@ Sutter St. (0.5). GOING W: 50 Exit 23 (Folsom Blvd.), L@ Folsom Blvd. (2.5), R@ Sutter St. (0.5).

OPEN M-Tu: 4 p.m.–closing, W-Su: 11:30 a.m.–closing

We wish this place were down the street from us. Their front signage, featuring a seemingly trustworthy cartoon gentleman in a fedora—which makes him seem extra trustworthy—indicates that you're entering "A 'Better Beer' Joint."
The proof backing up this claim is in the details: from tap lines cleaned after every keg to beer menus organized by the focal ingredient ("barley" for malty beers, "hops" for pale ales and IPAs, and "yeast" for German hefeweizens and Belgian styles), to expertly formulated beer-based cocktails and blends that are far more than the sum of their parts. Samuel Horne's is situated in a cozy, window-shopping section of Folsom, with knowledgeable staff and meticulously chosen draft and bottle lists; the latter included Lost Abbey, Jolly Pumpkin, Pretty Things, and Alesmith when we were last there. This is definitely one of the best beer joints in the region.

22 Sudwerk Restaurant & Brewery
Brewpub

WWW.SUDWERK.COM

9900 Greenback Ln., Folsom, CA 95630, (916) 989-9243—GOING E: 50 Exit 23 (Folsom Blvd.), L@ Folsom Blvd. (3.6), R@ Greenback Ln. GOING W: 50 Exit 23 (Folsom Blvd.), L@ Folsom Blvd. (3.4), R@ Greenback Ln.

OPEN M-Th: 11:30 a.m.–10 p.m., F-Sa: 11:30 a.m.–11 p.m., Su: 11 a.m.–10 p.m.

Second location (for details, see main listing: Sudwerk Restaurant & Brewery – Davis on page 211).

23 Manderes
Restaurant

WWW.MANDERES.COM

1004 E. Bidwell St., Ste 600, Folsom, CA 95630, (916) 986-9655—GOING E: 50 Exit 27 (Scott Rd./E Bidwell St.), L@ Scott Rd. (3.1). GOING W: 50 Exit 27 (Scott Rd./E Bidwell St.), R@ Scott Rd. (3.0).

OPEN M-Sa: 11 a.m.–11 p.m., Su: noon– 11 p.m.

A nicely appointed restaurant (dark modern styling, electric guitars, big-screen TVs) with a serious craft-beer focus. Friendly, knowledgeable owner whose expertise shows on the carefully chosen tap list—Bear Republic Racer 5, Anderson Valley Boont Amber, Franziskaner Hefeweizen, and Koningshoeven Quad are the regulars. The twenty-plus taps are supported by a hefty bottle list, and the menu included beer-centric entrees, including Old Rasputin Ribs and Chimay Glazed Chicken. Cozy, so get there early to guarantee a table.

24 The Tap Room
at Whole Foods Market
Beer Bar/Grocery Store

WWW.WHOLEFOODSMARKET.COM

270 Palladio Pkwy., Folsom, CA 95630, (916) 984-8500—GOING E: 50 Exit 27 (Scott Rd./E Bidwell St.), L@ Scott Rd., L@ Iron Point Rd., R@ Palladio Pkwy. GOING W: 50 Exit 27 (Scott Rd./E Bidwell St.), R@ Scott Rd., L@ Iron Point Rd., R@ Palladio Pkwy.

OPEN Su-Th: 8 a.m.–9 p.m., F-Sa: 8 a.m.– 10 p.m. (Tap Room hours may differ)

Second location (for details, see main listing: The Tap Room at Whole Foods Market – Coddingtown on page 76).

Beer versus Wine

You'll often see the talking heads of both the beer and wine industries arguing over which beverage is better and more complex, and much of this kind of attention is due to the comparatively recent resurgence of artfully crafted beer in this country. Restaurants hold "Beer vs. Wine" pairing dinners, entire books have been written on the subject (He Said Beer, She Said Wine by Sam Calagione and Marnie Old; Charles Bamforth's Grape vs. Grain), and it's hard to put beer and wine advocates in a room together for very long without a little bit of grumbling. Much like shopping for a new monocle or entering a golden trousers competition, however, most of the debate is usually an exercise in fanciness.

Wine can be deliciously complex. Beer can be deliciously complex. The major distinction that I find most interesting goes back to the ingredients going into these beverages. Winemakers typically purchase their grapes from growers, and much of the final complexity in the finished product hinges on how the grape harvest went that year. Brewers, in contrast, work with a much broader spectrum of ingredients (malts, hops, yeasts, spices, sugars, fruits, etc.), the majority of which don't really change all that much from year to year. Much of the complexity and nuance of the final product rests squarely on the shoulders of the person brewing it. In my mind, there seems to be more room for artistic expression.

Perhaps that's just my fanciness talking. Regardless, people can judge for themselves. Gold Hill Brewery and Vineyard in Placerville offers a gorgeous venue for comparing the two beverages side by side, while Napa Smith Brewery and Winery in Napa affords two adjacent tasting rooms in one of the more expansive beer-sampling spots out there. Pull on your shiniest trousers and decide for yourself if you're in wine or beer country.

erville Brewing ... pany
pub

WWW.PLACERVILLEBREWING.COM

155 Placerville Dr., Placerville, CA 95667, (530) 295-9166—GOING E: 50 Exit 44B (Placerville Dr.), R@ Placerville Dr. GOING W: 50 Exit 44B (Forni Rd.), R@ Placerville Dr.

OPEN Every day (except Tuesdays): 11 a.m.–9 p.m.

Placerville Brewing Company is one of the main beer stops in El Dorado County. While some of the beers tended to be on the sweet side (including their popular Strong Blonde Ale and their range of fruit beers), others were excellent. The Stout was creamy, dark, and delicious, showing plenty of chocolate and roast, with a light, nutty oiliness adding an extra layer of complexity. Their seasonals tend to rotate in and out pretty quickly, but hopefully the 425 (a dry-hopped pale ale) will be on tap when you stop in.

BREWMASTER: Steve Meylor
ESTABLISHED: 2005
BE SURE TO TRY: Stout

26 Brick Oven Pub
Restaurant

WWW.BRICKOVENPUB.COM

2875 Ray Lawyer Dr., Placerville, CA 95667, (530) 622-7420—GOING E: 50 Exit 44B (Placerville Dr.), R@ Placerville Dr. (0.6), R@ Ray Lawyer Dr. GOING W: 50 Exit 44B (Forni Rd.), R@ Placerville Dr. (0.5), R@ Ray Lawyer Dr.

OPEN M-Sa: 11 a.m.–closing, Su: generally noon–closing

Family-owned restaurant focused on brick-oven pizzas and featuring twenty-five taps. The majority are pouring craft beer, with regulars from Bear Republic and Lagunitas along with limited-release regional kegs.

27 Gold Hill Brewery and Vineyard
Brewery

WWW.GOLDHILLVINEYARD.COM

5660 Vineyard Ln., Placerville, CA 95667, (530) 626-6522—Plan ahead or GPS (20 min off Hwy 50; 40 min off I-80).

OPEN Th-Su: 10 a.m.–5 p.m. (and by appointment)

I guess one other distinction between wine and beer (Beer versus Wine sidebar on page 221) is that the former often takes one to scenic chateaus overlooking artfully landscaped vineyards, whereas beer venues tend to be more, well, not overlooking artfully landscaped vineyards. Gold Hill offers both house-made wine and beer, and might very well be the most scenic place to sample beer in the whole region, surrounded by rolling, bright green hills. One can see stacked kegs stored underneath the eaves holding up the property's solar panels.

Their beer lineup is pretty well handled. Gold Hill offers a standard line of

Jack Russell Brewing

approximately six beers, and their Gold Trail Pale Ale and Axe Pic'n Stout were our favorites of the bunch. The Stout shows an impressively complex nose of leather, dark fruits, cola, and chocolate. We made sure to bring some home to share. (They sell bottles, but BYO growler.) While they're currently working on getting bottles into stores in El Dorado County, at the time the only place outside the brewery to sample their work was on tap at Red Hawk Casino.

BREWER: Dan Lee
ESTABLISHED: 1999
BE SURE TO TRY: Axe Pic'n Stout
ELSEWHERE: Draft

Old Hangtown Beer Works
Nanobrewery

Placerville, CA

Old Hangtown is the area's only nanobrewery, producing small amounts of handcrafted beer for local festivals and Placerville beer spots (check The Wine Smith, Powell's Steamer Co., and The Cozmic Café; no listings). At festivals, look for the "Ale Camino" with its HOM BRU license plate and two functional tap handles.

BREWER: Michael Frenn
ESTABLISHED: 2010
ELSEWHERE: Draft

Jack Russell Brewing Co.
Brewery

WWW.JACKRUSSELLBREWING.COM

2380 Larsen Dr., Camino, CA 95709,

(530) 647-9420—GOING E: Hwy 50, L@ Carson Rd., R@ Carson Rd. (1.1), L@ Larsen Dr. (0.8), R@ Larsen Dr. (0.5). GOING W: 50 Exit 54 (Camino), R@ Carson (0.7), R@ Larsen Dr. (0.8), R@ Larsen Dr. (0.5).

OPEN M-Th: 11 a.m.–7 p.m., F: 11 a.m.–8 p.m., Sa: 11 a.m.–7 p.m., Su: 11 a.m.–6 p.m.

Jack Russell Brewing Co. is a bit off the beaten path, about halfway between Sacramento and South Lake Tahoe on Highway 50. But our experience here was unlike that at any other brewery we've visited. Passing lots of apple and pear farms along the way, you'll find the brewery itself is surrounded by berry patches, and their huge outdoor area in front affords plenty of space for relaxing and enjoying their impressive lineup of beers. They were in the process of expanding when we visited, hoping to produce wine, mead, and cider as well. While bottles of their beer will suffer if you wait too long or don't keep them cold, in our experience, tasting their beers on site established that this was most assuredly a packaging issue, not a problem in the brewing. Their fruit beers, particularly the Apple Ale and Blueberry Ale, are what we wish more fruit beers were like, as they showed a vibrant, crisp, and nicely dry whole-fruit character (attention other brewers: fruit syrup is meant for waffles, not beer). The Scottish Ale showed a nicely integrated peaty smokiness (think Islay-region Scotch), while the Strong Blonde seemed far drier and better focused than the one at Placerville. The All American Lager was another favorite, a toasty and honey-laden lager, but everything was good. We're definitely looking forward to making it back out to see how their renovations are coming along.

BREWERS: David Coody, Erik Schmid
ESTABLISHED: 1997
BE SURE TO TRY: Harvest Apple Ale
SEASONALS: Blueberry Beer (spring)
ELSEWHERE: Draft

30 El Dorado Brewing Company
Brewery

WWW.ELDOBREW.COM

Camino, CA

Like a handful of other breweries in the area, the El Dorado brand traces its complicated history back to the 1800s. The original brewery survived Prohibition by successfully producing a highly regarded "near beer" under 0.5% ABV, before closing its doors in the 1950s. The brand was revived in the 1990s, and their beers (including Real Mountain Ale, Gold Rush Lager, and Trailblazer Stout) can occasionally be found in bottles and kegs at local venues and beer festivals. The farthest away we've noticed their bottles was at Ledger's in Berkeley.

BREWMASTERS: Greg Upton, Allan Camillo
ESTABLISHED: 1853 (current operations begun in the 1990s)
ELSEWHERE: Bottles, Draft

31 The Original Home Brew Outlet, Inc.
Homebrew Shop

WWW.EHOMEBREW.COM

5528 Auburn Blvd., #1, Sacramento, CA 95841, (916) 348-6322—GOING E: 80 Exit 96 (Madison Ave.), R@ Madison Ave. (0.6), L@ Auburn Blvd. (0.8). GOING W: 80 Exit 98 (Greenback Ln./Elkhorn Blvd.), L@ Elkhorn Blvd./Greenback Ln., R@ Garfield Ave. (1.0), L@ Auburn Blvd.

OPEN M-Sa: 11 a.m.–6 p.m., Su: 11 a.m.–3 p.m. (Varies, call ahead)

Offering beer, wine, and cheese-making supplies in northeast Sacramento, about halfway between downtown and Roseville. It's your first major beer stop heading east on Interstate 80 out of Sacramento. The shop offers occasional homebrewing classes and hop rhizomes for sale seasonally. There's also a small shop down the street called German Deli (no listing), which offers a modest collection of refrigerated German imports.

32 Gordon Biersch
Brewpub

WWW.GORDONBIERSCH.COM

1151 Galleria Blvd., Space 9211, Roseville, CA, 95678 (916) 772-2739—GOING E: 80 Exit 105A (Atlantic St.) (0.7), L@ Roseville Pkwy. (1.2), R@ Galleria Cir. GOING W: 80 Exit 106 (Hwy 65 N) (1.0), Exit 307 (Galleria Blvd., keep left) (1.1), R@ Roseville Pkwy., R@ Galleria Cir.

OPEN M-Sa: 11 a.m.–9 p.m., Su: 11 a.m.–7 p.m.

Chain location (for details, see main listing: Gordon Biersch – San Jose on page 147).

Loomis Basin Brewing

back when I partook) and has a Wine & Brew Lounge with six craft-dedicated taps. Steady draft rotation and a tendency toward the big and barrel-aged ensure lots of pairing options to match one's cigar. Perfecto and Knee Deep Brewing were collaborating on a cedar-aged brew last time I checked in.

34 Total Wine & More
Bottle Shop

WWW.TOTALWINE.COM

5791 Five Star Dr., Roseville, CA 95678, (916) 791-2488—From Hwy 80, Exit 106 (Hwy 65 N) (~1.0), Exit 307 (Galleria Blvd./Standford Ranch Rd., keep right) (0.5).

OPEN Every day: 9 a.m.–10 p.m.

Total Wine has their beer aisles organized by style—that alone should offer a sense of how jaw-dropping the selection is. Huge craft-beer aisles, plus a wider selection of Oregon brews than just about anywhere else. This bottle warehouse ("shop" isn't quite adequate) also offers monthly beer education classes.

33 Perfecto Lounge
Cigar Bar

WWW.PERFECTOLOUNGE.COM

973 Pleasant Grove Blvd. #110, Roseville, CA 95678, (916) 783-2828—GOING E: 80 Exit 105A (Atlantic St.) (0.7), L@ Roseville Pkwy (2.1), R@ Pleasant Grove Blvd. GOING W: 80 Exit 106 (Hwy 65 N/Lincoln/Marysville) (2.1), Exit 308 (Pleasant Grove Blvd.), L@ Pleasant Grove Blvd., L@ Highland Pointe Dr.

OPEN Su-Th: 10:30 a.m.–10 p.m., F-Sa: 10:30 a.m.–midnight

Perfecto Lounge stocks only premium cigars (their house blend is rolled by the same gentleman who rolled the popular Opus X line, one of my favorite smokes

35 Loomis Basin Brewing Company
Brewery

WWW.LOOMISBASINBREWING.COM

3277 Swetzer Rd., Loomis, CA 95650, (916) 259-2739—GOING E: 80 Exit 110 (Loomis), R@ Horseshoe Bar Rd. (0.5), R@ Taylor Rd., L@ King Rd.,

R@ Swetzer Rd. GOING W: 80 Exit 110 (Loomis), L@ Horseshoe Bar Rd., R@ Taylor Rd., L@ King Rd., R@ Swetzer Rd.

OPEN Tu-Th: 3 p.m.–7 p.m., F-Sa: 3 p.m.–8 p.m.

Loomis Basin's Brewmaster, Jim Gowan, has plenty of experience in both brewing and brewery consulting. He's worked at Auburn Alehouse and Sacramento Brewing Company, as well as designed the systems at Gold Hill Brewery and Western Pacific, and that expertise shows through in the beers being produced here at his latest endeavor. Along with his son Kenny (the name alone is a sure sign of greatness), he's making some phenomenal brews. The Swetzer Pale Ale is an extra pale ale with citrusy hops and a crackery core, while their seasonal "Wet Hop" Harvest Ale is a showcase of exactly what freshly picked hops can bring to the table, showing pine, mint, and herbal qualities. Vindicator IPA was a full-on assault of tongue-numbing orange and grapefruit bitterness, and a delicious archetype of West Coast IPA. The tasting room itself, though in an industrial setting, was filled with a beer-loving after-work crowd—the fresh-popped popcorn was a nice touch—and Jim and Kenny were hard at work brewing beer and chatting with customers. A great addition to the local beer scene, and absolutely worth a stop. Casks soon, perhaps.

BREWERS: Jim Gowan (Brewmaster), Kenny Gowan (Brewer)
ESTABLISHED: 2011
BE SURE TO TRY: Vindicator IPA
SEASONALS: "Wet Hop" Harvest Ale (fall)
ELSEWHERE: Draft

36 Knee Deep Brewing Co.
Brewery

WWW.KNEEDEEPBREWING.COM

Lincoln, CA, (775) 750-8028

Jeremy Warren was one of the first folks we connected with back when we were staying out in the Reno area for a few months, and he's since gone from simply homebrewing to producing some really solid commercial products. The IPA and Hoptologist DIPA are both assertive hop bombs, and the Tanilla Porter (flavored with Tahitian vanilla beans) shows a chocolatey porter base with a vanilla contribution showing through softly. My personal favorite is Immigration Red Ale, which was just phenomenal the first time I sampled it on tap. We keep seeing more brews from Knee Deep appearing on the shelves, and plans are in the works to open up another brew site in Reno.

BREWMASTER: Jeremy Warren
ESTABLISHED: 2010
BE SURE TO TRY: Immigration Red Ale (IRA)
ELSEWHERE: Bottles, Draft

37 Auburn Alehouse Brewery and Restaurant
Brewpub

WWW.AUBURNALEHOUSE.COM

289 Washington St., Auburn, CA 95603, (530) 885-2537—GOING E: 80 Exit 119A (Maple St./Auburn), R@ Lincoln Way, R@ Park St., L@ Washington St. GOING W: 80 Exit 119B (Hwy 49 S/Placerville), R@ Lincoln Way, L@ Sacramento St.,

PuB
Specials) GOLD COUNTRY PILSN
AMERICAN River Pale A
Old Town Brown
Gold Digger I.P.A.
IPA ON NITRO!
Limited Release
Sierra GOLD
"CITRA" -5.8/.
Fool*s Gold Ale
Pu240 DOUBLE IPA 8.0/
EXPORT LAGER -5.0/.
Shanghai Stout

Auburn Alehou

R @ Washington St.

OPEN Su–Th: 11 a.m.–10 p.m., F-Sa: 11 a.m.–midnight+

Auburn Alehouse is pretty much the last beer stop heading east until Truckee, and there are some hotels within walking distance. Brian is making some absolutely phenomenal beers here, from the lighter lagers up to their über-dry-hopped imperial IPA, fittingly named after a nuclear-grade isotope. The Export Lager and Gold Country Pilsner tend to take turns on tap, and both are very clean (minimally fruity), crisp lager renditions, with the Gold Country Pilsner showing more of an American, citrusy hop character. It earned a Bronze at the Great American Beer Festival in 2010. Gold Digger IPA has a slight crystalline-sugar center and an explosive hoppiness. Their seasonals are similarly well-handed, and a cask-conditioned version is typically offered once a week. If you happen to be staying in town and are looking to try another local beer spot, Bootleggers Old Town Tavern & Grill (no listing) is just

Barrel Aging

Todd Ashman, Director of Brewing Operations at FiftyFifty Brewing Co., has been producing barrel-aged beer since before most U.S. craft beer drinkers knew what that meant. He made his first barrel-aged beer, Imperial Eclipse Stout, back in 1997, when he was brewing at Flossmoor Station in Illinois. Imperial Eclipse was an imperial stout aged in barrels that had previously been used for aging Jim Beam bourbon. In 1998, it received a gold medal at the Great American Beer Festival (entered in the Experimental Beer category). Todd was instrumental in pushing for a "Wood- and Barrel-Aged Beer" category at GABF, which was introduced in 2002. The following year, it was one of the categories with the most entries.

Aging beer in a barrel is delicate business, and different brewers take different approaches in how they choose to incorporate a barrel's character into a base beer. New oak barrels are used occasionally, but it's more common for brewers to use barrels that were previously used for aging a wine (Cabernet Sauvignon, Chardonnay) or liquor (Bourbon, rye, Scotch—even tequila barrels have been used). Beer transferred into a freshly emptied barrel will first pick up much of the alcohol character left behind from whatever was stored there previously, followed by a slower extraction of wood sugars and other barrel qualities. Todd typically allows a beer to age in a barrel for at least 225 days, and sometimes for up to two years. As he put it, "The secret ingredient in barrel aging is always going to be time."

Each year, FiftyFifty produces multiple versions of Imperial Eclipse Stout that have been aged in different types of barrels. 2011 saw seven different barrel treatments total, including versions aged in Elijah Craig twenty-year Bourbon barrels and Rittenhouse rye barrels—plus, for the first time, a Brewmaster's Grand Cru blend. Todd's been working on various other barrel-aged beers as well, including Rouge Baril Baltique, a Baltic porter aged in Cabernet Sauvignon French oak barrels, created to commemorate City Beer Store's fifth anniversary. Barrel aging can add various nuanced layers to a given beer, and, as FiftyFifty co-owner Andy Barr commented, "It's a good way to expand horizons in terms of what beer can be."

FiftyFifty Brewing

BARREL-AGED BEER
FIFTYFIFTY IMPERIAL ECLIPSE
STOUT

Whereas brewers in the past typically tried to minimize the aromas and flavors imparted by the wooden barrels in which beer was historically stored (before kegs became commonplace), many craft breweries have returned to barrel-aging beers with the opposite intent (see Barrel Aging sidebar on page 229). Whether using new barrels or those that previously housed a wine or spirit, aging beer in barrels lets brewers introduce additional layers to a given brew, including creamy vanilla notes from the wood's vanillin, caramelized or toasty notes offered up by the barrel's charring, and (in certain cases) even contributions from resident wild yeasts and microorganisms. The crux is getting these layers to work seamlessly with the base beer.

For beer aged in barrels previously housing spirits (booze, not ghosts), one of the prime examples is the Imperial Eclipse Stout from FiftyFifty. Their bourbon-barrel versions exhibit both richness and restraint, with lightly charred bourbon notes, chocolate-covered nuttiness, and caramelized sugars housed in a package that proves tempered in both alcoholic warmth and overt sweetness. Other breweries creating exceptional barrel-aged beer in Northern California include Russian River, Marin, High Water, and Dust Bowl.

around the corner.

BREWMASTER: Brian Ford
ESTABLISHED: 2007
BE SURE TO TRY: Export Lager or Gold Country Pilsner
SEASONALS: Oktoberfest Lager (fall)
ELSEWHERE: Bottles, Draft

38 Long's Bottle Shop
Convenience Store

420 Colfax Ave., Grass Valley, CA 95945, (530) 477-8803—From Hwy 80 in Colfax, Exit 135 (Hwy 174 W), follow Hwy 174 W (12.9).

OPEN M-Th: 7 a.m.–11 p.m., F: 7 a.m.–midnight, Sa: 8 a.m.–11 p.m., Su: 8 a.m.–10 p.m.

Long's Bottle Shop is a ways off Interstate 80 (the directions provided above are out and back for simplicity—plus, the other main option closes seasonally), but if you print out directions or use GPS, you could navigate here by taking Highway 49 and 20 without losing much time. Long's has a small but choice Belgian selection, nice regional representation (including a range from Russian River, plus things like Mammoth and Auburn Alehouse bottles), and some solid East Coast sixers, including Dogfish Head.

39 Sierra Moonshine Homebrew Supplies
Homebrew Shop

WWW.SIERRAMOONSHINE.COM

12535 Loma Rica Dr., Grass Valley, CA 95945, (530) 274-9227—From Hwy 80

in Colfax, Exit 135 (Hwy 174 W), follow
Hwy 174 W (9.8), R@ Brunswick Rd.
(1.7), R@ Loma Rica Dr. (0.8).

OPEN W–Su: 10 a.m.–4 p.m.

Heading east, Sierra Moonshine is one of
the last stops for homebrewing supplies
before Nevada. The shop carries beer,
wine, mead, and soda-making supplies,
and offers cider apples for sale in the fall.

40 FiftyFifty Brewing Co. ⭐
Brewpub

🍴 🥛 ☀️ 🍺 🍾

WWW.FIFTYFIFTYBREWING.COM

11197 Brockway Rd., Truckee, CA 96161,
(530) 587-2337—GOING E: 80 Exit 186
(Central Truckee), R@ Donner Pass Rd.
(0.6), R@ Bridge St./Brockway Rd. (1.3).
GOING W: 80 Exit 188 (Hwy 89/Hwy
267/Sierraville/Lake Tahoe), L@ Hwy
267 E/Hwy 89 S (1.5), R@ Brockway
Rd.

OPEN M–Th: 11:30 a.m.–9:30 p.m., F:
11:30 a.m.–10 p.m., Sa: 8 a.m.–10 p.m.,
Su: 8 a.m.–9:30 p.m.

Todd Ashman has been creating
exemplary barrel-aged beers for about
as long as anybody (see sidebars Style:
Barrel-Aged Beer and Barrel Aging), and
his latest versions of Imperial Eclipse Stout
have been stellar. The annual release of
Imperial Eclipse usually draws plenty of
attention from the beer-geek community,
perhaps to the point of overshadowing
much of the other work Todd's been doing
out here. My favorite FiftyFifty offering is
actually their Totality Imperial Stout, which

FiftyFifty Brewing

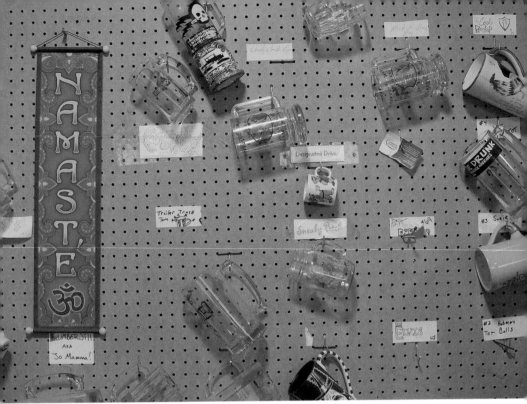

serves as the base beer for the Imperial Eclipse and recently became essentially a year-round offering. It also won a bronze medal at the 2011 Great American Beer Festival. The Rockslide IPA was recently redesigned with Calypso hops and shows even more charismatic hop character than before (it's evolved into a great beer), while the RyePA showed plenty of juicy orange and grapefruit hoppiness.

FiftyFifty recently started offering a few select guest taps and bottles, in addition to frequently rotating their own house seasonals. There are a number of hotels nearby (some right next door), and, at least outside of the snowy winter months, it's also a reasonable walk from the hotels in central Truckee.

BREWER: Todd Ashman (Director of Brewing Operations)
ESTABLISHED: 2007

BE SURE TO TRY: Totality Imperial Stout
SEASONALS: Imperial Eclipse (winter)
ELSEWHERE: Bottles, Draft

41 Desolation Brewing Company
Brewery

2060 Eloise Ave., South Lake Tahoe, CA 96150, (530) 541-7405—Near the intersection of Hwy 89 and Hwy 50 in South Lake Tahoe. GOING E: Hwy 50, L@ Dunlap Dr., R@ Eloise Ave. GOING W: Hwy 50, R@ Dunlap Dr., R@ Eloise Ave.

OPEN M–Su: 5 p.m.–7 p.m.+

The last time we checked in, Mt. Tallac Brewing Company was in the process of switching over to the name Desolation Brewing Company. Desolation is the westernmost of the three breweries in South Lake Tahoe, a block or two away from the intersection of Highways 50 and 89. The brews on tap switch through pretty regularly, and we got to enjoy the hoppy, lightly roasted Lake Tahoe Amber Ale and their 10th Anniversary Imperial Irish Red when we stopped by. We had a blast hanging out with the local crew, and games of cornhole (beanbags, to the uninitiated) and outdoor music are a frequent attraction. Be sure to say hello to the dog, Moo.

BREWMASTER: Jeff Walker
ESTABLISHED: 2001
ELSEWHERE: Draft

42 Roadrunner Gas & Liquors
Convenience Store

WWW.ROADRUNNERGAS.COM

2933 US Highway 50, South Lake Tahoe, CA 96150, (530) 577-6946—Directly off Hwy 50/Hwy 89, about 5 miles south of South Lake Tahoe (in Meyers).

OPEN Su-Th: 6 a.m.–10 p.m., F-Sa: 6 a.m.–11 p.m.

A beer oasis cleverly disguised as a gas station. When we last visited, we counted approximately two hundred craft bottles—everything from local mainstays to Goose Island's limited releases to Victory Prima Pils. You can buy single bottles and build your own six-packs here. Also check out King's Beverage (no listing) in South Lake Tahoe.

43 The Brewery at Lake Tahoe
Brewpub

WWW.BREWERYLAKETAHOE.COM

3542 Lake Tahoe Blvd., South Lake Tahoe, CA 96150, (530) 544-2739—Directly off Hwy 50/Lake Tahoe Blvd. in South Lake Tahoe.

OPEN Every day: 11 a.m.–closing

The Brewery at Lake Tahoe offers the broadest selection of house-made brews in South Lake Tahoe, and Head Brewer Steve Canali is doing some excellent work here. When the old brewer took off some years earlier, taking the recipes with him, it fell upon Steve to basically start from scratch. While it was hard to choose a favorite, pretty much all of the brews were stylistically solid. Their Killibrew Brown Ale was a robust, nutty brown, while the Bad Ass Ale (weighing in at 9.2%) is

e Brewery at Lake Tahoe

indeed "a style of its own," offering light caramel notes and vinous warmth, while hiding its potent alcohol content quite well.

My personal favorites were the Washoe Wheat Ale and White-Out Wit, partly for the lesson they taught. One of the things you'll occasionally hear from overly opinionated beer geeks is that lemon and orange wedges are simply an abomination, and they must be tossed aside immediately with a disgusted huff. For some German hefeweizens, sure, I can go along with that to a degree, but here the fruit wedges worked great. The lemon slice complimented a nice husky wheatiness in the Washoe, while the orange-adorned White-Out showed a refreshing orange character alongside the brew's light coriander note. Ignore what you've heard. Enjoy unabashedly.

HEAD BREWER: Steve Canali
ESTABLISHED: 1992
BE SURE TO TRY: Your favorite style

44 Stateline Brewery & Restaurant
Brewpub

WWW.STATELINEBREWERY.COM

4118 Lake Tahoe Blvd., South Lake Tahoe, CA 96150, (530) 542-9000—Directly off Hwy 50/Lake Tahoe Blvd. in South Lake Tahoe.

OPEN Every day: for lunch and dinner

For working with an extract-based brewing system (as opposed to the all-grain systems generally used), Bryan Parker brews some reasonable beers at Stateline, including an easy-drinking, lemony Pilsner and a lightly sweet American pale ale (Avalanche Ale). Stateline also offered a pretty nice selection of guest taps, including Mammoth's Double Nut Brown. From experience, I'd advise against the spicy and delicious Buffalo wings should you have any plans to use your taste buds later in the day.

BREWER: Bryan Parker
ESTABLISHED: 2008

UGLY KEGS BEAUTIFUL BEER

UT L BOWL

The Central Valley and Yosemite region consists of everything east of East Bay and south of the Highway 50 corridor. For us, this was essentially the final frontier of our travels: breweries we had never been to, and areas we hadn't yet explored much. Nearly half of the region is national parks and national forests.

The western approach to Calaveras Big Trees State Park passes by The Growler Craft Brewery, Alchemy Market & Cafe, and Snowshoe Brewing Company. Chappell Brewery sits near one entrance to Yosemite National Park, while Mammoth Brewing Company and various craft-beer stops await one on the other side. Additionally, the beer selection in Yosemite itself may surprise you. It surprised us. The Highway 99 corridor, from Sacramento south, shows a whole bunch of breweries and beer stops dotting its length. For pretty much every single brewery in this region, samples are available and you can buy beer to go. There's also a surplus of hotels and campsites.

While I stand by the conviction that almost anything is worth trying once, failing to give a nod to our regional favorites would be an oversight. This section's Beer Destinations include two of our favorite regional breweries and artists: Don Oliver's masterful work at Dust Bowl Brewing Company in Turlock, and the brilliant lineup headed by Jason Senior at Mammoth Brewing in Mammoth Lakes. Both stops offer an impressive diversity of spot-on beer. We were grateful to be staying locally.

A third Beer Destination, High Water Brewing, is expected to open soon in Stockton. For now, one can find Steve Altimari's delicious beer in bottles and kegs throughout Northern California. Particularly keep an eye out for Blind Spot and fresh No Boundary IPA.

If one times one's trip appropriately (or gets lucky), the Mammoth Festival of Beers and Bluesapalooza is a huge three-day festival held in Mammoth Lakes every August, while the NorCal Oktoberfest, hosted in Modesto's Vintage Gardens, offers great beer, a legitimate Oompah band, and outbreaks of yodeling.

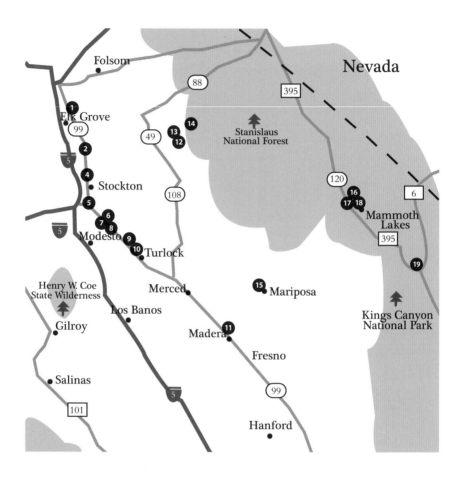

Folsom

Nevada

88

395

Elk Grove

99

14

13

12

Stanislaus
National Forest

49

2

4

Stockton

108

120

5

16

6

17 18

7 8

Mammoth
Lakes

Modesto

9

395

10 Turlock

Henry W. Coe
State Wilderness

Merced

15 Mariposa

19

Los Banos

Gilroy

Kings Canyon
National Park

Madera

11

Fresno

Salinas

5

99

101

Hanford

5 to try

Dust Bowl Hops of Wrath Dust Bowl Lager High Water No Boundary IPA
Lodi Tart Cherry Wheat Mammoth IPA 395

1. Handcraft Brewing – Elk Grove   Homebrew Shop
2. Lodi Beer Company – Lodi   Brewpub
3. High Water Brewing – Stockton   Brewery
4. Valley Brewing Company – Stockton   Brewpub
5. Kelley Brothers Brewing Company – Manteca   Brewpub
6. P. Wexford's Pub – Modesto   Beer Bar
7. Barley & Wine – Modesto   Homebrew Shop
8. St. Stan's Brewing Co./Hero's Sports Lounge & Pizza Co. – Modesto   Brewpub
9. Grizzly Rock Cafe & Grill – Turlock   Beer Bar/Restaurant
10. Dust Bowl Brewing Company – Turlock   Brewpub
11. Three Monkeys Brewing Company – Madera   Brewery
12. The Growler Craft Brewery – Murphys   Brewpub
13. Alchemy Market & Cafe – Murphys   Restaurant/Bottle Shop
14. Snowshoe Brewing Company – Arnold   Brewpub
15. Chappell Brewery – Mariposa   Nanobrewery
16. Mammoth Brewing Company – Mammoth Lakes   Brewery
17. Alpenhof Lodge's Clocktower Cellar Pub – Mammoth Lakes   Beer Bar
18. Angel's Restaurant – Mammoth Lakes   Restaurant
19. Manor Market – Bishop   Grocery Store

uncharted territory

Prospectors Brew Co. (Mariposa)

1 Handcraft Brewing
Homebrew Shop

WWW.HANDCRAFTBREWING.COM

9183 Survey Rd., Ste 104, Elk Grove, CA 95624, (916) 525-2739—GOING S: 99 Exit 284 (Grant Line Rd./Kammerer Rd.), L@ Grant Line Rd., R@ Survey Rd. GOING N: 99 Exit 284 (Grant Line Rd./Kammerer Rd.), R@ Grant Line Rd., R@ Survey Rd.

OPEN M-Th: 10 a.m.–5 p.m., F: 10 a.m.–6 p.m., Sa: noon–6 p.m.

One of the first beer stops heading south from Sacramento is Handcraft Brewing, offering homebrewing and winemaking supplies both online and at its retail location in Elk Grove. It also stocks a wide range of specialty ingredients (from juniper berries to vanilla beans) and hosts occasional Brewing 101 classes.

2 Lodi Beer Company
Brewpub

WWW.LODIBREWINGCOMPANY.COM

105 South School St., Lodi, CA 95240, (209) 368-9931—GOING S: 99 Exit 267A (Turner Rd./Lodi), Cherokee Ln. (1.0), R@ E Lodi Ave. (0.7), R@ S School St. GOING N: 99 Exit 264A (Cherokee Ln./Lodi) (0.8), L@ E Kettleman St. (0.8), R@ S School St. (1.2).

Lodi Beer

This is one of the highlights of the Highway 5/Highway 99 corridor. Located right in downtown Lodi, this brewery's previous existence as a bank is evidenced by many of the details overhead: high flat ceilings, intricate moulding around the edges, old metal arches, and dark wooden features under them. It's possible not to notice, however, with the copper and silver brewing kettles prominently gleaming at the center of the restaurant.

Two of the strongest renditions here are the Lodi Lite Lager and the Umna Hefeweizen, which outshine many of their other standard offerings (which often sway toward the sweeter side of things). The Lodi Lite Lager is a light, crisp American lager weighing in at 3.8% ABV and a fantastic example of what a lighter lager can be like, with plenty of fruitiness and mineral hop notes. The Umna Hefeweizen, while also on the more sugary end of the spectrum, is reminiscent of crème brûlée, with a creamy banana character.

The highlight, though, is the Tart Cherry Wheat, made with 100% local Berlat and Tartan cherries. It's a modestly but legitimately tart beer, and a nice glimpse into what's offered from a more intense Belgian lambic (which are generally much tarter and funkier; Lindemans Framboise, to repeat my earlier comment to this effect, doesn't count). The local cherries offer a vibrant red-fruit character. Imbibe with an open mind.

BREWMASTER: Peter York

ESTABLISHED: 2004

BE SURE TO TRY: Tart Cherry Wheat

High Water Brewing at Whole Foods Coddingtown

Ancient Yeast

Back in 1995, Dr. Raul Cano and his team of scientists at California Polytechnic State University reportedly managed to isolate dormant yeast cells from a 45-million-year-old piece of Burmese amber. Yeasts, of course, are the reason we have beer in the first place (perhaps the most simplified explanation of their role: they convert malt sugars into carbon dioxide and alcohol), and the team soon realized that the isolated yeast varieties had the potential to be used in baking and brewing applications. After running some initial tests to determine the fermentation characteristics of one particular strain, they found they could make some pretty solid beer with it. As Dr. Cano put it, "That was the beginning of Fossil Fuels Brewing Company."

Today, the revitalized yeast is being put to work at Kelley Brothers Brewing Company in Manteca, where the Fossil Fuels brand is currently brewed. While on the sweeter side (the prehistoric yeast doesn't have the ability to ferment the same range of sugars as most brewer's yeasts), Dr. Cano describes its flavor contributions as gingery, with clove and pineapple notes. The Fossil Fuels Wheat definitely had peppery and lemony attributes when we sampled it, while their Fossil Fuels Pale Ale was slightly less assertive. Mmm, science.

3 High Water Brewing
Brewery

WWW.HIGHWATERBREWING.COM

Stockton, CA, (866) 206-0482

Brewmaster Steve Altimari put Valley Brewing in Stockton on the beer-geek map with his phenomenal double IPAs and barrel-aged sours. Steve has amassed a collection of state and national brewing awards over the years, and was most recently recognized for his English-style barley wine, which received a gold medal at the 2009 Great American Beer Festival, and English dark mild, which received a silver medal at the 2010 World Beer Cup. After departing Valley Brew in 2010, Steve partnered with regional craft-beer distributor John Anthony to form High Water. While they're currently in the process of setting up a retail location in Stockton, High Water beer can be found in craft beer shops throughout Northern California.

Packaged in 22-ounce bottles with an iconic woodcut waterfall on the front, High Water's releases so far have been strongly hop-focused. Their Hop Riot IPA (7.3% ABV) and Retribütion Imperial IPA (9.5% ABV) are both immensely hoppy, vibrantly bitter, and full of citrusy and floral hop complexi The Retribütion even shows some var and toasted-marshmallow character at the center, providing just enough balar for the onslaught of hops. But our hea belong to the No Boundary IPA, whic is a bit lower in alcohol than Hop Rio and provides a perfectly dry frameworl a bracing bitterness, and soft, rounded orange notes.

Perhaps the most exciting thing about

brewing techniques on display in his new venture, High Water Brewing (see above).

⑤ Kelley Brothers Brewing Company
Brewpub

🍴 🥐 🥛 🍾 🛢️

WWW.KELLEYBREWING.COM

112 East Yosemite Ave., Manteca, CA 95336, (209) 825-1727—GOING S: 99 Exit 242 (120E/Yosemite Ave./Sonora), R@ E Yosemite Ave. (1.3). GOING N: 99 Exit 242 (120E/Yosemite Ave./Sonora), L@ E Yosemite Ave./120 W (1.4).

OPEN Su–Th: 11 a.m.–9 p.m.+, F–Sa: 11 a.m.–10 p.m.+

Kelley Brothers' cavernous brewpub is built on what was previously the site of the El Rey Theater, which burned down in 1977 in spooky parallel to that cinema's final showing of The Towering Inferno. The Fossils Fuels brand is the main pull here (see Ancient Yeast sidebar on page 246), and although the Fossil Fuels Wheat exhibits some of the same clove and peppery quality one would expect in German hefeweizens, there's a brisk lemony tartness hinting that this is something else entirely. The Four Towers IPA is their best seller, and shows candied oranges and a prominent bitterness. That said, I've heard multiple reports of very patchy beer selection as of late.

BREWMASTER: Joe Kelley
ESTABLISHED: 1997
BE SURE TO TRY: Fossil Fuels Wheat
ELSEWHERE: Draft
LAST-MINUTE UPDATE: Closed as of early 2012.

Hitting the Jackpot in Central Valley

While we found any number of hidden gems during our travels, the origin story behind Dust Bowl Brewing Company was one of our favorites. We had found incredible beer in what many would consider the middle of nowhere (not fairly, of course), and we wanted to know why.

In 2006, homebrewer Don Oliver won the highly competitive Samuel Adams Longshot National Homebrew Competition with his rendition of an Old Ale. Don had worked five years as a helicopter mechanic for the Marine Corps, and he was taking business classes in the hopes of eventually raising sufficient funds to go to UC Davis and become a professional brewer. Brett Tate, a Turlock-based entrepreneur with ambitions of opening a brewery in the area, had read about Don's win in a local paper. It took some time, but Brett eventually tracked down a distant acquaintance of Don's at a soccer game. As Don remembers the details of some of the early planning, Brett said to him, "Any schooling you need is a business expense."

At UC Davis, Don studied under both Charles Bamforth and Michael Lewis (see sidebar Beer Education on page 215). Brett recalls a bit of nervousness on Don's part early on, due to being "just a homebrewer." There were also the issues of expectation, which spurred Don to focus even more carefully on his coursework. He knew that he had to build a brewery when he was done. In 2008, Don completed UC Davis' Master Brewers Program. He also received the John S. Ford Award from the Institute of Brewing and Distilling for having achieved the highest score worldwide on their Diploma in Brewing exams that year.

The final piece fell into place with the arrival of Kevin Becraft, who'd previously served as the Assistant Head Brewer at Arcadia Ales in Michigan. While Don was receiving a ton of résumés from those seeking brewing positions, he joked that, "[Kevin's] résumé didn't have any spelling errors, and it said 'brewer' on it." Kevin's role and responsibility at Dust Bowl is expected to grow as the brewery builds its distribution.

Dust Bowl Brewi

6 P. Wexford's Pub
Beer Bar

WWW.PWEXPUB.COM

3313 McHenry Ave., Modesto, CA 95350, (209) 576-7939—GOING S: 99 Exit 230 (Standiford Ave./Beckwith Rd.), L@ Standiford Ave. (3.4), R@ McHenry Ave. GOING N: 99 Exit 230 (Standiford Ave./ Beckwith Rd.), R@ Standiford Ave. (3.3), R@ McHenry Ave.

OPEN Su-M: 11 a.m.–11 p.m., Tu-Sa: 11 a.m.–midnight

While the tap handles still have a significant BMC angle to them (from Bud Light to Blue Moon), this Irish pub has one of the best craft beer selections for miles. Local offerings frequently featured include Moylan's, Dust Bowl, and Rubicon, and pint nights are held every Thursday (though some of their selections can be a bit iffy).

250

Lone Palm Ave. GOING N: 99 Exit 227 (Kansas Ave.), L@ Kansas Ave. (0.5), R@ Lone Palm Ave.

OPEN Tu-F: 10 a.m.–6 p.m., Sa: 9 a.m.–5 p.m.

Just off Highway 99, Barley & Wine offers both brewing and winemaking supplies. A modest selection is available online, and the shop occasionally holds homebrewing classes for those new to the hobby.

8 St. Stan's Brewing Co./Hero's Sports Lounge & Pizza Co.
Brewpub

WWW.STSTANS.COM

821 L St., Modesto, CA 95354, (209) 606-2739—GOING S: 99 Exit 226B (Hwy 108/ Hwy 132/Maze Blvd.), L@ L St. GOING N: 99 Exit 226 (Hwy 132/Hwy 108/Vernalis Central Modesto), 6th St. (0.6), R@ L St.

OPEN Su-W: 11 a.m.–9 p.m., Th: 11 a.m.–10 p.m., F-Sa: 11 a.m.–midnight

While neither of us found a beer selection here we were especially fond of, the IPA (on the sweeter side, with plenty of candied fruitiness) enjoys a strong local following. St. Stan's and Hero's have something of a symbiotic relationship, with approximately six St. Stan's beers appearing on tap at any given point. The St. Stan's Tap Room, to the left upon walking into the restaurant, has limited hours. Call ahead for them.

BREWER: Bill Coffey
ESTABLISHED: 1984

Dust Bowl Brewing

7 Barley & Wine
Homebrew Shop

WWW.SHOPBARLEYANDWINE.COM

1125 Lone Palm Ave., Modesto, CA 95351, (209) 523-2739—GOING S: 99 Exit 227 (Kansas Ave.), R@ Kansas Ave., R@

9 Grizzly Rock Cafe & Grill
Beer Bar/Restaurant

🍴

4905 North Golden State Blvd., Turlock, CA 95382, (209) 250-0086—GOING S: 99 Exit 217 (Taylor Rd.), L@ W Taylor Rd., L@ N Golden State Blvd. GOING N: 99 Exit 217 (Taylor Rd.), R@ W Taylor Rd., L@ N Golden State Blvd.

OPEN M-Sa: 7:30 a.m.–11 p.m.+, Su: 8 a.m.–11 p.m.+

A rustic, casual stop at the northern edge of Turlock, Grizzly Rock offers about a dozen taps with a heavy California focus. The regional offerings included Lagunitas, Anchor, Rubicon, and Snowshoe the last time we stopped in, and this is one of the few places in the region where one can track down limited-release seasonal kegs. Though not a huge beer destination, the owner is quite knowledgeable about craft beer, and there's plenty of room outside to enjoy the occasional evening barbecues and live music.

10 Dust Bowl Brewing Company
Brewpub

🍴 🥛 🍶 🍾 🛢

WWW.DUSTBOWLBREWING.COM

200 W. Main St., Turlock, CA 95380, (209) 250-2042—GOING S: 99 Exit 213 (W Main St./Central Turlock), L@ W Main St. (1.3). GOING N: 99 Exit 213 (W Main St./Patterson), R@ W Main St. (1.2).

OPEN M-Th: 4 p.m.–10 p.m., F-Sa: 11 a.m.–11 p.m., Su: 10 a.m.–8 p.m. (approximately)

Dust Bowl Brewing Company in downtown Turlock is a perfect example of why one goes beer hunting in the first place (see sidebar Hitting the Jackpot page 249). Up until our initial visit to the newly opened brewpub in 2011, I'd never heard so much as an enthusiastic peep about the place. Their chalkboard list was jaw-dropping, especially for the region: thirteen beers on tap, including a doppelbock, a double IPA, a buckwheat beer, a dark Belgian ale (made using piloncillo sugar), and two different barrel-aged offerings from Zinfandel, Cabernet, and Chardonnay barrels. They had been open six weeks. Afterward, I frequently had to explain to people where Turlock was.

Dust Bowl is one of the main evening draws in the downtown area, and seats can fill up pretty quickly on the weekends. While a Dust Bowl/Great Depression theme runs through some of the beer nomenclature (Hops of Wrath, anyone?), the modern décor and youthful crowd won't have you thinking Steinbeck. An order of the Squeakers (Hilmar Cheese Company curds battered, fried, and served with a savory marinara sauce) is encouraged, and the entrees tend to be very reasonably priced, especially for us city folks.

The beers? Where to begin. The Lager is a magnificent take on the Munich Helles style, showing a rounded Pilsner-malt character (you'll know it when you taste it) that simply pops. Malty, but nothing hefty about it. The India Pale Ale, a.k.a. Hops of Wrath, is a textbook example of West Coast IPA, with tongue-numbing

orange and citrusy hop character atop a thankfully quiet malty center. The Fruit Wheat uses different fresh fruits throughout the year and makes you want to shake those brewers who use syrups instead. A stout made with oats and medium brown sugar rounds out the lineup: a creamy, chocolatey masterpiece. This is the sort of beer that makes you want to move here. Book a hotel room nearby. Start with a sampler.

BREWMASTER: Don Oliver

ESTABLISHED: 2009 (Tap Room in 2011)

BE SURE TO TRY: Lager or IPA (Hops of Wrath)

ELSEWHERE: Bottles, Draft

11 Three Monkeys Brewing Company
Brewery

WWW.3MONKEYSBREWING.COM

5 East Yosemite Ave., Madera, CA 93638, (559) 363-2709—GOING S: 99 Exit 154 (Central Madera), L@ N I St., L@ W Yosemite Ave. GOING N: 99 Exit 153B (Hwy 145 N/S/Madera Ave./Yosemite) (0.5), L@ S Gateway Dr., R@ E Yosemite Ave.

OPEN Check web site or call ahead

Three Monkeys' tap room just opened in early 2012. Previously, the best places to find Three Monkeys beers were convenience stores and bars in the Madera/Fresno area, which is where we'd managed to track them down. The Brown Barrel Ale is a nutty, chocolatey brown, and the cereal maltiness and spicy hops of the Tres Vaqueros Amber play out perfectly together. Both are a steal at $3 a bomber. We look forward to checking out the new place.

BREWMASTER: Matt McDougall

ESTABLISHED: 2009

BE SURE TO TRY: Tres Vaqueros Amber Ale

12 The Growler Craft Brewery
Brewpub

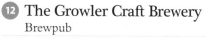

164 Highway 4, Murphys, CA 95247, (209) 728-1162—Directly off Hwy 4 in Murphys, 70 minutes E of Stockton.

The Art of Beer Travel

Did we really need to go all the way up to Eureka? There was always the option of just cobbling together information online, tracking down whatever bottles I could get locally, and soliciting some stock photos. Very few people would have noticed, and even fewer would have cared. What about Etna? Or Turlock?

I guess one could argue that our trip out to Yosemite and Mammoth Lakes, for instance, was all about a respect for the final artisanal product, about sampling beer as close to its source and in its most pristine condition. It sounds good and wholesome, right? Like multigrain bread. It's a perfectly good reason for venturing out to visit breweries, and plenty of people have suggested that it's the best reason to do so.

But I have a secret. The Mammoth beers I sampled on site weren't as good as they were in Yosemite.

This requires some careful explanation (as the Mammoth beers we sampled were all generally fantastic, and the employees and our fellow beer samplers were nothing less). You see, Mammoth re-labels some of their standard lineup for sale in Yosemite National Park. Their Paranoid Pale Ale becomes "Yosemite Pale Ale." Their Real McCoy Amber, which we first sampled at the bar in The Ahwahnee Hotel (located in the heart of Yosemite Valley), becomes "Ahwahnee Amber." Their Epic IPA becomes "Tuolumne Meadows IPA." Their Golden Trout Pilsner becomes…actually, that one stays the same. It's wholly a labeling issue, and there were no discernible differences in freshness or serving temperatures or anything fancy like that. We toted around plastic beer cups, so even the jazzed-up labels had no real influence. It couldn't have had anything to do with the naming, either, as even the Golden Trout seemed improved.

The beers were exactly the same each time. And yet, drinking them in those particular moments, with the best company I could ask for, in one of the most beautiful places on Earth, they just tasted better.

We hope yours do, too.

OPEN M-Th: 11 a.m.–9 p.m., F-Su: 11 a.m.–10 p.m.

The town of Murphys sits just outside Stanislaus National Forest and Calaveras Big Trees State Park, and Growler Craft Brewery provides an endearing afternoon stop on the way in, usually pouring five of their house-made beers. Our favorite by a fair margin was their Hefeweizen, which showed far more pepper than you normally get from this kind of yeast (it's normally focused on bananas and cloves) and seemed almost a hybrid between a German hefeweizen and a Belgian tripel. The brewpub appeared brand new when we visited, and the Hefeweizen certainly hit the spot in the relative calm of their outdoor patio. St. Charles Saloon (no listing), twenty minutes south in the town of Columbia, is the only other place to find their beer.

BREWMASTER: Rich Howell
ESTABLISHED: 2008
BE SURE TO TRY: Hefe
ELSEWHERE: Draft

⑬ Alchemy Market & Cafe
Restaurant/Bottle Shop

WWW.ALCHEMYMARKET.COM

191 Main St., Murphys, CA 95247, (209) 728-0700—GOING E: Hwy 4, L@ Main St., R@ Main St. GOING W: Hwy 4, R@ Main St., R@ Main St.

OPEN Hours change seasonally. Call ahead.

Alchemy has both a retail/market component and an upscale wine bar with seasonal hours. There are twelve rotating taps in the dining area, and about a hundred bottled beers that can be purchased either at the market (open on the weekends) or from the wine bar itself (for in-house consumption or to go). About thirty of the bottled beers rotate as part of their reserve list, highlighting Belgian selections and heftier U.S. releases.

14 Snowshoe Brewing Company
Brewpub

WWW.SNOWSHOEBREWING.COM

2050 Highway 4, Arnold, CA 95223, (209) 795-2272—Directly off Hwy 4 in Arnold, 90 minutes E of Stockton.

OPEN M: 4 p.m.–8:30 p.m., Tu-Th: 11:30 a.m.–8:30 p.m., F-Sa: 11:30 a.m.– 9 p.m., Su: 11:30 a.m.–8 p.m. (seasonal)

You're already in the woods by the time you get to Arnold. Snowshoe is the last beer destination before Highway 4 heads out into national forests, and the entrance to Calaveras Big Trees State Park is just two or three minutes further out. This cozy brewpub fittingly fills up with a mixture of locals and vacationers.
The most solid beers at Snowshoe, for us, tended to be their three standard offerings available in bottles: the Snoweizen Wheat Ale, Thompson Pale Ale, and Grizzly Brown. The Snoweizen is a fully American wheat, focusing on creamy wheat notes and lemony citrus—in

STYLE:

BROWN ALE
MAMMOTH DOUBLE
NUT BROWN

The brown ale style is one characterized by a solid central maltiness, offering flavors ranging from caramel to chocolate to roasted nuts. It will also be, well, brown: frequently a cola color or, at its lightest, a deep amber. Mammoth Brewing Company's Double Nut Brown, while pushing at that upper edge of darkness and dark-chocolate notes for the style (it's about halfway into Porter Land, which sounds like a fantastic place to live), perfectly showcases the nuttiness and rich malt character of the most generous browns.

That pronounced maltiness and color serve as the guiding principles. Beyond that, things labeled as brown ales will vary widely. Nut browns tend to be quite common, and are usually more malt-focused. Many of the more recent American versions, though, have been favoring higher hopping rates. Janet's Brown Ale from Russian River (created by Mike "Tasty" McDole) is a prime local example of a hoppy brown, while Uncommon Brewers Bacon Brown Ale takes the style in an entirely different, slightly smoky direction.

contrast to the more charismatic yeast character of German-style hefeweizens—and the large additions of malted wheat give this an especially creamy texture. The Grizzly Brown shows caramel, light roasted maltiness, and a touch of chocolate on the finish.

The Thompson Pale Ale, while probably more of an amber ale with its biscuity malt core and earthy hop bitterness, was delicious, and our general favorite of their lineup. The Apricot Wheat carries a devoted local following, but was too syrupy sweet for our tastes. The beer-battered fries are excellent, there's a children's menu and a video game room, and their one-gallon growlers (a rarity) are a sight to behold.

BREWMASTER: Tom Schuermann
ESTABLISHED: 1995
BE SURE TO TRY: Thompson Pale Ale
ELSEWHERE: Bottles, Draft

15 Chappell Brewery
Nanobrewery

5024 Highway 140, Mariposa, CA 95338, (209) 742-4500—Directly off Hwy 140 in Mariposa, 1 hour NE of Merced, 1 hour SW of Yosemite.

OPEN Th-Sa: 3 p.m.–7 p.m.

Considering its location, it's a little surprising that Chappell Brewery is open only a few days each week. Mariposa sits less than an hour outside two of Yosemite's west entrances, and the downtown area is a popular stopover for those traveling in and out of the national park. Chappell Brewery is on the main central strip. The brewery's tasting room, which doubles as the Chappell Winery tasting room, had three beers on tap last time I checked in, and it's very likely walking distance from your hotel if you're staying in town.

HEAD BREWER: Scott Chappell
ESTABLISHED: Circa 2008

16 Mammoth ⭐ Brewing Company
Brewery

WWW.MAMMOTHBREWINGCO.COM

94 Berner St., Mammoth Lakes, CA 93546, (760) 934-7141—From Hwy 395: take Hwy 203 W (4.0), R@ Minaret Rd., R@ Forest Trail, R@ Berner St.

OPEN Every day: 10 a.m.–6 p.m.

From the outset, I knew we had to travel out to Mammoth Brewing Company (see sidebar The Art of Beer Travel on page 254). Situated in the town of Mammoth Lakes—which is essentially an adult playground of fishing holes, mountain bike trails, and ski lifts—Mammoth Brewing was our most distant major Beer Destination.

We were not disappointed. This is one of the more elaborate craft beer tasting rooms we've seen, with a full lineup of standard and specialty releases, an impressive range of Mammoth merchandise (including a straw hat that I've regretted not purchasing ever since), some limited homebrew supplies, and— most importantly—free samples. (Though please don't yell at me or Mammoth if details regarding sampling fees have since changed!)

Having picked up a couple lackluster Mammoth bottles along the way (which had evidently sat on a shelf for far too long), this underscored the importance of sampling things fresh at the source. Their IPA 395, a double IPA that features locally harvested sage, was bursting with fresh hop character alongside herbal and spicy juniper notes—a unique, delicious double IPA. The Epic IPA showed smooth, orangey hops and pithy grapefruit, while the Golden Trout was a crisp, floral Pilsner. Their Double Nut Brown was textbook (sidebar Style: Brown Ale on page 255). Nothing but masterfully done beer across the entire lineup, yet the beer I went back to was the Lake Tahoe Red Ale, which Mammoth contract brews for the Lake Tahoe Brewing Company brand (no listing). The Irish Red style is rarely seen in perfect form like this, exhibiting lighter-bodied roast and red fruits.

The biggest beer show in town is the annual Bluesapalooza in August, pairing a wide range of music acts and sixty-plus craft breweries from across the country. Mammoth Brewing manages the beer side of things.

BREWMASTER: Jason Senior
ESTABLISHED: 1995
BE SURE TO TRY: Lake Tahoe Red Ale
SEASONALS: Annual beer for Bluesapalooza (2010: Imperial Stout; 2011: Blond Bourbon Bock)
ELSEWHERE: Bottles, Draft

17 Alpenhof Lodge's Clocktower Cellar Pub
Beer Bar

WWW.ALPENHOF-LODGE.COM

6080 Minaret Rd., Mammoth Lakes, CA 93546, (800) 828-0371—Directly off Hwy 203/Minaret Rd. in Mammoth Lakes.

OPEN Every day: 5 p.m.–midnight+

Even though recent changes have put the Clocktower Cellar Pub more into whiskey-bar territory (they showcase over one hundred different types), this is still the place to go for craft beer after Mammoth closes for the evening. Family-owned, with a cozy lodge feel to it, the pub offers twenty-five taps with plenty of Californian handles and a solid selection of imports (Köstritzer, Franziskaner, Spaten). They also have around fifty bottled beers, including some of the heftier dark Belgian ales. Every third Friday they host Cask Beer Night with Mammoth Brewing.

Keep in mind that the pub closes twice annually during the slow seasons, for three weeks at a time, starting in late May and early October. During peak season it can draw some pretty big crowds, particularly on the weekends. Should you not plan on going anywhere for a while, there's a 160-proof Austrian rum called Stroh that may end up in front of you. It tastes a bit like eggnog. Eggnog that makes your eyes wiggle.

18 Angel's Restaurant
Restaurant

WWW.ANGELSBBQ.COM

20 Sierra Blvd., Mammoth Lakes, CA 93546, (760) 934-7427—GOING W: Hwy 203, R@ Sierra Blvd. GOING E: Hwy 203, L@ Sierra Blvd.

OPEN Su-Th: 11 a.m.–closing, F-Sa: 11 a.m.–11 p.m.

Angel's Restaurant is a few blocks down the street from Mammoth Brewing and Clocktower Cellar Pub (see above). Their burger and wood-fired-barbecue-centric menu also offers a number of vegetarian options, and the limited (but well-chosen) taps are supplemented by a large bottled beer list mixing macro and craft.

19 Manor Market
Grocery Store

3100 W Line St., Bishop, CA 93514, (760) 873-4296—GOING S: Hwy 395, R@ Brockman Ln. (1.0), R@ W Line St. GOING N: Hwy 395, L@ Hwy 168/W Line St. (2.3).

OPEN M-Sa: 6 a.m.–9 p.m., Su: 6 a.m.–8 p.m.

Should one accidentally make a wrong turn heading out of Mammoth Lakes (and not notice for an hour), Manor Market's hundred-plus craft bottles and multiple shelves of Belgian beer might help make it feel like the right turn. One of the most remote corners of the Northern California beer map, and the best bottle shop for miles.

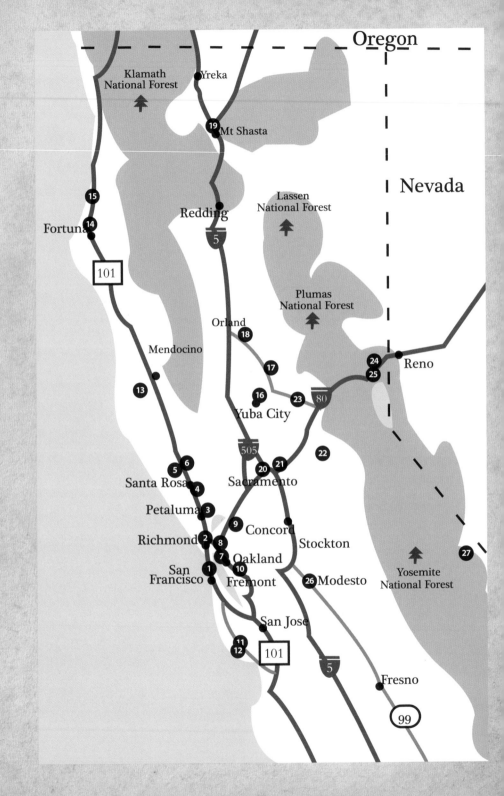

January

The Brewing Network's Winter Brews Festival – Berkeley **8**
WWW.THEBREWINGNETWORK.COM/EVENTS/

February

Double IPA Festival – Hayward (held at The Bistro) **10**
WWW.THE-BISTRO.COM

Sacramento Beer Week – Sacramento (held at many venues) **21**
WWW.SACRAMENTOBEERWEEK.COM

San Francisco Beer Week – San Francisco (held at many venues) **1**
WWW.SFBEERWEEK.ORG

WINTER

March

Fairfax Brewfest – Fairfax
WWW.FAIRFAXBREWFEST.COM

April

San Francisco International Beer Festival – San Francisco
WWW.SFBEERFEST.COM

Oroville Beer Fest (April-May) – Oroville **17**

May

Great Petaluma Chili Cook-off, Salsa and Beer Tasting – Petaluma
WWW.CINNABARTHEATER.ORG/CHILI/

Legendary Boonville Beer Festival – Boonville **13**
(held near Anderson Valley Brewing Company)
WWW.AVBC.COM

Raley Field Brewfest – Sacramento **21**
WWW.RALEYFIELD.COM

West Coast Brew Fest – Sacramento **21**
WWW.MATSONIAN.COM/WCBF/HOME.HTML

June

Beerfest - The Good One! – Santa Rosa **4**
WWW.F2F.ORG/EVENTS2.HTML

Bell Tower Brewfest – Placerville **22**
WWW.PLACERVILLE-DOWNTOWN.ORG/EVENTS.HTML

Davis BeerFest – Davis (held at Sudwerk Brewery) **20**
WWW.DAVISBEERFEST.ORG

Soroptimist Microbrew Festival – Chico **18**
WWW.SIBIDWELLRANCHO.ORG/INDEX.PHP?PG=MICROBREW

Truckee Brew Fest – Truckee **24**
WWW.TRUCKEEOPTIMIST.COM/TRUCKBREWFEST.HTM

SUMMER

July

The BreastFest Beer Festival – San Francisco **1**
WWW.THEBREASTFEST.ORG

California Beer Festival – Santa Cruz **12**
WWW.CALIFORNIABEERFESTIVAL.COM

Santa Cruz Hop N' Barley Festival – Scotts Valley **11**
WWW.HOPNBARLEY.ORG

State of Jefferson Brewfest (late summer) – Mt. Shasta **19**
WWW.SKIPARK.COM

SUMMER

August

Brews, Jazz & Funk Fest – Olympic Valley
WWW.SQUAW.COM

Hops in Humboldt – Fortuna
WWW.HOPSINHUMBOLDT.COM

IPA Festival – Hayward (held at The Bistro)
WWW.THE-BISTRO.COM

Mammoth Festival of Beers and Bluesapalooza – Mammoth Lakes
WWW.MAMMOTHBLUESBREWSFEST.COM

Russian River Beer Revivaland BBQ Cookoff – Guerneville
(held at Stumptown Brewery)
WWW.STUMPTOWN.COM/REVIVAL/

Sierra BrewFest – Grass Valley
WWW.MUSICINTHEMOUNTAINS.ORG/BREWFEST.PHP

September

Beer in the Plaza – Healdsburg **6**
WWW.SIHEALDSBURG.ORG/BEERINTHEPLAZA.HTML

Brews on the Bay, presented by the San Francisco **1**
Brewers Guild – San Francisco
WWW.SFBREWERSGUILD.ORG

California Brewers Festival – Sacramento **21**
WWW.CALBREWFEST.COM

Biketoberfest Marin (early fall) – Fairfax **2**
WWW.BIKETOBERFESTMARIN.COM

Oktoberfest By the Bay (early fall) – San Francisco **1**
WWW.OKTOBERFESTBYTHEBAY.COM

StrangeBrew BeerFest (early fall) – Eureka **15**
WWW.EUREKATHEATER.ORG

FALL

October

The Bay Area Craft Beer Festival – Martinez **9**
WWW.BAYAREACRAFTBEERFESTIVAL.COM

California Beer & Wine Festival – Yuba City **16**
WWW.CALIFORNIABEERANDWINEFESTIVAL.COM

NorCal Oktoberfest – Modesto **26**
WWW.NORCALOKTOBERFEST.COM

Oaktoberfest in the Dimond – Oakland **7**
WWW.OAKTOBERFEST.ORG

Oktobrewfest 5K – Davis (held at Sudwerk Restaurant and Brewery) **20**
WWW.CHANGEOFPACE.COM/OKTOBREWFEST.HTML

Village Oktoberfest – Olympic Valley **25**
WWW.SQUAW.COM

Wet Hop Festival – Hayward (held at The Bistro) **10**
WWW.THE-BISTRO.COM

November

West Coast Barrel Aged Beer Festival – Hayward (held at The Bistro) **10**
WWW.THE-BISTRO.COM

GLOSSARY

ABV: Alcohol by Volume. The standard U.S. measure of how much alcohol is in a beer. The standard ABV of beer (if there is such a thing) is around 5%, but craft beers range from significantly lower than that to way higher. In terms of keeping oneself out of trouble, this is a useful number to pay attention to.

ADJUNCT: Broader definitions can include any atypical ingredient one puts into beer (coffee, etc.), but more often this refers to brewing ingredients that will ferment (corn, rice, sugar, fruit, etc.) but that aren't malted grains.

BARLEY WINE: A complex, higher-alcohol beer style of British descent. Not made from grapes. See Barley Wine/Old Ale/Stock Ale sidebar on page 170.

BARREL: One barrel of beer corresponds to approximately 31 gallons in the U.S.

BEER: Most often: water + malted barley + hops + yeast. But not always. See also: Malt, Hops, Yeast.

BEER GEEK: Generally a term of endearment (other less-flattering terms exist for pretentious beer geeks). A beer geek enjoys learning about beer and tends to think a little bit more carefully about what's in his or her glass.

BMC: Bud-Miller-Coors. The big guys, the behemoth brands, the insipid mass-market lagers. See also: Macro.

BOMBER: A 22-ounce bottle of beer. Not an airplane.

CASK-CONDITIONED BEER: See cask-conditioned beer discussion in

Explanation of Symbols sidebar on page 20.

CICERONE: The craft-beer equivalent of a wine sommelier, managed by the Cicerone Certification Program.

CRAFT BEER: A variety of definitions exist, with the Brewers Association's definition being the most established and highlighting "small, independent, and traditional" breweries. Almost all of the breweries in this guidebook adhere to the Brewers Association definition, with the very few exceptions evaluated and included at my discretion. These are generally breweries that don't satisfy the "independent" clause but that are still making uncompromised beer.

DRY HOPPING: A slight misnomer (the hops still get wet), dry hopping is a process in which hops are added after the wort has been boiled and cooled, as opposed to the more traditional practice of adding them during the boil. This results in greater fresh-hop aroma and flavor characteristics (often grassy), while adding minimal actual bitterness.

ESTER: A group of yeast byproducts from fermentation, often providing fruity notes such as apple or banana.

FLAGSHIP BEER: Term used to describe a brewery's best-selling or most representative beer.

GASTROPUB: An arguably uppity name for a pub serving fancier food than standard pub fare.

GROWLER: Typically a half-gallon (64-ounce) glass container used for taking draft beer home with you. Growlers are usually filled directly from the tap and sealed with a metal lid. Keep them refrigerated and drink promptly.

GUEUZE: Typically a blend of one, two, and three-year-old lambic. A pleasantly funky, tart, effervescent style.

HOPS: The flowers of the Humulus lupulus plant that generally provide the bitterness in beer to balance the malts' sweetness. (Other occasional sources of bitterness can include a variety of herbs and darker specialty malts.) In the simplest explanation, the amount of time that hops are boiled during the brewing process determines whether they predominantly contribute to aroma, flavor, or bitterness. See also: Dry Hopping.

IPA: India Pale Ale. A hop-centric beer style. See India Pale Ale (IPA) sidebar on page 69.

KRIEK: Typically a lambic with cherries added.

LAMBIC: A traditional Belgian beer style spontaneously fermented with naturally occurring yeast and bacteria. This style can take some getting used to—it's often challengingly sour, acidic, and funky—but most serious beer geeks eventually come to love its complexity and refreshing qualities. See also: Gueuze and Kriek.

MACRO: The opposite of micro. A beer produced by one of those delightful mega-corporations. See also: BMC.

MALT: Almost always refers to malted barley (though other grains can be malted as well). Malts provide, among other

things, the sugars that yeast will ferment into alcohol and carbon dioxide. There are many different kinds of malts available, and how they are handled and kilned will determine their flavors, aromas, and other contributions.

MICROBREWERY: Previously used to describe the artisanal U.S. brewing industry, it's been largely replaced by "craft brewery" as the dominant phrasing in recent years. See also: Craft Beer.

NANOBREWERY: An exceptionally small commercial brewery. See Nanobrewing sidebar on page 85.

NOBLE HOPS: An American-based categorization that refers to a small subset of European hop varieties, including Saaz from the Czech Republic and Hallertauer Mittelfrueh, Spalter, and Tettnanger hops from Germany. These hops tend to be highly aromatic and only modestly bittering, offering herbal, floral and spicy notes. Noble hops tend to be quite distinct from many of the heavily bittering, citrus-focused American hop varieties.

SAISON: Traditional Belgian-style farmhouse beer. Often peppery, reasonably hopped, and golden-orange in color.

Tank Cleaning at Loomis Basin Brewing

SESSION BEER: While a variety of definitions exist, generally a lower-alcohol (<4.5% or so, at least by U.S. standards) beer that one can drink a fair amount of over an extended period of time without getting smashed. We love these and wish we saw more of them, particularly from craft brewers.

SOUR BEER: A good thing, at least as the term is used in this book. (The term "infected beer" would be used if a beer isn't intentionally sour.) Tart, acidic, often magical. See Sour/Wild Ale sidebar on page 71.

WORT: The unfermented (non-alcoholic) mixture of malt sugars, hops, water, etc. that yeast will ferment into beer.

YEAST: The microorganisms responsible for fermenting wort into beer. The saying often goes, "Brewers make wort. Yeast makes beer." There are an incredible number of yeast strains out there, and certain strains, such as those used in Belgian-style beers and German-style hefeweizens, tend to provide significant flavor and aroma contributions.

ACKNOWLEDGMENTS

Getting to all of this involved a long and convoluted path, and I'm grateful that it's also involved so many good people. Our family—Mom, Russ, Dad, Kelly, Phil, Grandma, Diana, Joe, Ron, Tammy, Vanessa, Omar—has been supportive at every single turn, even when those turns appeared somewhat batshit crazy. Thank you thank you thank you, and take some solace in the fact that I haven't made it any easier for those mentioned after you. Kyle Fleit will back me up here, as my college roommate, a dear friend to this day, and the person who introduced me to good beer.

Kyle also saved my life this one time. I totally forgot to mention this at his wedding.

Dr. Stephen Garoff and Dr. Kunal Ghosh, my physics advisors at Carnegie Mellon, are two of the very few people who laughed in a good way when I told them I was quitting physics to pursue writing. Dr. Richard Galik, my thesis advisor at Cornell, guided me through those last couple years. Rest peacefully, Richard.

John Dawe was my first editor, and the first person who helped me get started and doing what I needed to do. No one's influenced and helped shape my writing more than Maud Casey, who taught me (among numerous other, more nuanced teachings) that it ultimately comes down to making a hat. I made a hat, Maud.

While on the accessory theme: Russ Owens somehow rigged up an umbrella to keep me safe and sound during the many corporate downpours at my old consulting gig. Russ, you made that transition so much easier, and I hope you've found your own better place in the world by the time you read this.

Greg Kitsock gave me my first paychecks as a beer writer (for tiny articles in Mid-Atlantic Brewing News), which set the stage for everything afterward. Joe Tucker, Mario Rubio, and the community at Ratebeer.com have taught me so many things about the beer world and given me a place inside it that I consider home. Greg Barbera and Daniel Bradford at All About Beer have been hugely supportive of Ali and me from the very beginning of our freelance careers, and we couldn't have asked for a better publication to work with.

Many beer writers have proven time and again that what we do is ultimately an artistic pursuit. Michael Jackson (forever the beer hunter at the front of the pack), Lew Bryson, Stan Hieronymus, Randy Mosher, Jay Brooks, Eric Asimov, and others have both served as an inspiration and made books like this possible. In the same breath go endless thanks to the craft brewers—the artists and visionaries who continue to inspire us all.

To my Word Pirates and Redwood Writers: for so much, especially early on when I needed it most.

To folks like Rick Sellers, Brian Stechschulte, Peter Estaniel, and other area beer hunters: for keeping me on top of the latest bits and pieces in their local beer scenes. To Pam D'Angelo, Deborah Taylor-French, and Susan Willow: for the edits and endless encouragement. To Patrick Walsh and Michelle Dotter: for polishing up my prose and helping me sound like a quasi-normal human being. To Mike Persinger: for his generous editing and support throughout. To Gwendolyn Meyer: for reminding us book design is its own art form. To Chris Gruener at Cameron + Company: for bringing us into this project, assembling a fantastic book team, and (somehow) knowing that we could actually pull this off.

To our wonderful friends: for your support when we needed it (we always need it), for your floor space and your futons, and for your kind company. To Ali: for being so much of what went into this—the photographs, feedback, reality checks, Reality Czecks…for everything, and all of this, and way more.